Auditing Theory

Auditing Theory provides a theory of auditing that underpins auditing practice. A key aim of the book is to identify the objectives of auditing in the context of corporate financial reporting, to explore the underlying beliefs about what kind of practices will fulfil these objectives and to explain how the concepts that are used in developing these practices arise out of these objectives and beliefs and how they in turn are used in developing and applying the rules that govern auditing practice.

The book is innovative in providing an explanation of the idea of a theory of auditing that draws upon modern philosophical explanations of rule-governed practices that can be applied to the practice of auditing. This perspective provides an understanding of what it is to provide reasons for adopting rules of the kind expressed in a theory of auditing. Philosophical ideas about the social construction of reality are used to explain the other role of theory in developing the concepts of auditing that arise out of the objectives and beliefs that underpin audit practice.

Auditing Theory gives new insights into the nature of materiality, evidence, professional judgement and scepticism in auditing. This is achieved through the method of conceptual enquiry, conceived as a particular kind of philosophical investigation that is explained in the book, into the concepts of auditing. The insights provided in this book should assist standard setters in their standard setting decisions and practitioners in following auditing standards.

Ian Dennis is Senior Lecturer and was formerly Head of the Accounting Department at Oxford Brookes University Business School, UK. He is also an Adjunct Associate Professor at the Norwegian School of Economics.

Routledge Studies in Accounting

Auditing Theory

Ian Dennis

Routledge
Taylor & Francis Group

NEW YORK AND LONDON

First published 2015
by Routledge
711 Third Avenue, New York, NY 10017

and by Routledge
2 Park Square, Milton Park, Abingdon, Oxon OX14 4RN

First issued in paperback 2018

*Routledge is an imprint of the Taylor & Francis Group,
an informa business*

Library of Congress Cataloging-in-Publication Data
Dennis, Ian.
    Auditing theory / by Ian Dennis.
        pages cm. — (Routledge studies in accounting ; 17)
    Includes bibliographical references and index.
    1. Auditing. I. Title.
    HF5667.D43 2015
    657'.4501—dc23   2015003256

Typeset in Sabon
by ApexCoVantage, LLC

ISBN 13: 978-1-138-59970-3 (pbk)
ISBN 13: 978-1-138-79201-2 (hbk)

For Sally Ann and George with thanks for their love and encouragement

Contents

Acknowledgements

I would like to thank the Business School of Oxford Brookes University for releasing me from my teaching commitments for a semester to enable me to write this book.

I would also like to thank the Association of Chartered Certified Accountants (ACCA) for their support for, and encouragement of, a research study on professional judgement in auditing from which a number of ideas in this book were developed.

1 The Nature of Auditing Theory and of Conceptual Frameworks in Auditing

A book on auditing theory is confronted with an immediate problem. There is a perception that such a book is unnecessary. It has been suggested that 'auditors on the whole are very practical people and . . . there is, of course, a danger that some practitioners will believe that they do not need a philosophy or set of unifying theories that explain what they do or should do' (Gray and Manson, 2011, p. 31). This lack of interest was observed by the authors of one of the seminal works on auditing theory who observe that 'many think of auditing as a completely practical, as opposed to theoretical, subject. To them, auditing is a series of practices and procedures, methods and techniques, a way of doing with little need for the explanations, descriptions, reconciliations, and arguments so frequently lumped together as "theory"' (Mautz and Sharaf, 1961, p.1). A later writer on auditing theory notes that 'in spite of the social importance of auditing and the fact that it constitutes a significant part of the work of the accountancy profession throughout the world, there has been little interest in the study of its theory or in the development of research' (Flint, 1988, p. 3). The result is that 'auditing has developed in a very practical way. Perhaps surprisingly, given . . . the effort devoted to developing a coherent theory (or conceptual framework) of *accounting*, little attention has been given to developing a theory of *auditing*' (Porter, 2003, p. 42). Although there are plenty of books on auditing practice, there are very few books on the theory of auditing. A conceptual framework is equated with a theory of accounting, but there is no conceptual framework for auditing.

The lack of interest in a theory or conceptual framework for auditing is confirmed by the fact that the International Audit and Assurance Standards Board (IAASB) rejected a proposal to develop 'fundamental principles of auditing', of the kind that might be expected in a conceptual framework, as part of the Clarity Project (Dennis, 2010a, p. 299). One reason for this decision was that the IAASB believed that developing a framework would take up too much time and would deflect from the goal of clarifying auditing standards (Dennis, 2010a, p. 299). Theory appears to be too far removed from the exigencies of practice to warrant the expenditure of time. Another possible explanation is that it is difficult to understand the nature of conceptual frameworks, something that is a legacy of their development in the area of financial reporting (Dennis, 2010a, p. 301). There is still residual dissatisfaction, expressed in some of the comment letters on the exposure draft of clarified ISAs (International Standards on Auditing), that such a framework was not developed.

The IAASB has published the *International Framework for Assurance Engagements* (IAASB, 2005). It relates to *all* assurance engagements, of which auditing is one example. What kind of 'framework' is it? It states the objectives of assurance engagements and identifies five 'elements' of such engagements, namely that there is a three party relationship; a subject matter, or what the engagement is about; criteria, or what is evaluated or measured; evidence; and what kind of assurance report is required. It is not a theory or conceptual framework for auditing but, rather, a kind of 'pro-forma' for thinking about developing it or something that suggests what needs to be thought about in theorising or conceptual frameworking. This book starts off by thinking about the kind of 'theory' that might be developed from the 'pro-forma'. Chapter 2 examines the objectives of auditing against the background of a three party relationship that exists in an auditing situation. Chapter 3 considers the 'subject matter', financial statements, and the nature of the opinion about them. The specific evidence required to give an audit opinion and the concept of materiality used in expressing the opinion are explained in chapters 4 and 5. Although the IAASB chose not to develop a conceptual framework for auditing, they bowed to pressure to develop some principles of auditing in a revision of ISA 200 (Dennis, 2010a, p. 304).

Notable examples of books on auditing theory are Mautz and Sharaf's *The Philosophy of Auditing* (1961), Flint's book *Philosophy and Principles of Auditing: An Introduction* (1988) and Lee's book *Corporate Audit Theory* (1993). 'Theory' has been defined as 'a framework of logically connected statements which assist in organizing, explaining and predicting observations of the so-called real world' (Lee, 1993, p. 1). Explaining and predicting accounting practice is the objective of positive accounting theory, and auditing practice, a kind of accounting practice, could be a species of positive or scientific (Watts and Zimmerman, 1986, p. 2; Sterling, 1979). An important strand in the philosophical literature rejects philosophical enquiry as a scientific investigation. The fact that two of the books on auditing theory have 'philosophy' in the title suggests that they may not be concerned with making a contribution towards the 'science' of auditing. A second problem with a book on auditing theory is that its nature is unclear. There are different views about auditing theory and its objectives, and readers may have different expectations about it.

Perhaps this explains the paucity of such books in the literature. It is important to explain the kind of theory in the book. This is done by starting with considering the implications of conceiving of auditing as a practice. Conceptual frameworks, as a theory of a practice, will then be examined. The role of concepts and of conceptual enquiry within theorising of this kind is explained. The idea of a philosophy of auditing is considered. Theorising about a practice, what might be called normative theorising, is differentiated from scientific theorising, or positive accounting theorising. Normative theorising of the kind developed in a conceptual framework for auditing is described. Problems with the practice of auditing may be solved by such a theory, which should 'provide a basis for determining professional action' (Mautz and Sharaf, 1961, p. 13). Assuming, for the moment, that such an enquiry is justified, what is involved in changing a practice? Examining the idea of practices throws some light on what is involved.

PRACTICES

Practices involve regularities in behaviour where there is an intention to conform to a pattern. It is possible to identify acts that are in conformity with the practice and those that are not. An important starting point in understanding a particular kind of auditing theory, one that develops the practice of auditing, is the observation that auditing is *a rule-governed practice*. Rules exert a 'dominating influence' on the practice of accounting (West, 2003, p. 66). The same can be said about auditing. Accounting and auditing are *activities of following rules*. Rules are prescriptions that guide conduct and explain and justify actions of following rules. These prescriptions are not narrow, 'rules-based' prescriptions to be contrasted with 'principles-based' ones. Rules, in the sense intended here, prescribe and guide types of behaviour in types of situations (Dennis, 2014, p. 15). A *practice* is *an activity of following rules* (Dennis, 2014, p. 19).

Auditing, like accounting, is today an *institutional practice*. This means that auditors follow rules that are promulgated by an *institution*, the International Audit and Assurance Standards Board, and set out in International Standards on Auditing. At least part of the reason why auditors follow such rules is that they accept the authority of the standard setter and want to follow the rules promulgated by them (Dennis, 2014, p. 21). When questions are asked about audit practices, what is wanted is an answer which explains why the *standard setter* promulgated the rules that are followed, not why auditors follow them. This is the focus of auditing theory. This underlies practitioners' perception that theory is not something *they* need to engage with because it is a concern of *standard setters*.

One way of understanding the nature of auditing theory is to understand it as something that assists standard setters in making decisions about what rules to promulgate in standards. This is the kind of thing that conceptual frameworks for financial reporting were developed to achieve. They provide 'a coherent frame of reference to be used . . . in the development of accounting standards' (Accounting Standards Board [ASB], 1999, §2). They have been characterized as some kind of 'theoretical basis' for financial accounting (Archer, 1993, p. 62). This suggests that looking at the nature of a conceptual framework may shed some light on the nature of the kind of auditing theory that underpins practice.

CONCEPTUAL FRAMEWORKS

One important purpose of conceptual frameworks is 'to play a role in decision-making, in particular in assisting standard setters in making *rational decisions* about which accounting standards to promulgate' (Dennis, 2014, p. 25). The Financial Accounting Standards Board (FASB) acknowledges that the 'Concepts Statements', which constitute the conceptual framework in the U.S., 'will guide the Board in developing accounting and reporting guidance by providing the Board with a common foundation and basic reasoning on which to consider merits of alternatives' (FASB, 2010, p. 5). This is also recognised by the International Accounting Standards Board (IASB) and the Accounting Standards Board (ASB) in the UK. This ties in closely with Mautz and Sharaf's conception of auditing theory as something which considers 'the reasons for the use of various procedures as well as the steps in the procedures themselves, the "why" as well as the "how"' (Mautz and Sharaf, 1961, p. 3).

The model of a conceptual framework for financial reporting could be used for a framework for an auditing theory. In financial reporting accounting standards are promulgated for reasons, and the purpose of a conceptual framework is to provide such reasons (Dennis, 2014, ch. 3). The 'principles' in such frameworks constitute sentences that appear in reasoning that has as its conclusion a desire to promulgate standards that include rules that are to be followed in practice. Two kinds of reasoning have been identified as relevant in standard setting decisions. One starts from general rules, sometimes understood as conventions of accounting, and derives more specific rules of accounting from them. These rules may be referred to as 'principles', and the reasoning has been referred to as a 'logic of appropriateness' (Dennis, 2014, p. 20). Another starts with desires to achieve certain ends or objectives from which a desire to promulgate standards that are believed will fulfil these objectives is derived. These desires may also be referred to as 'principles', and the reasoning has been referred to as a 'logic of consequences' (Dennis, 2014, p. 20). Both of these kinds of 'principle' and reasoning have been used in developments of accounting theory and conceptual frameworks in the previous century. Both might provide a model for the development of auditing theory of the normative kind. However, interest in developing the conceptual framework has shifted from conceiving of the framework as the expression of accounting conventions to a decision-useful approach where the framework expresses objectives, that is, what is wanted from a system of financial reporting (Dennis, 2014, p. 36). The shift involves a change from a logic of appropriateness to a logic of consequences.

Setting standards is an *intentional action* of standard setters (Dennis, 2014, p. 25). Intentional actions are done for reasons. These reasons are used to make decisions about what to do. The reasoning involved is 'practical reasoning', another name for a 'logic of consequences'. In reasoning of this kind, the person deciding to act starts with a premises that express a desire that the action is to achieve and from other premises that express beliefs that a certain action will fulfil this desire from which a conclusion is derived that expresses a desire to act. If, as a result of wanting to perform an action, the action is undertaken, then the desire and beliefs expressed in the premises give reasons for performing that action (Anscombe, 1957, §5). A reason for acting thus involves '(a) having some sort of pro attitude toward actions of a certain kind, and (b) believing (or knowing, perceiving, noticing, remembering) that his action is of that kind' (Davidson, 1980, p. 3). Given the purpose of a conceptual framework as something that assists standard setters in deciding what standards to promulgate, such a framework is something that gives reasons for standard setting actions. They include expressions of the underlying desires and beliefs that constitute reasons for setting standards. The statements of objectives and qualitative characteristics are to be understood as statements expressing what is wanted from the action of financial accounting and reporting (Dennis, 2014, ch. 3). The decision-usefulness approach that underpins the conceptual framework states that what is wanted is to provide information that is useful to users that is expressed in the objectives chapter of the conceptual framework (CF). The chapter on qualitative characteristics states that what is wanted is information that has certain qualities that users find useful. Standard setters undertake practical reasoning by starting with desires of this kind and then look around for standards that when followed will result in financial reporting that meets the desires expressed. They need to undertake research to identify such standards. If standard setters want to achieve these desires and believe that by promulgating certain standards that will be followed these desires will be achieved, then they may conclude that they want to promulgate these standards.

If the model of a conceptual framework for financial reporting is to be used as a model for a conceptual framework for auditing, then such a framework needs to include statements about the objectives of auditing, or what is wanted from the practice of auditing. These are sometimes referred to as 'principles', but the nature of principles is unclear (Dennis, 2006). The *statements* that appear in the conceptual framework are used to derive other statements included in the standards. There is a logical relationship between these statements. Again, it is unclear whether this is meant to be a deductive logical relationship or whether it involves logic of some other kind. It is suggested that this is a logic of practical reasoning (Dennis, 2014, ch. 3). The conceptual framework is explained as a series of 'concepts statements'. To understand this involves understanding the word. It is important to realise that the term 'concept' covers different kinds of things.

WHAT ARE CONCEPTS?

The FASB and the IASB quote the definition of 'concept' from the *Oxford English Dictionary* as 'a general notion or idea . . . of a class of objects' and go on to quote Sir W. Hamilton's definition of a conception as 'the act of comprehending or grasping into unity the various qualities by which an object is characterised' (FASB/IASB, 2005, p. 1). There is no recognition that these are definitions of two different kinds of thing. The latter is the definition of an act or action whereas the former is the definition of a notion or class. Acts are not the same kind of thing as notions or classes. Loose talk of this kind is endemic in discussions about the conceptual framework for financial reporting. It would not take much effort to resolve a confusion of this kind. One could talk of a concept as the outcome of an *act* of conceiving. 'Conceiving' in this context would appear to be an act of defining objects or, more accurately, defining words or expressions used to denote objects. This would render a concept as the outcome of this kind of activity and something that thus gives the meaning of a word or expression. This ties in with the notion of concepts in the philosophical literature, which are equated with the *meanings of words* (Craig, 2005, p. 135). An example of a concept that the FASB/IASB identifies is that of an asset. The meaning of the word 'asset', as explained in the conceptual framework, is, at least in part, 'a source of future economic benefits'. The concept of an asset is thus explained by explaining the meaning of the word 'asset'.

The claim is made that a concept differs from a convention in that the latter, again defined by the *Oxford English Dictionary*, is 'a rule or practice based upon general consent' (FASB/ IASB, 2005, p. 1). Wittgenstein argues that definitions give rules for the meaning of expressions (Baker and Hacker, 1980, p. 35). It would seem that these rules are also conventions if, as is presumably the case given that language is a shared practice, they are based upon 'general consent'. It is a little unsettling to see them set out in something the FASB refers to as 'concepts statements' when, according to the FASB, concepts are meant to be different from conventions. The example of a convention given by the FASB/IASB is the rule of straight-line depreciation. This is also a rule, but it is different from a rule for the use of an expression. It is not that the one is a rule and the other is not, but that one is a rule for the meaning of an expression whereas the other, a convention, provides another kind of rule, that is, a rule that requires one to do something other than to use an expression in a certain way.

A conceptual framework is meant to provide 'fundamental concepts' that are used to 'root' standards (FASB/IASB, 2005, p. 1). It has already been suggested that the concepts statements dealing with objectives and qualitative characteristics express desires or what is wanted from financial reporting. There are also concepts in the conceptual framework which are definitions of the meaning of expressions like 'asset' and 'liability' which give rules for the use of these expressions. There are also general rules in the other sense of rules requiring something to be done such as the recognition and measurement principles which are meant to guide the standard setter in deriving more specific rules for particular accounting elements. The FASB and the IASB do not have a clear idea of what concepts are and have not successfully differentiated them from conventions. This is one illustration of the failure of standard setting bodies to undertake adequate enquiry into the concepts they make use of before undertaking a conceptual framework project. There has been a failure to properly explain the concept of a concept, that is, the meaning of the expression 'concept'! Past confusions are simply recycled.

This failure is part of a more general failure to properly explain the idea of a conceptual framework, that is, the meaning of the expression 'conceptual framework'. It has been suggested that 'while massive financial resources have been expended by the . . . FASB . . . in developing a CF, little attention has been given to the *idea* of such a CF' (Power, 1993, p. 44). There are, of course, explanations of the expression, but these are explained in terms that themselves require explanation. Power suggests that 'little attention has been given to the role and status of what might be called "conceptual considerations" in financial reporting' (Power, 1993, p. 44). What is needed in dealing with problems like this is *conceptual enquiry*. Before the conceptual framework for financial reporting is used as a model for developing auditing theory, it is necessary to undertake an enquiry of this kind into the nature of the concepts or principles in such a framework. What is a conceptual enquiry?

CONCEPTUAL ENQUIRY

The method of conceptual enquiry has been explained by Dennis and used in auditing research and in research in financial reporting (Dennis, 2008; Dennis, 2010b; Dennis, 2014). Given that concepts are the meaning of words or expressions, a conceptual enquiry is an enquiry into the meaning of those words or expressions. There are three kinds of conceptual enquiry. A 'descriptive' conceptual enquiry identifies the meaning of expressions as they are used by practitioners (Dennis, 2008, p. 261). A brief conceptual enquiry into the expression 'conceptual framework' and 'concepts' has already been conducted. Other expressions that need to be examined have already been mentioned. Explanations of the conceptual framework mention 'principles', an expression in need of further examination. The objective of such enquiries is to identify the rules for the use of expressions that are followed in using the expressions. Such enquiries aim to determine whether there is an agreed understanding of the use of these expressions in discourse or whether there is no precise meaning and they are vague or ambiguous. An expression is vague if there is, 'in the practice of its application, significant disagreements about what uses of it are correct' (Baker and Hacker, 1980, p. 218).

Concepts are important. Wittgenstein once wrote that 'concepts lead us to make investigations; are the expression of our interest, and direct our interest' (Wittgenstein, 1953, §570). He also observes that 'concepts help us to comprehend things. They correspond to a particular way of dealing with situations' (Wittgenstein, 1978, p. 431). The concept of a conceptual framework or of principles and the idea that such a framework provides guidance to standard setters whose standards are rooted or flow from the framework directs conceptual frameworkers to construct a framework of a particular kind. Without an agreed meaning, different users of these expressions might have their interest 'directed differently' and end up with different frameworks or different interpretations of their nature (Dennis, 2008, p. 263). The need for such enquiries is evident, and yet, according to Power, they are not undertaken in thinking about conceptual framework projects or, as will be considered throughout this book, in thinking about theorising about auditing. The same need for conceptual enquiry is evident in the area of standard setting in general. If a standard includes a prescription to do something, then what is meant by the expression that describes what is to be done needs to be both understood and understood in the *same* way that the standard setter understands it if the professional is to end up doing what the standard setter want him or her to do. An example from the area of auditing will make this clear. If auditors are directed by standard setters to exercise professional judgement and adopt a sceptical attitude in the search for evidence, then it is important that they understand the expressions 'professional judgement', 'sceptical' and 'evidence' in the same way and also in the way intended by standard setters. If not they may do different things in following the requirements of standards and not act as standard setters intend.

The need for conceptual enquiry arises because the investigation of practices in important areas of financial reporting and auditing is conducted *in language*. Language has been described in the legal literature as 'an imperfect instrument which is often imperfectly used' (Twining and Miers, 1976, p. 119). Vagueness is a major problem that a rule-maker faces (Twining and Miers, 1976, p. 122). Observations about the vagueness of language are made in the philosophical literature and have inspired consideration of the issue in the accounting literature (Brown et al., 1993; Penno, 2008). It has been suggested that 'accounting standards give practicing accountants only incomplete direction, necessitating the application of professional judgment' (Brown et al., 1993, p. 275). Conceptual enquiry is needed where there are significant disagreements about what uses of language are correct. This would be demonstrated by the fact that those using the expression in practice give different explanations of the meaning of the expression or use the expression in different ways. This shows that there is no agreed practice in using the expression (Baker and Hacker, 1985, ch. 5). It is not necessarily the case that there are always disagreements about what uses of language are correct (Dennis, 2014, ch. 5). Whether or not expressions are vague is something revealed by a descriptive conceptual enquiry.

Where the descriptive conceptual enquiry identifies meanings that are imprecise or ambiguous, another kind of enquiry seeks to *evaluate* concepts by trying to understand the ends or objectives of the practice in which concepts are developed and considers how the concepts that are used in the practice contribute to meeting these ends or objectives (Dennis, 2008, p. 263). This kind of enquiry assumes, using Wittgenstein's term, a 'naturalistic' view of language. Lyas explains this as the idea that language 'develops over millennia to fit our needs. As something arises that we need to mark off, so we develop, by a linguistic reflex, as it were . . . to mark distinctions that it seemed important to us to make'. It follows that 'to understand the meaning of any term is to understand those human interests, needs and practices in the context of which it arose and into which it fits' (Lyas, 1993, p. 163). One implication of this approach is that concepts are *created* and do not just happen. To understand why a concept has been created, why a certain meaning or rule for the use of the expression has been established, it is important to grasp the 'human interests, needs and practices', interests, in short, which constitute the objectives or desires that prompted its creation. This is the role of an evaluative conceptual enquiry. The idea that concepts are created is a key assumption in the literature on the *social construction of reality*. This has been expressed in the accounting literature as the idea that the concepts we use are shaped by us and not found in nature (Young, 2006, p. 581; Hines, 1988). An evaluative conceptual enquiry seeks to understand the interests and needs that the concept is meant to assist in fulfilling. The reasons for constructing a concept are the same ends or objectives of the practice within which the concepts are developed. These are the kind of thing expressed by objectives statements in the conceptual framework. In the area of auditing, the concepts used in thinking about auditing need to be understood as being useful to achieve the objectives of auditing.

A further kind of conceptual enquiry is a 'prescriptive' conceptual enquiry. The objective of this enquiry is to consider whether, in the light of the findings of a descriptive conceptual enquiry, there is vagueness or ambiguity in the meaning of expressions used in practice. Given the identification of the ends or objectives that underlie the adoption of concepts, it might be better to abandon certain meanings in favour of others and to seek the agreement of users on a preferred meaning of expressions that are used in a practice.

Conceptual enquiries of these kinds are a species of *philosophical* enquiry. As Lyas suggests, 'philosophy, in this sense, is a matter of conceptual analysis, and any discipline which uses concepts, including accounting, will have a philosophical dimension' (Lyas, 1993, p. 156). The same is true of auditing. If philosophical analysis is understood in this way, then it is possible to grasp why a certain kind of thinking about auditing might be referred to as a *philosophy of auditing*. If this is the kind of enquiry envisaged by Mautz and Sharaf, and also by Flint, then it looks reasonable to include the reference to philosophy in the titles of their books. As Lyas observes, 'no discipline worth bothering about can seek to evade such conceptual enquiries'.

They 'constitute the hygiene of the reasoning of a discipline. Without them we are prey to the loose, the ambiguous, the down-right slovenly', and they are 'essential to the well-being of accounting' (Lyas, 1993, p. 156–157). There is little interest in conceptual enquiry in the accounting literature. Perhaps this is another manifestation of the lack of interest in theoretical matters in practical disciplines like accounting and auditing rather than a manifestation of 'slovenly' behaviour. Philosophy is often dismissed as divorced from practice. This attitude arises from a misconception of the nature of philosophy. To illustrate this misconception, Mautz and Sharaf's idea of philosophy will be examined.

MAUTZ AND SHARAF ON PHILOSOPHY

The first chapter of Mautz and Sharaf's book is called 'Toward an Auditing Philosophy'. The first sentence introduces the subject as an attempt to outline the theory of auditing. This suggests that an 'auditing philosophy' is a 'theory of auditing', and the chapter uses these terms interchangeably. Mautz and Sharaf say that their book sets out 'a number of basic assumptions and a body of integrated ideas, the understanding of which will be of direct assistance in the development and practice of the art of auditing' (Mautz and Sharaf, 1961, p. 1). The focus on developing the practice of auditing and to solving the problems in practice suggest that such theorising seeks to change what is done in practice. There should be 'an eagerness to uncover the basic "laws" that govern its organization and activities. As an organized body of knowledge there must be some rhyme and reason to its system . . . there is indeed something incongruous about a profession with no visible support in the form of a comprehensive and integrated structure of theory. We need a philosophy of auditing' (Mautz and Sharaf, 1961, p. 5). Seeking what *ought* to be done rather than to identify what currently *is* being done suggests that they wanted to develop a *normative* theory. Academics have been told that they should not be concerned with theories of this kind (Watts and Zimmerman, 1979; Watts and Zimmerman, 1986). This raises a third problem for a book on auditing theory. Even if such a book is useful and the nature of the subject is understood, should accounting academics be involved in writing it?

Although there are disagreements on the purpose and methods of philosophy, Mautz and Sharaf suggest some basic ideas about the nature of philosophy. It 'gets back to first principles' and provides a 'rationale behind the actions and thoughts which tend to be taken for granted'. It organises knowledge and 'provides a basis whereby social relationships may be moulded and understood'. Philosophy is 'the most general science' and 'the science of first principles of being', a 'science of sciences' (Mautz and Sharaf, 1961, p. 8). There is the 'necessity of an integrated analytic and valuational approach in this study' which involves 'a doctrine concerning the nature of man, desirable goals of human life, principles by which we may guide our conduct' (Mautz and Sharaf, 1961, p. 11). The 'analytic' approach asks 'How do you know?' and 'What do you mean?' Brennan is quoted as saying that 'many problems of philosophy will be solved if inquiry is made into the meaning of the terms of the argument' (Mautz and Sharaf, 1961, p. 12). In auditing 'we have two kinds of problems requiring two different methods of study: problems of fact and problems of value' (Mautz and Sharaf, 1961, p. 12). Finally, 'if a philosophy, an underlying structure of reason and purpose, can be developed, it should provide a basis for determining professional action', and 'the foundation of a philosophy of auditing necessarily starts with the nature of auditing itself' (Mautz and Sharaf, 1961, p. 13).

It is not surprising that the auditing practitioner might feel little need to embark on a philosophy or theory of auditing. These explanations scarcely make it clear what is involved in such a study. It seems to involve a number of different kinds of activity. It is a kind of science, it explains and uncovers laws, it considers assumptions, it involves values and purposes, identifies principles and gives rational explanations and reasons. What kind of 'assumptions' are made, though? Are they assumptions about matters of fact or value? What kind of 'reasoning' or 'rational explanation' is involved? What are 'principles' of auditing? What kind of 'science' is undertaken? What kind of 'laws' are uncovered? It is unrealistic to expect a full consideration of these matters in Mautz and Sharaf's book, located, as it is, in the auditing literature rather than in the literature of philosophy or methods of enquiry. It also has to be remembered that the book was written in 1961 and is thus based on the ideas about philosophy and theory that were prevalent at the time. These ideas have changed since then.

Mautz and Sharaf are correct in their observation that philosophers disagree about the purpose and methods of philosophy. It has been observed that 'among intellectual disciplines, philosophy occupies a unique and peculiar position. There is a wide-spread disagreement about what activities it is legitimate for philosophy to pursue . . . Characterisation of the nature of philosophy is itself a philosophical issue' (Baker and Hacker, 1980, p. 259). Mautz and Sharaf are thus engaged in a philosophical discussion of what is involved in a philosophy of auditing. Bertrand Russell suggested that philosophy is really a branch of science. It seeks to develop theories 'with the maximum explanatory power using the minimum of assumptions (primitive propositions) and theoretical concepts (primitive ideas)' (Baker and Hacker, 1980, p. 261). Mautz and Sharaf characterize it as a science which seeks to uncover basic 'laws'. These laws may be hypotheses that are conjectured and possibly refuted by experience (Popper, 1963). These might be described as 'assumptions' if to conjecture is to assume something to be the case. Russell treated philosophy as 'the most general science, the supreme form of theory construction' (Baker and Hacker 1980, p.259) and saw it as 'the Queen of the Sciences, or perhaps more accurately the foundation of all the sciences' (Baker and Hacker 1980, p. 262).

This view of philosophy was disputed by Wittgenstein. He thought that 'the sciences are totally different in nature and pursued for very different purposes' and that 'consequently science is irrelevant for philosophy' (Baker and Hacker 1980, p. 259). Philosophy is not concerned with explaining empirical phenomena. Instead 'philosophy is a critique of language' (Baker and Hacker 1980, p.268). It considers the meaning of expressions in our language and 'explains nothing, but only describes' (Baker and Hacker 1980, p. 280). It describes the use of expressions in our language in an attempt to dissolve philosophical problems that arise out of a misunderstanding of their meaning. The focus on language, or the 'linguistic turn . . . of most of the important philosophy this century' (Blackburn, 1984, p. 6), is very important. It has been said that 'a philosophy of a discipline such as history, physics, or law seeks not so much to solve historical, physical, or legal questions, as to study the concepts that structure such thinking, and to lay bare their foundations and presuppositions' (Blackburn, 1994, p. 286).

Mautz and Sharaf's description of philosophy is something of a mixture of Russell's and Wittgenstein's ideas. It is some kind of science but also guides the development of a practice. It asks about the meaning of expressions, the kind of conceptual or philosophical enquiry undertaken by Wittgenstein. The result is that their conception of auditing theory and of a philosophy of auditing is muddled. Similar muddles are evident in discussions of the nature of theories in accounting in general. This undermines understanding of what a theory of auditing might be. A descriptive conceptual enquiry into 'accounting theory' reveals this lack of understanding.

A DESCRIPTIVE CONCEPTUAL ENQUIRY INTO 'ACCOUNTING THEORY'

It would be nice to think that looking to theories of accounting would throw light on the nature of auditing theory. One is quickly disabused of this idea when one reads 'the actual state of accounting . . . is not that it has no theories, but that it has a vast number of implicit or partial theories which are not necessarily consistent with each other. As a result, accounting lacks a coherent theory by reference to which established, new and proposed practice may be appraised' (Matthews and Perera, 1996, p. 51). This is the also the conclusion of an influential pamphlet published by the American Accounting Association (AAA). It states that 'a single universally accepted basic accounting theory does not exist at this time. Instead, a multiplicity of theories has been—and continues to be—proposed' (AAA, 1977, p. 1). What follows is a series of definitions of 'theory' followed by a catalogue of '. . . ives' (deductive, inductive, positive, normative, prescriptive, descriptive) that are used as adjectives of different kinds of theories. These do little to assist in the understanding of the nature of theories in accounting.

A descriptive conceptual enquiry into the expression 'accounting theory' looks at the explanations and use of the expression. One review reveals that 'its nature, scope and purpose are vague' (Higson, 2003, p. 34). In other words, there is no agreement on whether it should be applied to certain phenomena and no agreement in the explanations of the meaning of the expression. Even where there is apparent agreement on explanations, the meaning of the expressions used in the explanation may be variously understood. A good example of this is to be found in a definition of 'theory' as 'a set of interrelated constructs (concepts), definitions and propositions that present a systematic view of phenomena by specifying relations among variables with the purpose of explaining and predicting the phenomena' (Kerlinger quoted in Matthews and Perera, 1996, p. 51). It has already been suggested that the idea of a concept is not clearly understood. One way of understanding it is that it is something that gives the meaning of an expression and so is not different from a definition. If this is the meaning, then including 'definitions' in the explanation of the term 'theory' is redundant. If it is not redundant, then 'concept' means something else, but the explanations given by the IASB/FASB are not clear. It has been suggested that theorists may have 'different starting points' in developing theories of accounting and different purposes. These may include explaining and predicting practice, explaining accounting alternatives, providing guidelines for practitioners, justifying practice and explaining 'the impact of accounting data on users' (Higson, 2003, p. 35). A descriptive conceptual enquiry reveals differences in the use of the expression. The suggestion that this may be because those who construct theories have different purposes is the outcome of an evaluative conceptual enquiry that seeks to understand the objectives of developing a concept within the context in which it is constructed. One conclusion that might be drawn from these enquiries is that 'there may even be a question as to whether it is appropriate to talk about "accounting theory"' (Higson, 2003, p. 35). This is, in effect, a conclusion of a prescriptive conceptual enquiry. A moral from enquiries into the concept of theory in the accounting context might be that using the expression 'auditing theory' at all might be counterproductive.

A less radical conclusion would be to accept that 'theory' has different meanings determined by different starting points and purposes and go on to identify the purposes of constructing a concept of theory in a particular context and to explain the expression in light of these purposes. One way in which this approach may be facilitated is the suggestion that theorising is to be understood as an *activity* with certain *purposes*. A theory is to be understood as something that is the *outcome* of this activity. Theorising, as an activity, has objectives whereas theories do not.

THE ACTIVITY OF THEORISING

A review of the different meanings of 'accounting theory' suggests that the problem in understanding this expression is that the *activities* from which theories emerge are various and different from each other. Two different activities, positive and normative theorising, have outcomes that constitute different kinds of theory. These adjectives are often used in relation to theories, but it may be more useful to apply them to different activities of theorising. Unfortunately, these adjectives terms are used with 'various meanings in the literatures of philosophy and accounting' (Archer, 1998, p. 298). In this philosophical literature, 'normative' is used to mean 'value laden', as opposed to 'value free', whereas 'writers on accounting often use it to mean "prescriptive" as opposed to "descriptive" or "predictive"' (Archer, 1998, p. 301). Normative theories prescribe what *ought* to be the case (Hendriksen and van Breda, 1992, p. 17, Matthews and Perera, 1996, p. 58) and tell 'practitioners what accounting procedures they ought to use' (Kam, 1990, p. 491). The objective of accounting theories that are positive or descriptive is 'to *explain* or *predict* accounting practice' (Watts and Zimmerman, 1986, p. 2). One problem with these adjectives is that sometimes they are applied to theories and sometimes to the activity of theorising. It may be clearer if the terms 'normative' and 'positive' are used as adjectives of the *activity* of theorising rather than on their *outcomes*.

Activities or actions, in so far as they are intentional, are done for reasons. The quotes cited earlier suggest that normative theorising prescribes practices rather than describing or predicting and explaining them. Prescribing a practice is a matter of establishing rules that are to be followed by practitioners. Today this is something done by standard setters. Standard setting is an activity that involves deciding to promulgate rules either by deriving the rule from a more general rule using a 'logic of appropriateness' or using practical reasoning or a 'logic of consequences'. Even where a 'logic of appropriateness' is used, the general rules must be decided upon using a 'logic of consequences'. The standard setters thus need to determine what it is they want to achieve in the activity of promulgating a rule. Only then can they look around for rules, general or specific, that will fulfil this desire and make a decision to promulgate such rules. The explanations of normative theorising give rise to another question. Is normative theorising the activity of promulgating rules or the activity of determining something that will assist in the activity of promulgating a rule or does it cover both?

Promulgating a rule is *prescribing* a rule that is to be followed in practice. Prescribing a rule might also be described as determining what practitioners *ought* to do in certain situations. Both prescribing and determining what ought to be the case might be described as *normative activities*. Prescribing rules uses practical reasoning as described earlier. This reasoning includes premises that express what is wanted and might be said to involve *values*. For all of these reasons, promulgating a rule might be described as normative. This appears rather odd, though. It would mean that standard setting is an activity of normative theorising. It would also mean that standards, something that are the outcome of such theorising, are normative theories. It has been pointed out that 'theory consists of the reasoning and logic used to justify, or arrive at, a method, procedure, or rule. It is quite important to understand that rules themselves are not theory; rather, they are, or should be, the result of applied theory' (Hylton quoted in Higson, 2003, p. 22). However, even this looks rather strange. Reasoning is an activity, but theory is not an activity but the outcome of an activity.

Theorising is not an activity of promulgating rules. Academic accounting has been said to be an 'applied science'. It is 'the application of law-statements . . . to practical goals' (Mattessich, 1995, p. 263). This makes it sound as though an 'applied science' is something that includes promulgating rules. If by 'law-statements' is meant statements expressing what is generally wanted from a practice, then academic accounting as an 'applied science' is something that applies these desires in coming to decisions about practice and the rules that govern it. In other words, applied science is an activity of promulgating rules. It would be better to say that a theorising about accounting is something that *helps* in promulgating rules. Theorising determines what is wanted from promulgating rules or determines values. It is not an activity of promulgating rules. Promulgating rules is 'value laden' only in so far as it uses premises that express what is wanted, or values, in practical reasoning to the desire to promulgate rules. Promulgating rules does not determine what is wanted but only uses conclusions about what is wanted in order to determine what rules to promulgate. The distinction between promulgating rules and determining something that will assist in promulgating rules, that is, theorising, is apt to be lost in the rather crude characterisation of normative theorising as being concerned with prescription, with what ought to be the case and with values.

A fuller description of the reasoning to the promulgation of rules clears up confusions and shows that normative theorising is concerned with determining what is wanted from a rule but does not itself prescribe the rules. Given the aforementioned description of conceptual frameworking, it counts as normative theorising in so far as it determines what is wanted from rules. The outcome of this activity is the conceptual framework itself, and as such it is a theory. It is not just concerned with determining what is wanted from financial reporting, though. It also determines certain general rules, such as measurement and recognition rules, that may be used to derive specific rules in accounting standards. It is prescriptive only in the sense that it may determine these general rules. It does not determine the rules that practitioners are to follow. It counts as normative theorising in so far as it is *not* prescribing rules for practice, does not say what practitioners ought to do, but does something that *helps* to determine what rules are to be promulgated.

Promulgating rules requires not just premises expressing what is wanted from rules but also premises that express beliefs about what rules will fulfil the desires in question. This involves predicting the effect of following rules. Discovering the effect of rules uses generalisations derived from another kind of theorising, positive theorising. In the literature on the philosophy of science, predicting involves the use of the 'covering-law model', or 'deductive-nomological' reasoning. On this model an explanation explains a fact by deducing it from a general law. An explanation is thus a *deductive argument*. To be an adequate 'scientific' explanation, there *must be at least one true general law*, and this and the statements of 'initial conditions' must be *empirically true* (Salmon, 1992, p. 17). Hempel claims that there is symmetry between *prediction* and *explanation*. On the 'hypothetico-deductive' method of prediction, an event is predicted from laws and initial conditions if the event is *deduced* from statements of the law and initial conditions. Explaining and predicting phenomena requires laws. Positive theorising concerns itself with the activity of finding such laws. Not all scientific explanations conform to this model, though. Statistical laws are important in science and are not of the deductive-nomological variety (Salmon, 1992, p. 23). The kind of explanations involved using an 'inductive-statistical' pattern of argument 'can be described as an argument to the effect that the event to be explained was to be expected by virtue of certain explanatory facts'. This is not a deductive inference, but the conclusion has 'inductive probability' (Salmon, 1992, p. 25). It is important to realize that finding laws or generalizations in the activity of positive theorising is not, in itself, predicting or explaining events or states of affairs. Positive theorising is an activity that *assists* in explaining and predicting practice. It is not itself an activity of explaining or predicting just as normative theorising is not the activity of promulgating rules but of finding something that assists in the activity of promulgating rules.

Standard setting, involving as it does the promulgation of rules, uses or applies the results of both normative and positive theorising. Reasoning to rules involves general statements about what is wanted in practice, the outcome of normative theorising, as well as general statements about the effect of promulgating a rule to achieve the ends desired, the outcome of positive theorising. Mattessich acknowledges the use of positive theorising in considering means-end relations. He says that standard setting needs a 'purpose-orientation' and must consider means-end relations but admits that 'rarely are such means-end relations discussed explicitly in the accounting literature' (Mattessich, 1995, p. 259). In effect, he is saying that standard setting needs to use the results of both normative and positive theorising. Failure to recognize the importance of using normative theorising in standard setting is due to the impact of the 'positive trend in accounting' with its avoidance of value-laden premises (Mattessich, 1995, p. 260). Standard setters cannot avoid value-laden premises, those derived from normative theorising, in promulgating rules since they are required in the practical reasoning involved in promulgating rules.

Accounting academics can avoid the use of value-laden premises by not getting involved in standard setting. This squeamishness on the part of academics seems unnecessary. Although promulgating rules requires engagement with desires, academics are not required to approve such desires, or make any kind of value judgement in respect of them, in order to undertake such an activity. Mattessich refers to this as the application of a 'conditional-normative accounting methodology', or 'CoNAM' for short (Mattessich, 1995, p. 262). He envisages that the academic presents the practitioner with prescriptions for alternative ends, that is, with 'means-end relations'. He says that *'the very essence of an applied science lies in preparing "in advance" theoretical solutions for an entire battery of alternative objectives'* (Mattessich, 1995, p. 266). The academic is not represented as saying that these ends or objectives are to be wanted but merely saying that if someone wants these ends, then these rules are a means to, or will fulfil, them. Accepting the rules derived is conditional on accepting the ends or desires that are involved in the reasoning to these rules.

Instrumental hypotheses state that if one event occurs, that is, the action M, then another event B, the fulfilment of a desire, will occur. Mattessich refers to instrumental hypotheses as conditionally normative, or a 'conditional prescription' (Mattessich, 1995, p. 266). In the philosophical literature, conditional-normative or conditional prescriptions are called 'hypothetical imperatives'. They appear in the moral philosophy of Kant in contrast with 'categorical imperatives', which are things one *has* to do rather than things where if one wills an end the one wills the means to the end. The logic of such statements is not that clear (Hare, 1952, p. 33). One suggestion is that such imperatives say no more than an indicative statement, that is, to say 'To attain end E, under circumstances C, choose means M' says no more than 'M will bring about E under circumstances C'. Another suggestion is that the imperatives, the end that is willed and the means to the end, 'cancel one another out' (Hare, 1952, p. 37). If the former is the case, then Mattessich's 'conditional-normative' statements are simply positive statements in disguise. The contrast between instrumental hypotheses and positive ones is thus illusory. However, setting them out in the 'conditional-normative' form does emphasis one of the ends of positive theorising. CoNAM is not a research methodology, a method of doing research, but an attempt to apply certain kinds of research method to a context where the objective of the research activity is made explicit. Predicting that following a rule will achieve an end is useful given a context where one wants the end in question. There are plenty of other contexts where using the results of positive theorising to predict that something will happen or explain what has happened is also useful. One might want to predict what will happen if a certain medicine is administered because one wants to find a cure for a disease. If researchers did not want certain ends, promulgating rules or finding cures for diseases, then they would not undertake positive theorising and apply the results. It is not clear why wanting to find cures for diseases is a scientific activity whereas promulgating rules that achieve certain ends is not. Both use the results of positive accounting theorising.

Positive accounting theorising may be useful in the activity of predicting and explaining events. This activity is used in promulgating rules. In so far as promulgating rules involves using the results of positive accounting theorising, it would appear to count as 'scientific activity'. Normative theorising does not have as its objective finding something of use in predicting or explaining events. However, it is misleading to call this activity 'unscientific'. This has the implication that the activity is something that *should* have the objectives of scientific activity but *does not*. It is rather that the activity of doing something that assists in promulgating rules is *not-scientific* in so far as it does not have the objective of providing something that is useful in explaining or predicting events. There is no implication in saying that it is not-scientific that it ought to have these objectives but does not.

If rules are to be promulgated, then it is necessary to determine what is wanted from following these rules. This is the kind of theorising that goes on in constructing conceptual frameworks. What arguments might be put forward against getting involved in such activity? Watts and Zimmerman suggest that the literature referred to as financial accounting theory is predominately prescriptive, that is, it is concerned with 'what the contents of published financial statements should be; that is, how firms should account' (Watts and Zimmerman, 1979, p. 273). As argued earlier, this is not accurate. Theorising is not prescribing rules but determining something that will assist in the activity of prescribing rules. If this is its role, then it is strange that, according to Watts and Zimmerman, it has had little impact on accounting practice or policy. Researchers are 'unable to agree on the objectives of financial statements' and also 'disagree over the methods of deriving the prescriptions from the objectives' (Watts and Zimmerman, 1979, p. 274). It is claimed that these prescriptions do not satisfy all practicing accountants and are not accepted by standard setting bodies. Given that theorising does not itself make prescriptions, this presumably means that the prescriptions that are made using the results of theorising are not accepted.

The explanation for the limited impact on practice given by Watts and Zimmerman is that the setting of accounting standards is the product of political action rather than 'flawless logic or empirical findings'. In this context 'political' is taken to mean 'self-interested considerations or pleadings by preparers and others that may be detrimental to the interests of investors and other users' (Zeff, 2002, p. 43). They predict that theory will be used to 'buttress preconceived notions'. This can be interpreted as meaning that what is wanted in rules of accounting is that they should result in the acceptance of the rules which currently govern practice. This is the sense in which Glover states that the 'normative exercise' of setting standards may have a 'positive orientation' whereby 'observed practice serves as the starting point we try to understand, abstract from, and generalize' (Glover, 2014, p. 18). This is in contrast to a 'normative orientation' that attempts 'to prescribe what practice should be without reference to existing practice' (Glover, 2014, p. 18). Another interpretation is that it means that what is wanted is to fulfil self-interests, which are 'preconceived notions'. These two interpretations are not mutually exclusive. Standard setters may decide what they want on the grounds that they want what is the case as this fulfils their self-interest. Watts and Zimmerman argue that the theorising and theory come afterwards to justify these decisions rather than providing grounds for making the decision in the first place (Watts and Zimmerman, 1979, p. 288). If interests are diverse, there will be no agreement on theory, and different justifications will be given.

If normative theorising involves agreeing on objectives, or what is wanted in financial statements, but no agreement is possible because what is wanted is motivated by self-interest, then, as Watts and Zimmerman claim, no theory of this kind would appear to be acceptable. The lack of agreement on objectives has been evident in the debate about the objectives chapter in the conceptual framework. However, it would appear that there is fairly widespread agreement on the need to provide information that is useful in making decisions. The question of which decision makers are to be taken into account was the subject of debate. There was also argument as to whether the information provided was for the purpose only of resource allocation decisions or whether there was the need for a separate stewardship objective. Other disagreements over what is wanted from financial statements manifested themselves in the debate over qualitative characteristics, that is, on whether reliability or faithful representation was the appropriate characteristic of useful information (Dennis, 2014, pp. 48–53). That there are residual worries over these matters is evident in the Comment Letters on the 2013 Discussion Paper *A Review of the Conceptual Framework for Financial Reporting* (IASB, 2013). Not all practitioners may agree on the prescriptions which follow from the use of the desires expressed by the objectives and qualitative characteristics chapters. However, the IASB appear to think there is sufficient agreement reached following due process for these desires to be used by the IASB in its standard setting activities. It may no longer be the case that those interested in these debates are unable to agree on the objectives.

Is it still the case that theories have little impact on practice given that one of the reasons for this is the previous lack of agreement on objectives? Standard setters such as the IASB, the FASB and the ASB in the UK repeatedly assert that the conceptual framework is used in reasoning towards the promulgation of accounting standards, and members of these boards individually assert that this is the case (see Dennis, 2014, pp. 24–27 for a review of this literature). Scepticism about these claims arises from evidence that statements of objectives, like those expressed in the conceptual framework, have *in the past* had no effect on standard setting decisions and are, hence, *unlikely to do so in the future* (Dopuch and Sunder, 1980, p. 18). The reason for this is that standard setting decisions are political in nature. This means, given Zeff's explanation of 'political', that decisions are made from self-interest. Examples of politics affecting decisions can be given (Zeff, 2002). There is a further argument that even if there is agreement on a conceptual framework and objectives, the framework is itself the product of a political process and is agreed out of self-interest.

The argument is that even if it appears that a conceptual framework is used to make decisions, this merely masks the real reasons for decisions which are made from self-interest. The underlying reason for this idea is the assumption, supposedly derived from economics, that practitioners make decisions that maximize utility, which means that they are egotistic and are motivated only by self-interest (Sterling, 1990, pp. 102–104). Another way of dealing with this problem is to agree that the conceptual framework desires to motivate standard setting decisions but that the conceptual framework itself is accepted out of self-interest and so the assumption of self-interest still applies. Standard setting or constructing a conceptual framework is not something academics should get involved with as they will only end up pandering to the self-interest of those who do get involved. This is the idea behind Watts and Zimmerman's idea that if academics do get involved, they are merely supplying excuses or justifying the choices made by powerful groups on the grounds of self-interest.

One of the problems with the assumption of self-interest is that it is not a scientific hypothesis. It might be assumed that the idea that standard setting decisions and decisions about what is included in conceptual frameworks are political decisions made from self-interest is justified by a careful examination of the evidence of particular decisions that underpin the generalization that all decisions are prompted by self-interest. The reasons given for decisions would need to be examined to see whether they support the decision, in the sense that the decision follows in accordance with some logic from the premises expressing the reasons, and whether the reasons express some kind of self-interest motive. Sterling suggests that the self-reports, like those of standard setters suggesting that they do use the conceptual framework in decision-making, that appear inconsistent with the self-interest motive are actually ignored (Sterling, 1990, p. 106). The claim that all actions are motivated by self-interest is not the product of any kind of scientific activity. He suggests that this claim is not a *scientific* hypothesis because it is not *falsifiable*. It does not meet the test of scientific hypotheses put forward by Popper. It is used to 'test the acceptability of evidence rather than the other way around' (Sterling, 1990, p. 104). The evidence that standard setters claim to be using the conceptual framework to make standard setting decisions is dismissed because the 'hypothesis' states that such decisions *must* be motivated by self-interest.

The 'must' suggests that it has the *necessity* of a law-like statement. The law in question is something like 'all decisions to act are motivated from self-interest'. This has a certain plausibility given the empirical fact that *many* actions appear to be so motivated. It appears a short move from the statement that many actions are self-interested to the statement that all are self-interested. In fact the necessity of such a statement is a move from an empirical generalization, 'all decisions are self-interested/political', to a *definition*, 'all decisions are self-interested/political'. This is an example of a phenomena that Wittgenstein observes that 'what to-day counts as an observed concomitant of a phenomenon will to-morrow be used to define it' (Wittgenstein, 1953, §79). The statement that all decisions are self-interested becomes a definition and not a scientific statement. As such, it has a necessity which derives from the fact that it gives a rule for the meaning of an expression. Its 'necessity' arises from *our determination* to be *bound* by such a rule. As Wittgenstein puts it, 'the emphasis of the "must" corresponds to the inexorability of our attitude towards our techniques of representation (Zettel §299)' (quoted in Baker and Hacker, 1985 p. 269). Because it is a definition, it is not falsifiable. It can, nonetheless, be useful or not useful. It defines what is meant by a decision. Any evidence against it can only be met with the rejection of it as a decision, for all decisions, in so far as they are decisions, are self-interested by *definition*. In fact, nothing can count as evidence against it because it is not a statement that is capable of truth or falsity, hence not something that is falsifiable.

If something appears to be what we want to call a decision but is not done from self-interested motives, then the definition of 'decision' as something that must be self-interested is not useful. Given that something can be a decision that is not self-interested, it makes sense to ask about the desires that are involved in the decision. It also makes sense to ask about what desires *ought* to be involved. This is precisely the question that is asked about standard setting decisions by those who construct conceptual frameworks. The fact that many actions are self-interested means that one needs to be sceptical about avowed desires. This is important if it is thought that self-interest is not a good motive for standard setting decisions. This is, presumably, the case and underlies Watts and Zimmerman's observation that 'individuals . . . do *not* want a normative theory which has their self-interest as its stated objective' (Watts and Zimmerman, 1979, p. 275). A 'normative theory' in this sense is one that states that a particular desire is *good*. One of the objectives of the conceptual framework is not just to identify desires that underpin standard setting decisions but to express approbation of such desires by identifying them as *good*, that is, as something that *should* or *ought* to be desired. In this sense, a normative theory is concerned with ought, as was maintained by certain writers, but this does not indicate a prescription about what *should be done*, a point that was made before in distinguishing normative theorising from promulgating rules, but a prescription about *what ought to be desired* in deciding what to do. It would make *no sense* to reject self-interest as something that ought to be wanted in making decisions if decisions had to be made from such a motive. Those who maintain the necessity of self-interest *cannot* engage in normative theorising that evaluates desires. It is no wonder that Watts and Zimmerman reject normative theorising. However, if the assumption of self-interest in the definition of decision-making is rejected, then it makes sense to undertake empirical investigations of motives and also to pronounce on the desirability of motives identified. Agreement on what should be desired is one of the objectives of the kind of normative theorising that goes on in constructing a conceptual framework. Can there be agreement on what ought to be wanted?

AGREEMENT ON WHAT OUGHT TO BE WANTED

It is important to agree on what is wanted in making prescriptions for a practice and that those affected should agree on the desires that the standard setter is going to use in making standard setting decisions through practical reasoning. What is not necessary is that the *reasons* for wanting these desires be agreed. There is no need for agreement on what might be called the assumptions that underlie what is wanted or, in the terminology that has been used in theorising about practice, on the 'postulates' of practice. Of course, if agreement on what ought to be wanted is not achieved, then it may be that debate about the reasons for wanting something is required. As suggested, this may involve considering the context in which the practice operates and its social and economic context. However, agreement on what ought to be wanted may be achieved without agreement on the postulates or assumptions of the practice that are made.

This possibility undermines the argument of Watts and Zimmerman that agreement on a normative theory for a practice is not possible because it is prompted by self-interest. Even if this is true, the claim that there can be no agreement on postulates or assumptions and hence no agreement on theory is not proven. There is the possibility that there can be agreement on what ought to be wanted even if the reasons for wanting it are different. Different groups may want the same thing, something that they might think to be in their self-interest, where their self-interests are different. 'Due process' might operate to achieve agreement on what is wanted and expressed in a theory without underlying agreement on postulates. Watts and Zimmerman point to the fact that there has been no agreement on what is wanted. In fact, the agreement on an objectives statement in the conceptual framework for financial reporting is evidence that at least *some* agreement is possible. All right, not everyone agrees, and the extent of agreement can be disputed, but the standard setter believes there to be *sufficient* agreement to justify the use of objectives in deciding on prescriptions.

Part of the scepticism about the objectives of, the expression of what is wanted from, a practice is due to a misconception of the nature of the desires in the practice. If these are conceived as universal desires, that is, as expressing what is to be wanted in all circumstances where the desires are used to make prescriptions and where the prescriptions have to be believed to fulfil these desire in all cases where they are followed, then it is difficult to think that agreement on such desires is possible. However, on an alternative conception, they may only express what is generally wanted. Judgement may be required in making decisions about prescriptions in practical reasoning by weighing them up. Agreement on what is generally wanted may not be so daunting. Before agreeing on them, it is not necessary to deduce *all* the consequences of wanting them and then to determine that one does, indeed, want them. One does not have the prospect of continually revising them if it turns out that something not wanted is deduced from them. Instead, one identifies certain things that are generally wanted and uses these to determine the prescriptions that will, generally, but not necessarily universally, fulfil them.

This throws a new light on normative theorising. It is, as suggested earlier, doing something that will assist in making decisions. It identifies what should or ought to be wanted in deciding actions. It is not using these desires to prescribe what should or ought to be done. These desires are used in practical reasoning to decisions about setting standards, that is, in prescribing rules. An auditing theory, in the sense of a normative theory as explained earlier, is one that expresses what ought to be wanted in the practice of auditing, that is, what desires ought to appear in premises of practical reasoning to decisions about what rules will govern the practice of auditing. How can academics contribute to the activity of normative theorising?

There is some distaste in the thought that academics should say what ought to be wanted. This is part of the general idea that academics, who should be involved in scientific activity, should not be dictating what ought to be the case. Their preserve is supposed to be the 'is', not the 'ought'. This needs to be clearly understood. It might mean that academics should not prescribe rules that govern practice. This might be readily accepted given that accounting is an institutional practice where it is the role of standard setters to prescribe rules. It might also mean that academics should not be involved in deciding what ought to be wanted by standard setters in deciding on the rules of practice. These are obviously value judgements, in the sense of judging values or, as it might also be expressed, desires. This is something the academic is not supposed to do. In other words, 'the academic . . . must not impose any objective upon the user' (Mattessich, 1995, p. 269). It is the 'users', the standard setters, who must decide what they ought to want, that is, what desires they will argue from in deciding on the rules for practice. If academics are proscribed from imposing objectives, what role can they have in conceptual frameworking?

THE ROLE OF ACADEMICS IN CONSTRUCTING CONCEPTUAL FRAMEWORKS OR NORMATIVE THEORIES

If scientific theorising is doing something that is useful in predicting and explaining events or states of affairs, then it has to be admitted that deciding what ought to be wanted from a practice is not scientific theorising. If accounting academics should only be involved in scientific theorising, then they have no business deciding what ought to be wanted from a practice, that is, getting involved in 'unscientific musings'. When Watts and

Zimmerman published their 'market for excuses' paper and their book on positive accounting theory, this spawned a considerable literature on the question of what being scientific amounts to (Laughlin, 2007). This is really a literature that considers the definition of 'science' or 'scientific theorising'. If language is 'naturalistic', as explained earlier, it is important to understand what is at stake with definitions and what 'human interests, needs and practices' prompt their creation. It is interesting to observe that if definitions prescribe rules for the use of expressions, then Watts and Zimmerman's definition of 'scientific theorising' is prescriptive. They would claim that it is merely describing the use of the term. This use is disputed by Laughlin. The suspicion, though, is that they go beyond description to prescription and that their musings are 'unscientific' in their proscribed sense.

It is interesting to reflect on the 'human interests' that underlie their decision to define 'scientific theorising' as they do. Under the influence of developments in finance and economics and the science of decision after the Second World War, the importance of undertaking scientific activity and the attempt to connect standard setting with science was recognized in the 1960s (Watts and Zimmerman, 1986, p. 5; Young, 2006, pp. 584–586). Accounting research shifted towards empirical research with its emphasis on predicting and explaining by the 1980s. This was fuelled by funding by the Ford Foundation and Carnegie Corporation and the availability of computer databases to support such research (Zeff, 2014, p. 44). Since Watts and Zimmerman's 1979 paper, 'a particular school of positive accounting theory was born . . . almost everything published in the leading accounting journals since that time can be characterized as positive accounting research' (Glover, 2014, p. 20). This has also been influential in countries developing the accounting discipline, although there are some signs of the re-appearance of a 'normative streak' in consideration of fair value (Macve, 2014, p. 34). As Watts and Zimmerman observe, 'researchers have non-pecuniary incentives to be well-known, and this reputation is rewarded by a higher salary and a plenitude of research funds' (Watts and Zimmerman, 1979, p. 286). Given the importance of publication to researchers in the U.S. and the importance of funding, it is perhaps not surprising that accounting researchers, and PhD students (Macve, 2014, p. 34), have 'followed the money' and gone the route of scientific theorising understood along the lines of Positive Accounting Theory (PAT). This may also account for the desire to define 'scientific theorising' only to include research of the PAT variety and exclude other kinds of research from the battlefield of funding.

If it is accepted that normative theorising is doing something that helps in determining what ought to be wanted from a rule, what arguments, other than those which depend upon a particular definition of 'scientific theorising', are there to say that accounting academics should not get involved in such theorising? A criticism that has been directed against normative theorising is it is 'subjective, hence "unscientific"', because 'value judgements, underlying every normative theory, are neither objective nor accessible to empirical refutation or verification' (Mattessich, 1995, p. 264). It can be readily agreed that deciding what ought to be wanted in standard setting is not accessible to empirical refutation or verification since expressing what is wanted is not expressing a proposition that is either true or false. Saying 'I want X' or 'I ought to want X' is not reporting an empirical proposition such as 'The proposition "I want X" is true' or 'It is true that I want X' but *expresses* a desire. This point is often made about moral judgements. They do not report autobiographical remarks (Williams, 1972, p. 30). If they did, then there would be no moral disagreements, for all that would be said by the parties to a disagreement is that one party had one attitude and another had a different one. The correct response to such a statement is not 'Are you really sure you want it?' but 'Why do you want it?', that is, one is not doubting that someone does want something, but one is enquiring as to the reasons for the desire, which one may, or may not, take issue with. Given that such statements do not express propositions that are true or false, they are not subject to empirical refutation or verification but can be questioned to identify reasons.

The idea that statements expressing such desires are not objective might be interpreted as saying that such statements are not capable of truth or falsity but might also be interpreted as saying that there are no reasons that can be given for wanting what is desired. Although the former can be readily agreed, the latter is not generally the case. Indeed, if the outcome of normative theorising is a statement 'I ought to want X', this has the implication not only that one does want X, that it expresses one's desire, but that there are *reasons* for wanting it. Implying that a desire is *subjective*, that is, not objective, may appear to have the implication that there can be no argument against it and that it is simply wanted, for no reason. The view that 'philosophers have taught that anything can be an object of desire; so there is no need for me to characterize these objects as somehow desirable; it merely so happens that I want them' has been dismissed as 'fair nonsense' (Anscombe, 1957, §37). This might be described as the view that desires are subjective. It is part of the meaning of 'want' that either reasons can be given or what is desired has a 'desirability characterisation', that is, something that 'gives a final answer to the series of "What for?" questions that arise about an action' (Anscombe, 1957, §38). What is desired, that which is used to explain any action for which reasons are given, can be understood as *desirable*. It is important to realize that this does not imply that everyone has to agree that it is, in fact, desirable, but rather than the desire is something that can be understood as desirable. Characterising some things as 'suitable' or 'pleasant' involves using terms that characterize what they apply to as desirable. Interestingly, the term 'should' is also a term that has the consequence that 'no further questions "what for?", relating to the characteristic so occurring in a premise, require any answer' (Anscombe, 1957, §37). A similar word 'ought' might also be used, but if so it is important to realize that it has no connotation of *moral* approbation (Anscombe, 1957, §38).

This throws an interesting light on the objective of normative theorising. Such theorising is designed to identify what ought to be wanted in a practice, that is, something that is characterized as desirable and which can be used as the *final answer* in a series of questions about the actions of those who determine rules for practice, that is, in the context of accounting practice, standard setting actions. That there is a final answer does not require that it be an answer that everyone will agree with, and, therefore, the search for what ought to be wanted in a practice is not the search for something that everyone, without exception, will agree with. Having said that, it does not follow that what is required is that everyone set out what they want and then some poll is taken where the desires of the majority or of the most powerful are then taken as the final answer. The point is that in arriving at a desire with the requisite desirability characterisation questions may be asked of the candidates, 'Why do you want X?' or 'Why do you think you ought to want X?', in order to arrive at the final answer. Questions like this are asked precisely because what is expressed as something to be wanted in determining a practice may not appear to everyone as having a desirability characterisation. The question of why this is wanted is naturally asked in such circumstances.

The kind of practical reasoning involved in standard setting or in reasoning to prescriptions is often portrayed as reasoning to actions rather than to desires. In fact, practical reasoning is reasoning from what is wanted to a *desire to act* in a way that is believed to achieve these desires. It is thus reasoning from desires to desires. If one wants to act, then the action results *causally* from this desire. What makes it *practical* is that it is eventually used to reason to a desire to act. What is wanted is not wanted idly. The desire is to *do something* that will have a certain result. In financial reporting the decision-usefulness approach starts with the desire to provide information that is useful to users. Providing information is an action that has the result that something that is useful to users is provided. If one asks the question of the premise that expresses a desire to act 'Why?', the answer mentions another desire and a belief that an action which meets this other desire will result in an action that meets the original desire. In conceptual frameworks for financial reporting, the reasoning is usually presented the other way around. It starts with a desire to 'provide financial information about the reporting entity that is useful to existing and potential investors, lenders and other creditors in making decisions about providing resources to the entity' (IASB, 2010, §OB2). There then follows beliefs that decisions about providing resources involve decisions about 'buying, selling or holding equity and debt instruments, and providing or settling loans and other forms of credit'. To make these decisions, information is needed 'to help them assess the prospects for future net cash inflows to an entity' (IASB, 2010, §OB3). A further belief states that this information is 'about the resources of the entity, claims against the entity, and how efficiently and effectively the entity's management and governing board have discharged their responsibilities to use the entity's resources' (IASB, 2010, §OB4). From this a desire is derived for 'general purpose financial reports' to 'provide information about the financial position of a reporting entity, which is information about the entity's economic resources and the claims against the reporting entity' (IASB, 2010, §OB12). This is an example of practical reasoning, in this case from the objectives statement to further desires for statements to contain certain information. It is also possible to reason in reverse by starting with a desire and asking the question 'Why do you want X?' So, if what is wanted is to provide information about the financial position and the question 'Why?' is asked, the answer is that what is wanted is information about resources and claims and that one believes that providing information about the financial position will fulfil this desire. If one asks why one wants information about resources and claims, then the answer is that one wants information that is useful to users in making decisions about providing resources to the entity and that one believes that information about the financial position will fulfil this desire. At this point no further questions may be asked because wanting information that is useful to users in making certain decisions has a desirability characterisation. It forestalls any further questioning. Normative theorising comes to an end with the identification of a desire with a desirability characterisation or of something that ought to be wanted.

Asking the question 'Why?' is something that the accounting academic is capable of doing. Although the objective of the questioning is to identify something that ought to be wanted, in the sense of a desire with a desirability characterisation, it does not follow that the academic is making a value judgement that such desires are desirable. They may well have a view on this, but it is not essential for them to air such a view. The point of their question is to elicit the reasons for others, the standard setter or interested parties in financial reporting, wanting particular ends or objectives or desires with a desirability characterisation. This assists in the identification of such desires, which are then to form the basis of promulgating rules. This is not necessarily directly from the desires identified, but these may need further reasoning, of the kind outlined in the conceptual framework, to identify further desires which do then form the premises in practical reasoning to standard setting decisions. These desires may be at some remove from the initial statements of objectives or desires in the conceptual framework. The reasoning in the conceptual framework for financial reporting can be represented as moving forward from the objectives to other statements in the framework. It uses practical reasoning to do so. The reasoning can also be used in arguing backward from desires for a practice to other desires in order to reach more 'fundamental' desires that have a desirability characterisation, which is also something the academic can explore.

There is another way in which the academic can make a contribution to normative theorising. The standard setter or other interested parties need to know what they want in a practice and so can be led to recognize these fundamental desires as something that underpins their decision-making. This raises the question of whether one always knows what one wants until one has seen what follows from such desires in the process of practical reasoning. This is particularly problematic where the kind of desires expressed in objectives statements of a practice, such as those in chapter 1 of *The Conceptual Framework for Financial Reporting*, are conceived as *universal* desires that represent something that is *always wanted* and are used in *deducing* standard setting decisions (Dennis, 2014, pp. 39–47). There is a similar assumption of universalism and deductive reasoning in some systems of moral reasoning. An example from the area of financial reporting would be where the desire for information that has the qualitative characteristics of reliability is taken to be something that is always wanted in standard setting decisions. What happens if the standard setter decides, on other grounds or for other reasons, that he or she wants information in financial statements based on fair values? A problem arises that such information may not always be reliable. If the decision is taken that some of the elements in financial statements are to be shown at fair value, this would be either a standard setting decision or a decision about a general rule of measurement, then the universal desire premise that is supposed to be used in deductive reasoning to standard setting decisions needs to be rejected. If other principles are used to deduce a conclusion that fair value is to be used, then the principle of wanting information that is reliable has to be rejected. It is arguable that just this kind of 'reverse engineering' has actually occurred in the move away from reliability to faithful representation in the conceptual framework. An alternative non-deductive view of the use of principles in the conceptual framework may also be adopted. If so, then what is wanted is not universally desired but only *wanted in general*, and it is possible that, on occasion, it will not be wanted. Reasoning from desires to decisions is not deductive with desires of this kind (Dennis, 2014, pp. 46–55). There may still be a reconsideration of what is generally wanted in the light of the consequences of wanting it, if sufficient examples of instances where what is supposed to be generally wanted is not, in fact, wanted. With universal desires one counter-instance of not wanting the consequence is enough for the rejection of the desire, but with general desires a number of counter-instances are required, the precise number being a matter of judgement. The academic has a role in pointing out the consequences of wanting certain things by showing what standard setting decisions may follow from such desires. The standard setter or interested parties can then consider whether they really want such things, whether universally or generally.

A similar process of exploring reasons is evident in the area of morality. It was suggested that in giving a moral judgement one is not simply reporting attitudes that one may have to certain events. There is the assumption that some argument might be advanced in support of a moral judgement and not just an impasse where one person states he or she has an attitude and another person states that he or she has a different attitude. If two people agree that something is wrong, there is little incentive to ask for justification of their point of view, although this could be done. There is more point where there is disagreement. Take an example where one person says, 'Killing people is always wrong', and another disagrees by saying, 'Killing people is sometimes right'. It would not be expected that the two would simply leave it at the observation that 'he has an attitude that killing people is always wrong, and I have an attitude that says that killing people is sometimes right, and so we have different attitudes'. Moral judgements are simply statements of attitude, questions of fact, and, in fact, we have different attitudes. It is more likely that these opposing attitudes would give rise to the thought that some argument was required and that reasons for these attitudes should be explored. The point of this is to see whether the two parties can reach some agreement on whether killing is always wrong or may, in some circumstances, be right. This argument might proceed by taking one of the attitudes and exploring whether it would be acceptable in various circumstances. The person who thinks killing is sometimes justified might give an example where someone was threatening to kill your child and the only way to save your child's life would be by killing this other person. You might conclude that it was right to kill the person threatening to kill your child. Underlying this judgement is an attitude that it is right to protect your child's life. Now there is a clash of attitudes. It is wrong to kill, but it is right to protect your child's life, therefore killing people is sometimes right if this is the only way to save your child. In presenting the argument in this way, the person who says that killing is always wrong is now supposed to see that because of something else that may be wanted, this attitude does not really express his or her moral position. The person might agree that in the circumstances, because of his or her belief that protecting the child is right, it may be that killing someone is also right. It may be that the person changing his or her point of view may wish to rephrase his or her attitude by saying, 'Killing people is always wrong except where it is necessary in order to protect the life of one's child'. This may give rise to further argument. What if your child was Hitler and, somehow, you know what he will become? Would it be right to protect your child's life in these circumstances? This illustrates the fact that it is difficult to devise a moral principle of the kind that includes the word 'always' and that is, hence, universal in that it applies in all of the circumstances covered by the principle in question. Maybe the principle includes the phrase 'generally' rather than always. One leaves it open that there may be circumstances where it will not apply, and judgement has to be exercised to determine whether certain circumstances constitute an exception or not. The important point is to realize that there may be conflicting principles leading to conflicting moral judgements, and it is important to explore such conflicts in determining the principles that will be accepted. In undertaking argument it is hoped that the parties may be able to reach an agreement on a principle that incorporates circumstances where conflict appears possible.

The process by which agreement is reached on what is wanted in a practice has been characterized, using a term invented by Rawls (1999), as 'reflective equilibrium'. The context in which the conceptual framework was developed was one where there was an emphasis on the 'scientific' approach to accounting theorising as noted earlier. An important account of the scientific method at this time was the account of science given by Popper, who conceived of it as a process of conjecturing hypotheses which were then subject to empirical testing by deducing consequences which were then tested with a view to possible refutation. These conjectures related to matters of fact and involved generalizations about what was the case. The first mistake that was made in applying this kind of idea to standard setting, or indeed any activity of prescribing rules, is that such activities do not proceed from generalizations about facts alone. They also require statements that express what is wanted from the rules prescribed. Theories that are used in the activity of standard setting do not identifying generalisations of fact that are used to derive empirical consequences that are then to be tested to see if they can be falsified. The reasoning to decisions about rules in standards requires that the standard setter starts with premises that express what is universally or generally wanted or express a rule to do something that is universally or generally to be followed. From these premises and beliefs about the effect of a prospective rule a desire to prescribe a particular rule in a standard is derived. If one does not really want the rule derived, then, assuming the belief premise is correct, what is 'falsified' is a desire rather than a generalization about matters of fact. The expression 'falsified' is not really appropriate to statements of this kind, for statements of desires are not statements that are capable of truth or falsity. It would be better to say that if a consequence is derived from the statement of a universal desire that is not wanted, then the desire is shown to be *unacceptable* rather than falsified. 'Unacceptable' merely means that it is not really wanted. The analogy with moral reasoning gets closer to what is really going on.

One system of moral reasoning that follows a Kantian model is that of Hare (1952). He recognises that moral principles are always capable of being reformulated in light of the conclusions about what action is wanted that are derived from the principle. He interprets the derivation as a matter of deduction of the consequences from the principle. It is suggested that 'we are always setting precedents for ourselves . . . decision and principles interact throughout the whole field . . . suppose that we have a principle to act in a certain way in certain circumstances. Suppose then that we find ourselves in certain circumstances which fall under the principle, but which have certain other peculiar features, not met before, which make us ask 'Is the principle really intended to cover cases like this, or is it incompletely specified—is there here a case belonging to a class which should be treated as exceptions?' Our answer to this question will be a decision, but a decision of principle . . . If we decide that this should be an exception, we thereby modify the principle by laying down an exception to it' (Hare, 1952, p. 65).

If we decide that we do not actually want what is supposed to be generally desired because the consequences that may be deduced from it are not acceptable, then we change the 'principle'.

Rawls's idea of 'reflective equilibrium' is meant to overcome the problem of *provisionality*. One begins by identifying moral judgements, or what might be called 'intuitions' or an 'original position', and then tries to construct 'principles' that provide the best fit with these judgements. The judgements or intuitions themselves may be modified until they reach some kind of 'equilibrium', or 'reflective equilibrium'. This idea has found favour in the accounting literature in understanding the role of the conceptual framework. Power suggests that 'the function of such a framework for financial accounting is loosely analogous to the process of finding Rawls's 'reflective equilibrium'. He suggests that a conceptual framework 'is not an ultimate foundation in any classical sense but a point of reference in the network of accounting standards and practices that serves to "organize" thinking about them' (Power, 1993, p. 53). The *process* of working out what general desires one really wants appears to be one of 'trial and error'. This is characterized, following Rawls, as 'forward' and 'backward' arguments that correspond to certain theories of accounting (Power, 1993, p. 56). It might be more accurate to say that they correspond to various activities involved in theorising about accounting. As described earlier, a conceptual framework is meant to be used to derive standard setting decisions, that is, desires for certain rules to be promulgated. This might be described as a 'forward' argument. However, if the conclusion derived in the argument is not really wanted, then the general desires from which it is derived are revised. This might be described as the 'backward' argument or as 'reverse engineering'. What is really happening in this process is that one starts with something desired and then looks for the reasons why this is wanted by considering the practical reasoning that concludes with the desire in question. If one does not want what is concluded, then one may wish to reject the premises that constitute reasons for wanting it. This suggests that theorising about what is wanted from a practice cannot be divorced from considering what decisions about setting standards for a practice follow from accepting such desires.

This process needs to be fleshed out with more detail about the nature of the arguments backward and forward and with a clear grasp of the components in the equilibrium. Practical reasoning, unlike deductive reasoning, is not 'erosion-proof'. Being 'erosion-proof' means that 'if new premises are added to an argument . . . the argument remains valid' (Salmon, 1992, p. 11). Although this is true of deductive reasoning, it is not true of practical reasoning. The introduction of premises expressing other desires can undermine practical reasoning from one desire to another. What is going on with this kind of argument is the process of 'reflective equilibrium'. Desires are assumed and the consequences of wanting something drawn out. It may be found that the conclusion is something that is not wanted. If the argument is taken as deductive, the original desire is modified. If the argument is not deductive but an instance of practical reasoning, the original desire is not changed, it is still *generally* wanted, but the new desire results in the original conclusion being rejected. 'Reverse engineering' in deductive reasoning results in a change in the original desire. In practical reasoning it results in the recognition of other desires that are important in an argument, and there is a requirement to exercise judgement in drawing conclusions from the desires identified. As suggested, it is important to clarify whether the statements of desire are meant to be taken as universal and used in deductive reasoning, that is, they are always to be wanted, or merely genera and used in practical reasoning.

This suggests that the process of theorising is the process of 'forward' and 'backward' argument towards a 'reflective equilibrium'. This process relies on using the desires assumed and then drawing out consequences by considering beliefs about what will achieve the desired end. It also involves going backward and drawing out the reasons for wanting what is assumed. The results of this process are expressed in the 'theory', the outcome of the process. A conceptual framework is a theory of this kind. A number of activities in which the academic can get involved within the overall activity of normative theorising have now been identified.

THE ACTIVITY OF NORMATIVE THEORISING

Asking the question of what is involved in the activity of normative theorising is another way of asking the question of what kind of enquiries are undertaken in such theorising. It was suggested that the overall objective of such an activity was to determine something that will assist in promulgating rules. Given that promulgating rules is an action and is the outcome of a decision to act and that this involves practical reasoning from a desire or objective to a desire to act, then one activity involved in normative theorising is to determine what is wanted in a practice. This means starting from some desire that has a desirability characterisation. This characterizes the desire as something that ought to be wanted and constitutes the starting point in practical reasoning to other desires and ultimately to the desire to promulgate rules in standards that determine practice. The activities involved in normative theorising of the kind that is useful in promulgating rules that determine a practice are:

- Identifying the objectives of the practice, or what is desired in the practice and, hence, of the rules that determine the practice;
- Identifying the objectives in backward argument to consider why these desires are wanted, i.e. reasons for wanting, with a view to arriving at something that is wanted that has a desirability characterisation; this involves considering other desires that may be wanted and beliefs that wanting something else will fulfil these objectives;

- Using these objectives in forward argument to determine the consequences of wanting these objectives, and beliefs about how these objectives are to be fulfilled, to determine whether they are really wanted;
- Determining what it *means* to want something (conceptual enquiry) so that what is involved in objectives or desires is understood;
- Possibly prescribing general rules that are to be followed that achieve the objectives identified where following these rules are believed to achieve what is wanted as expressed in the objectives.

The outcome of these activities constitutes a normative theory of the practice. The nature of auditing theory in this book, what is meant by the expression 'auditing theory', can now be understood.

WHAT IS MEANT BY 'AUDITING THEORY' IN THIS BOOK

The kind of theory that is investigated in this book is the kind of normative theory expressed in a conceptual framework. Conceptual frameworking is normative theorising that includes the activities listed in this chapter. The overall aim of such a framework is to express things that are useful in making standard setting decisions that establish rules for the practice. This involves practice reasoning from premises derived from the conceptual framework to decisions to promulgate rules in standards. The experience of constructing a conceptual framework for financial reporting can be used as a template for normative theorising relating to the practice of auditing. This template, and the nature of theorising and theories set out here, is used to construct a normative auditing theory. This might also be called a conceptual framework for auditing if the nature of such a framework is understood as set out in this chapter. This proviso is important because, as was stated at the beginning of this chapter, the nature of conceptual frameworks is not well understood.

This is the kind of auditing theory that will be explored in this book. If a practice is a rule-governed activity, then to establish the practice the rules that govern the practice must be determined. Given that auditing is an institutional practice, in the sense explained, these rules are determined by standard setters. They need a theory that identifies what is wanted from the practice and that can be used to look for rules that will fulfil what is wanted. Standard setting decisions proceed from premises that express what is *generally* wanted from a practice. Rules apply to situations generally, and so what is wanted must also be wanted generally, at least, on the various occasions when the rule is to be followed. Theories include statements with the requisite generality. The kind of theory envisaged in this book expresses generalisations, but not of facts, as with scientific theories, but of what is desired. An auditing theory of the kind in this book thus starts with identifying objectives of the practice in order to determine what is wanted, that is, desires that have a desirability characterisation. Such a theory underpins standard setting decisions but also enables practitioners to understand the reasons why standard setters promulgate the standards that they do. Understanding the role of such a theory is important if practitioners are to have input into the construction of such a theory through something equivalent to a conceptual framework for auditing. A grasp of such a theory will also assist them in the due process involved in setting standards and will assist them in commenting upon proposed standards.

This chapter also illustrates why an auditing theory has sometimes been referred to as a philosophy of auditing. 'Philosophy' is understood in this book as a form of conceptual enquiry. The aim of such an activity is to consider the meaning of expressions. The importance of conceptual enquiry has been illustrated in this chapter. It was suggested at the outset that the nature of an auditing theory was not clearly understood. This means that the expression 'auditing theory' is vague and not clearly explained. This chapter has undertaken a conceptual enquiry into the meaning of this expression in order to clarify what the book is about. The lack of clarity in the meaning of expressions has been commented upon a number of times in this chapter. The meaning of 'normative theorising', 'conceptual framework', 'concepts', 'philosophy' and 'scientific activity' have all been shown to require conceptual enquiry in order to clarify the meaning of these expressions. It has been shown that the explanations of these expressions are sometimes explained by using expressions that themselves stand in need of explanation. Power's observation that little attention has been given to conceptual considerations in financial reporting can be generalized to the discussion of theoretical matters in accounting, including auditing. Theoretical discussion of auditing stands in need of conceptual enquiry or a philosophy of auditing. This kind of enquiry is needed in the development of an auditing theory itself. It is likely that similar enquiries will be required in developing auditing theory. This book could well have included 'philosophy of auditing' in the title. However, it is important to grasp that an auditing theory is not restricted to conceptual enquiry. The identification of what is wanted from the practice of auditing, looking for possible general rules of auditing, is not an exercise in philosophical enquiry, understood in the sense of conceptual enquiry. An auditing theory involves more than a philosophy of auditing. The rest of this book will develop an auditing theory that considers what is wanted from the practice of auditing and examines the concepts used in talking about auditing practices.

SUMMARY

The nature of the kind of auditing theory explored in this book is examined. Conceptual frameworks are used by standard setters to determine the practices of accounting. A practice is an activity of following rules, and standard setters use such frameworks in making rational decisions about which rules in standards they wish to promulgate. Rational decisions are made using practical reasoning. This starts with premises that express what is wanted from the practice and considers beliefs about what rules, if followed, will fulfil these desires. A conclusion expressing a desire to promulgate these rules is derived. The idea of a concept expressed in conceptual frameworks is explored. Concepts in the philosophical literature which are equated with the meanings of words and conceptual enquiries explore the meaning of expressions used in a practice. A conceptual enquiry is a species of philosophical enquiry. Without such enquiries the expressions used in making decisions about promulgating rules and the rules themselves may be differently understood. The consequence is a lack of agreement about standard setting decisions that are made. A conceptual enquiry is undertaken into the meaning of 'accounting theory'. Theorising, in this book, is understood as something that will assist in promulgating rules. This is normative theorising and it involves agreeing on what is wanted in making prescriptions or rules for a practice. The distaste of accounting academics for such theorising is examined. The desires identified by such theorising have a desirability characterisation. Getting agreement about what is wanted and undertaking conceptual enquiry are two activities involved in the kind of auditing theory considered in this book. This provides some justification for thinking about this kind of theory as a conceptual framework for auditing and for the characterisation of the book as some kind of philosophy of auditing.

REFERENCES

AAA (1977) *Statement on Accounting Theory and Theory Acceptance.* Evanston, Ill.: AAA.

Anscombe, G.E.M. (1957) *Intention.* Oxford: Basil Blackwell.

Archer, S. (1993) 'On the Methodology of Constructing a Conceptual Framework for Financial Accounting' in M. Mumford and K. Peasnell (eds.) *Philosophical Perspectives on Accounting.* London: Routledge.

Archer, S. (1998), 'Mattessich's Critique of Accounting: A review article', *Accounting and Business Research*, Vol. 28 (3), pp. 297–316.

ASB (1999) *Statement of Principles for Financial Reporting.* London: ASB.

Baker, G. & Hacker, P. (1980) *Wittgenstein Meaning and Understanding.* Oxford: Blackwell.

Baker, G. & Hacker, P. (1985) *Wittgenstein Rules, Grammar and Necessity.* Oxford: Blackwell.

Blackburn, S. (1984) *Spreading the Word.* Oxford: Clarendon Press.

Blackburn, S. (1994) *The Oxford Dictionary of Philosophy.* Oxford: Oxford University Press.

Brown, G.A., Collins, R. & Thornton, D.B. (1993) 'Professional judgment and accounting standards', *Accounting, Organizations and Society*, Vol. 18 (4), pp. 275–289.

Craig, E., ed. (2005) *The Shorter Routledge Encyclopedia of Philosophy.* New York: Routledge.

Davidson, D. (1980) 'Actions, Reasons and Causes' in *Essays on Actions and Events*. Oxford: Oxford University Press.

Dennis, I. (2006) *A Philosophical Investigation into the Conceptual Framework for Accounting*. PhD Thesis, London School of Economics, University of London. Accessible at: http://ethos.bl.uk/OrderDetails.do?did=1&uin=uk. bl.ethos.433646 [Accessed 13 January 2015].

Dennis, I. (2008) 'A conceptual enquiry into the concept of a "principles-based" accounting standard', *British Accounting Review*, Vol. 40 (3), pp. 260–71.

Dennis, I. (2010a) ' "Clarity" begins at home: An examination of the conceptual underpinnings of the IAASB's Clarity Project', *International Journal of Auditing*, Vol. 14 (3), pp. 294–319.

Dennis, I. (2010b) 'What do you expect? A reconfiguration of the Audit Expectations Gap', *International Journal of Auditing*, Vol. 14 (2), pp. 130–146.

Dennis, I. (2014) *The Nature of Accounting Regulation*. New York: Routledge.

Dopuch, N. & Sunder, S. (1980) 'FASB's Statements on Objectives and Elements of Financial Accounting: A review', *Accounting Review*, Vol. 55 (1), pp. 1–21.

FASB (2010) *Statement of Financial Accounting Concepts No.8 Conceptual Framework for Financial Reporting, Chapter 1. The objective of general purpose financial reporting, and Chapter 3. Qualitative characteristics of useful financial information*. Norwalk, Conn.: FASB. Accessible at: http://www.fasb.org/resources/ccurl/515/412/Concepts%20Statement%20No%208.pdf [Accessed 13 January 2015].

FASB/IASB (2005) *Revisiting the Concepts: A New Conceptual Framework Project*. Norwalk, Conn.: FASB. Accessible at: http://www.ifrs.org/NR/rdonlyres/E5B8A298-6179-4FAA-985A-42416EB597F5/0/8_1455_0602sob04a.pdf [Accessed 12 January 2012].

Flint, D. (1988) *Philosophy and Principles of Auditing*. Basingstoke, UK: Macmillan Education.

Glover, J. (2014) 'Have academic accountants and financial accounting standard setters traded places?' *AEL: A Convivium*, Vol. 4 (1), pp. 17–26.

Gray, I. & Manson, S. (2011) *The Audit Process*. 5th edn. London: South-Western Cengage Learning.

Hare, R.M. (1952) *The Language of Morals*. Oxford: Oxford University Press.

Hendriksen, E.S. & van Breda, M.F. (1992) *Accounting Theory*. 5th edn. Homewood, Ill.: Richard D. Irwin.

Higson, A. (2003) *Corporate Financial Reporting: Theory & Practice*. London: SAGE Publications.

Hines, R. (1988) 'Financial accounting: In communicating reality, we construct reality', *Accounting, Organizations and Society*, Vol. 13 (3), pp. 251–261.

IAASB (2005) *International Framework for Assurance Engagements*. New York: International Federation of Accountants.

IASB (2010) *The Conceptual Framework for Financial Reporting*. London: IASB.

IASB (2013) *A Review of the Conceptual Framework for Financial Reporting*. London: IASB.

Kam, V. (1990) *Accounting Theory*. New York: John Wiley & Sons.

Laughlin, R. (2007) 'Critical reflections on research approaches, accounting regulation and the regulation of accounting', *British Accounting Review*, Vol. 39, pp. 271–281.

Lee, T. (1993) *Corporate Audit Theory*. London: Chapman and Hall.

Lyas, C. (1993) 'Accounting and Language' in M. Mumford and K. Peasnell (eds.) *Philosophical Perspectives on Accounting*. London: Routledge.

Macve, R. (2014) ' "Trading Places": A UK (and IFRS) Comment', *AEL: A Convivium*, Vol. 4 (1), pp. 27–40.

Mattessich, R. (1995) 'Conditional-normative accounting methodology: Incorporating value judgements and means-end relations of an applied science', *Accounting, Organizations and Society*, Vol. 20 (4), pp. 259–284.

Matthews, M. & Perera, M. (1996) *Accounting Theory and Development*. 3rd edn. Melbourne, Australia: Nelson.

Mautz, R.K. & Sharaf, H.A. (1961) *The Philosophy of Auditing*. Sarasota, Fla.: American Accounting Association.

Penno, M. (2008) 'Rules and accounting: Vagueness in conceptual frameworks', *Accounting Horizons*, Vol. 22 (3), pp. 339–351.

Popper, K. (1963) *Conjectures and Refutations: The Growth of Scientific Knowledge*. London: Routledge and Kegan Paul.

Porter, B. (2003) *Principles of External Auditing*. 2nd edn. West Sussex: John Wiley & Sons.

Power, M. (1993) 'On the Idea of a Conceptual Framework for Financial Reporting' in M. Mumford and K. Peasnell (eds.) *Philosophical Perspectives on Accounting*. London: Routledge.

Rawls, J. (1999) *A Theory of Justice*. Oxford: Oxford University Press.

Salmon, W. (1992) 'Scientific Explanation' in *Introduction to the Philosophy of Science*. Indianapolis, Ind./Cambridge: Hackett Publishing Company.

Sterling, R. (1979) *Toward a Science of Accounting*. Houston, Texas: Scholars Book Co.

Sterling, R. (1990) 'Positive accounting: An assessment', *Abacus*, Vol. 26 (2), pp. 97–135.

Twining, W. & Miers, D. (1976) *How to Do Things with Rules*. London: Weidenfeld and Nicolson.

Watts, R. & Zimmerman, J. (1979) 'The demand for and supply of accounting theories: The market for excuses', *Accounting Review*, April, pp. 273–304.

Watts R. & Zimmerman, J. (1986) *Positive Accounting Theory*. Englewood Cliffs, N.J.: Prentice Hall.

West, B. (2003) *Professionalism and Accounting Rules*. London: Routledge.

Williams, B. (1972) *Morality: An Introduction to Ethics*. Middlesex, UK: Penguin Books.

Wittgenstein, L. (1953) *Philosophical Investigations*. Oxford: Basil Blackwell.

Wittgenstein, L. (1978) *Remarks on the Foundations of Mathematics*. Oxford: Basil Blackwell.

Young, J. (2006) 'Making up users', *Accounting Organizations and Society*, Vol. 31 (6), pp. 579–600.

Zeff, S. (2002) ' "Political" lobbying on proposed standards: A challenge to the IASB', *Accounting Horizons*, Vol. 16 (1), pp. 43–54.

Zeff, S. (2014) 'Some historical reflections on "Have Academics and the Standard Setters Traded Places?" ' *AEL: A Convivium*, Vol. 4 (1), pp. 41–48.

2   The Objectives of Auditing

It was suggested in the previous chapter that theorising about auditing involves identifying what is wanted from the practice of auditing. What is wanted is meant to have a 'desirability characterisation'. It answers the question 'Why audit?' in a way that identifies something that is agreed to be desirable. This is used in the practical reasoning involved in promulgating rules for auditing practice. A reason of this kind forestalls further questioning of the desires used in reasoning to rules of a practice. In this chapter a start is made on constructing an auditing theory by considering the objectives of auditing which express, as in the objectives chapter of the conceptual framework, what is desired from the practice. It was noted that the IAASB did not choose to undertake a project to develop a conceptual framework for auditing, an auditing theory, as part of the Clarity Project. Instead they chose to revise ISA 200. This is entitled *Overall Objectives of the Independent Auditor and the Conduct of an Audit in Accordance with International Standards* (IAASB, 2010). Given the explanation of the kind of auditing theory explored in this book, it is clear that this auditing standard is really part of an auditing theory. A start in developing an auditing theory can be made by considering the objectives of auditing in ISA 200.

THE OBJECTIVES OF AUDITING IN ISA 200

ISA 200 identifies the overall objectives of the auditor as '(a) To obtain reasonable assurance about whether the financial statements as a whole are free from material misstatement, whether due to fraud or error, thereby enabling the auditor to express an opinion on whether the financial statements are prepared, in all material respects, in accordance with an applicable financial reporting framework; and (b) To report on the financial statements, and communicate as required by the ISAs, in accordance with the auditor's findings' (IAASB, 2010, ISA 200, §11). Given that objectives express what is wanted from the practice of auditing, these objectives can be rephrased, assuming that it is standard setters who are using these objectives to promulgate rules, as 'We want auditors to obtain reasonable assurance . . .' and 'We want auditors to report. . .'

As a proxy for a theory of auditing, ISA 200 might have been expected to have a definition of an audit. Power recognises that a logical place to start a study on auditing is with a definition of 'auditing' (Power, 1997, p. 4). Most books about auditing do so and quote various definitions given by academic, professional or regulatory bodies. Flint (1988) and Porter (2003) both quote the AAA definition. Gray and Manson (2011) mention a definition of auditing by the UK Auditing Practices Committee (APC) that states that 'an "audit" is an independent examination of, and expression of opinion on, the financial statements of an enterprise' (quoted in Gray and Manson, 2011, p. 58). Some writers define 'auditing' and some 'audit'. This is not a problem as long as auditing is understood as an activity whereas an audit is the outcome of this activity. Power says that a definition of auditing is 'not easy or even desirable' given the lack of 'precise agreement about what auditing really is . . . It is wiser to speak of a cluster of definitions which overlap but are not identical'. He goes on to say that 'the production of official definitions of a practice like auditing . . . is an idealized, normative projection of the hopes invested in the practice, a statement of potential rather than a description of actual operational capability. Defining auditing is largely an attempt to say what it *could* be' (Power, 1997, p. 4). Another way of expressing this is to say that a definition attempts to say what the objectives of auditing should be.

Hayes et al. point out that 'there is no definition of an audit, *per se*, in the International Standards on Auditing' (Hayes et al., 2005, p. 10). The word 'audit' is not defined in either the glossary of terms of the *Handbook of International Quality Control, Auditing, Review, Other Assurance, and Related Services Pronouncements* or in the 'Definitions' section of ISA 200. Rather inconsistently Hayes et al. say that there are 'two problems with the ISA 200 definition', which suggests that this *is* understood, at least by them, as a definition of an audit. What they presumably mean by 'per se' is that the 'definition' in ISA 200 is a definition but not a definition *of a certain kind*. Definitions that set out necessary and sufficient conditions for the application of an expression are sometimes taken as the *ideal* kind of definition, but there are other kinds (Baker and Hacker, 1980, p. 37). Definitions provide *explanations* of the meaning of an expression, but there are different kinds of explanation. Hayes et al. point to a 'better' definition of 'auditing' provided by the AAA in 1973: 'a systematic process of objectively obtaining and evaluating evidence regarding assertions about economic actions and events to ascertain the degree of correspondence between these assertions and established criteria, and communicating the results to interested users'. Perhaps it is better in that it gives necessary and sufficient conditions whereas the ISA 200 definition does not.

If definitions are viewed as an attempt to say what is *wanted* from the activity of auditing, what one is trying to achieve from it, then a statement of its *objectives* might constitute a definition of 'auditing'. The AAA definition could be rephrased as, 'We want auditors to undertake a systematic process of objectively obtaining and evaluating evidence . . .' The APC definition would be, 'We want auditors to undertake an independent examination of, and expression of opinion on, the financial statements of an enterprise'. Different definitions express different things that are wanted from the activity of auditing and give rise to different conceptions of what an audit is. It was suggested in chapter 1 that language is *naturalistic*. Expressions like 'auditing' develop in a context where certain things are wanted, and the term invented identifies something that is useful in fulfilling these desires. Power's point is that different people may want different things and so the term 'audit' is understood differently. It applies to different activities and embodies desires that may not be actually fulfilled by the practices that develop under such a term, particularly when it develops in different contexts. The idea that 'definitions are attempts to fix a practice within a particular set of norms or ideals' (Power, 1997, p. 5) really means that, like all language, meanings have to be understood in the context of the desires that prompt their development. Objectives and definitions are developed together. An audit *is* something that achieves certain ends, and grasping the objectives helps to understand what is meant by 'audit'. The meaning of 'audit' is contested because there are disagreements on what is wanted from auditing (Dennis, 2010, pp. 143). This helps in understanding a particular kind of 'expectations gap'.

THE EXPECTATIONS GAP

Although the term 'expectations gap' is widely used in discussions involving regulators, preparers of financial statements, the auditing profession and academics about auditing, the nature of the gap is not always clear. Sometimes it is characterised as the gap between what certain parties *believe* auditors do and what they *actually* do. It is sometimes characterised as the gap between what one party wants auditors to do and what they want or think they ought to do (Dennis, 2010). In this sense there is a gap 'between what the public expects from an audit' and 'what the auditing profession prefers the objectives to be' (Sikka et al., 1998, p. 299). If 'expects' is understood as 'wants', and objectives express what is wanted, then the gap is between what one party wants auditors to do and what auditors themselves want to do. Examples of differences are legion in the literature (for a review of some of the issues see Gray and Manson, 2011, ch. 18). Some users of financial statements may want auditors to detect all fraud/all major frauds whereas auditors may not want to do so unless the fraud results in material misstatement in the financial statements, as required by ISA 240. Some users may want auditors to warn them of going concern problems in a company whose financial statements they are using. Auditors may want to report only where there is material uncertainty about the entity's ability to continue as a going concern, as required by ISA 570. Parties on both sides of the gap appear to want different things. This is a different kind of gap to one in beliefs. One party may believe auditors do something when they actually do something else. One party may believe that auditors have to do something in order to meet a desire, and auditors may believe they have to do something else. Arguing about what auditors should do may involve arguing about what is wanted from the action or about what is believed to achieve desired ends. Both can give rise to 'expectations gaps'.

It is important to get clear about the nature of the expectations before trying to tackle the gap. If the gap is one of beliefs, then the solution to the problem is to get clear about matters of fact. If the gap is about what is wanted, then the way to overcome this is to argue about what is desired from the activity of auditing. This is the kind of argument that occurs when conceptual frameworks seek agreement on the objectives and qualitative characteristics of information. One way of tackling the expectations gap in auditing would be to agree on the objectives of auditing as part of the development of a conceptual framework for auditing or, what is taken as equivalent in this book, an auditing theory.

IDENTIFYING THE OBJECTIVES OF AUDITING

It was suggested in the previous chapter that what was wanted in undertaking normative theorising was to identify what is to be wanted in a practice. Something that has a *desirability characterisation* provides a *final answer* to a series of questions 'Why?' which is asked about the rules that determine the practice. The objectives of the auditor in ISA 200 do not strike one as identifying something with a desirability characterisation. Why should one want the auditor to obtain reasonable assurance about whether the financial statements as a whole are free from material misstatement and to express an opinion and report on the financial statements? An answer to these questions is actually given in the earlier section of the standard where the *purpose* of an audit is set out. The words 'purpose' and 'objective' appear to be interchangeable. A purpose is an 'idea or aim kept before the mind as the end of effort . . . an end desired'. This is scarcely different from an objective which is 'the point to which the operations . . . are directed' (both from *Chambers Twentieth Century Dictionary*). Both refer to something that is wanted from an action. The purpose identified in ISA 200 is 'to enhance the degree of confidence of intended users in the financial statements'. This is achieved by 'the expression of an opinion by the auditor on whether the financial statements are prepared, in all material respects, in accordance with an applicable financial reporting framework' and whether they are 'presented fairly, in all material respects, or give a true and fair view in accordance with the framework'. The opinion can be given by 'an audit conducted in accordance with ISAs and relevant ethical requirements' (IAASB, 2010, ISA 200, §3).

The structure of the argument is important to understand. It starts with a desire—to enhance confidence of users in the financial statements. A belief as to how this is achieved is then expressed by saying that confidence is enhanced by the auditor expressing an opinion on the financial statements. From these premises a conclusion of a desire for auditors to express an opinion can be derived. From this desire a desire for promulgating a rule to require auditors to express an opinion can be derived. The nature of the opinion is then set out in the sentence that explains, or gives the meaning of, the kind of opinion required. Another conclusion of a desire for auditors to give such an opinion and a prescription that they do so can be derived. A belief about what has to be done in order to give this opinion is then stated. To give such an opinion, an audit has to be conducted in accordance with ISAs and ethical requirements. The statements in this part of the standard are thus excerpts from an argument using practical reasoning to draw certain conclusions about what is wanted in an audit. Reasoning of this kind is normative theorising to desires from which decisions are made to promulgate rules. It is not presented in this way, though. This is a kind of 'forward argument' from certain desires identified in a conceptual framework or theory of auditing to a desire to promulgate rules that fulfil these desires. The theory provides premises that standard setters can use to set standards. These standards determine the work required to give an opinion that gives credibility to the financial statements. ISA 200 is a contribution to a normative theory of auditing. It is strange to call it an auditing standard. If the objective of such standards is to set out requirements in the form of rules that govern auditors, then ISA 200 is not a standard.

In fact, the beliefs and desires implicit in ISA 200 are not used in this way. The requirement for auditors to express an opinion of a certain kind has already been mandated by law in many jurisdictions. In the UK this is a requirement of the Companies Act 2006 set out in sections 495–498. The nature of the opinion to be presented is also often set out in legislation. It is redundant for standard setters to promulgate rules of this kind. ISA 200 does provide a *rationalization* of rules that have already been promulgated. It gives the reasons why the legislature *might* have decided to establish requirements of auditors. It provides *a* justification of the rules, but not necessarily the one that was actually used by legislators. This might be characterised as a 'backward argument'. Given the desire to promulgate rules of this kind, ISA 200 explains why there is such a desire by providing the premises in practical reasoning that enable the derivation of the desire in question.

As with the objective in ISA 200, the purpose 'enhancing the degree of confidence of intended users in the financial statements' does not appear to have a desirability characterisation that forestalls further questioning. Asking 'Why do you want to enhance confidence?' seems perfectly reasonable.

ISA 200 does not itself provide an answer to this question. The answer lies somewhere 'behind' the statement of purpose.

WHAT LIES 'BEHIND' THE PURPOSE?

In order to explain why there is a desire to enhance confidence, it is necessary to consider the economic and social roles of auditing. Auditing is said to 'provide a useful service in the community to individual and organizations in need of assurance and comfort because of prior doubts and uncertainties about the state of "things" in the real world in which they have an interest' (Lee, 1993, pp. 27–28). It does so by 'preventing or identifying any human carelessness or deceit which could damage individual and organizations with an interest in the "things" concerned' (Lee, 1993, pp. 27–28). These generalized remarks can be given substance by relating them to the context of financial reporting. Flint begins his book on auditing theory by observing that 'there is no general answer to the question of what is the purpose of an audit or why the procedures and practices that are adopted are seen to be adequate and appropriate in relation to the perceived objective' (Flint, 1988, p. 4). It states that it can be answered by considering the 'social concept' of audit. Auditing develops within a social context.

This idea is well covered in the literature and will not be laboured here. Investors and other stakeholders provide capital or resources for a business, and the business is accountable to them for its use. Financial reporting must provide financial information to existing and potential investors, lenders and other creditors to assist them in making decisions about providing resources to the entity. Given information asymmetry, management have information that these other users do not have access to, and the problem arises that management might not provide reliable information in the financial statements, either through 'carelessness or deceit'. There is a need to make this information *credible* so that it can be relied upon in making decisions. If it is believed that conducting an audit will result in making information reliable a desire for an audit may be derived. This kind of justification for auditing is set out more fully in the books on auditing theory such as Lee (1993, ch. 2), Flint (1988, ch. 1) and Mautz and Sharaf (1961, ch. 3). This gives reasons for wanting what is expressed in the purpose of auditing.

Auditing adds credibility to financial statements, but this is 'only one manifestation of the social function of auditing, although, no doubt, a very important one' (Flint, 1988, p. 6). Flint suggests that theories of auditing provide 'a coherent set of propositions about the activity which explains its social purpose and objectives, which furnishes a rational foundation and justification for its practices and procedures, relating them to the purposes and objectives, and which explains the place of the activity in the context of the institutions of society and the social, economic and political environment' (Flint, 1988, p. 9). Auditing is 'an evolving process, reacting with changing expectations', and 'is designed to monitor compliance with specified norms of what is acceptable behaviour', and hence 'it is clearly culturally, socially and politically dependent' (Flint, 1988, p. 13). Auditors and audit policy-makers should 'seek to find out what is the societal need and expectation for independent audit and to endeavour to fulfil that need within the limits of practical and economic constraints, remembering at all times that the function is a dynamic, not a static one' (Flint, 1988, p. 17). The investigation into the 'social concept' of auditing is an investigation designed to explain why certain things are wanted from auditing. The assumption is that the auditor and policy-maker should want what society wants from an auditing function. The idea of audit as an evolving process also implies, given a 'naturalistic' view of language explained in chapter 1, that the concept of an audit changes with changes in what is wanted from it.

As it has been represented here, the social or economic context of auditing gives the context in which what is wanted from auditing makes sense. It assists in understanding why certain things are wanted from auditing and why these things have a 'desirability characterisation'. Providing this background against which the objectives or purposes of auditing can be appreciated is sometimes identified in the literature as setting out the 'postulates' of auditing. This has created a certain amount of confusion as to what is going on. To see this the idea of a postulate as it has been explained in the literature will be examined.

THE POSTULATES OF AUDITING

There is quite a history behind the idea of postulates in accounting and auditing. Paton's book *Accounting Theory* (1922) introduces accounting postulates. They are said to be 'a series of general assumptions' upon which a theory is built (Paton, 1922, p. 417). They are 'fundamental premises . . . few if any of which are capable of complete demonstration' (Paton, 1922, p. 471). Chambers suggests that Paton provides the promise of a deductive derivation of a set of rules from a *set* of postulates (Chambers, 1966, p. 25). This idea was taken up by a Special Committee on Research Program set up by the American Institute of Certified Public Accountants (AICPA). They produced a report that stated that the problems of financial accounting should be 'visualized as requiring attention at four levels: first, postulates; second, principles; third, rules or other guides for the application of principles in specific situations; and fourth, research'. 'Postulates' were said to be 'few in number and are the basic assumptions on which principles rest. They necessarily are derived from the economic and political environment and from the modes of thought and customs of all segments of the business community' (AICPA Research Committee, 1958, p. 63, quoted in Zeff, 1972, p. 171).

Mautz and Sharaf explain 'postulates' as assumptions that cannot be directly verified. The propositions deduced from them can be directly verified, and this provides 'evidence of the truth of the postulates themselves' (Mautz and Sharaf, 1961, p. 37). They were writing at the time of the 'postulates/principles' debate, and they inherited some of the confusions in this debate. It is not surprising that the nature of postulates in auditing is not clear (for a fuller account of the debate see Dennis 2006). One problem with this debate was the lack of any clear analysis of the logical nature of sentences expressing 'postulates' or 'principles'. The 'terms such as axiom, postulate, principle, standard, procedure, canon, and rule, among others, are widely used, but with no general agreement on their precise meaning' (Moonitz, 1961, p. 1). Later they were said to be some kind of general truth about the environment of accounting (Moonitz, 1963, p. 43). They were said to be statements in the indicative mood and were used in deriving other statements' (Chambers, 1964, p. 39). The postulates of Moonitz were a mix of indicative statements and imperatives. The notion of a 'principle' was not actually explained in a second study, Accounting Research Study No. 3 (ARS 3), *A Tentative Set of Broad Accounting Principles for Business Enterprises*. The idea of a 'hierarchy' and of a 'frame of reference' for the practice of financial reporting was not explained. Chambers criticised the study on the grounds that there was little attempt to demonstrate how principles flow from the postulates (Chambers, 1964, p. 52) and questioned how the principles are deductively derived from the postulates and definitions (Chambers, 1966, p. 33).

Theorising about financial reporting turned away from thinking of theorising as a process of identifying postulates and then deriving principles which, in turn, would allow the derivation of prescriptions. The need for a different kind of accounting theory that started with the purposes and objectives of accounting was taken up by *A Statement of Basic Accounting Theory* (ASOBAT) (AAA, 1966). As Zeff observes, the 'explicit orientation toward users of information was a breath of fresh air' (Zeff, 1999, p. 96) and came to dominate thinking about accounting and underpins the conceptual framework approach described in chapter 1. In particular, this approach attempts to identify desires that have a 'desirability characterisation'.

This idea would appear to lie behind Mautz and Sharaf's idea that postulates are 'fundamental' or 'obvious truths' that are 'indemonstrable'. They quote Aristotle as claiming that 'demonstrable science' must 'start from indemonstrable principles, otherwise, the steps of demonstration would be endless' (Mautz and Sharaf, 1961, p. 37). In fact, this is true of practical reasoning. The chain of reasons from premises that express desires eventually gives out. Although one can ask 'Why do you want . . . ?' of such desires, this questioning comes to an end in desires that have a 'desirability characterisation' (Anscombe, 1957, §37). Such desires are not 'indemonstrable', in the sense that they are 'obvious truths' that cannot be deduced from anything else. Statements expressing such desires are *not truths at all*. Saying 'I want

X' is not stating a truth that stands in need of verification. If asked 'Why do you want X?' the correct answer is not to provide evidence that what you say is true, that you do actually want it, but to answer the question that is asking for reasons why you want it. It expresses a desire and does not state a factual statement that you have such a desire. If a statement that expresses a desire is a 'postulate', it is not an 'indemonstrable truth', or a statement that cannot be directly verified as true. It is not a statement of fact at all. It is the expression of a desire that has a 'desirability characterisation' that forestalls further questioning. It was suggested that identifying statements expressing such desires, that is, expressing what is wanted from a practice, constitute the objective of theorising about a practice. Calling them 'postulates' and equating them with assumed truths obscures their real nature. Mautz and Sharaf have adopted the jargon of the postulates/principles debate without adequate clarification of the nature of postulates and principles.

The kind of thing identified as postulates of auditing by Mautz and Sharaf amount to a rather motley collection of statements. They set out eight 'tentative' postulates of auditing in chapter 3 of their book. They note that there may be difficulty in accepting them as 'fundamental assumptions'. However, they are supposed to be used 'as the basis for deductions with respect to auditing theory' and can be integrated in such a theory (Mautz and Sharaf, 1961, p. 42). The first 'postulate' is 'financial statements and financial data are verifiable' (Mautz and Sharaf, 1961, p. 42). They explain its importance by noting that 'unless financial data are verifiable, auditing has no reason for existence' (Mautz and Sharaf, 1961, p. 43). 'Postulates' of this kind are supposed to be accepted 'a priori'. They are not hypotheses for which evidence can be found to support them, and yet 'this does not mean that postulates have no foundation in fact or truth'. They are supposed to 'support or prove all of the terms and theorems of the system for which they are the foundation' (Mautz and Sharaf, 1961, p. 38). This is not exactly very clear. The reason why auditors have to assume that that financial data are verifiable is that, as a matter or meaning, they cannot want to verify such data unless it possible that such data are verifiable. If they want credible information, and this is information that is verified, then they want verifiable information. This cannot be wanted unless the information is believed to be verifiable. This follows from the meaning of 'want'. The 'primitive sign of wanting is *trying to get*' (Anscombe, 1957, §67). This postulate does not identify a desire but what is implied by the *meaning* of having such a desire. It does not provide support for the desire that is identified in the theory of auditing, nor does it 'prove' the desire. It is assumed, for without the assumption, the desires in the theory make no sense.

Other postulates developed by Mautz and Sharaf are of this kind. The second postulate is 'here is no necessary conflict of interest between the auditor and the management of the enterprise under audit' (Mautz and Sharaf, 1961, p. 42). The importance of this postulate is explained by pointing out that if there was such a conflict, then the auditor could not perform his or her work in the required timescale. Again, if the auditor wants to give credibility, then he or she must believe it to be possible. If to be possible requires cooperation with management, then the auditor must believe in this cooperation and that no conflict of interest will undermine it. Assumptions of this kind constitute the background against which certain desires are possible. This confirms the idea that setting out postulates is setting out the background against which the desires identified in the theory of auditing make sense.

The same point can be made about the postulates mentioned by Flint. His first postulate is that 'the primary condition for an audit is that there is a relationship of accountability for a situation of public accountability' (Flint, 1988, p. 23). This describes the context in which the desire to give credibility makes sense. The second postulate identified by Flint is that 'the subject matter of accountability is too remote, too complex and/or of too great significance for the discharge of the duty to be demonstrated without the process of audit' (Flint, 1988, p. 26). This also provides the context in which the desires for auditing make sense. What is wanted from auditing is related to the social or economic context of auditing against which the desires need to be understood. If the desires constitute, in effect, 'principles' of auditing, that is, in one of the senses of 'principles' identified in chapter 1, the postulates represent the backdrop against which these principles are understood as desirable.

Having identified these principles, the desires that have a desirability characterisation and constitute the bedrock in auditing theory in the sense that no further questioning of them is required, they can be used to argue forward to other desires that auditing should fulfil.

THE FORWARD ARGUMENT

The desires identified in theorising can be used to argue to new desires which underpin standard setting decisions. This is illustrated in ISA 200. What is wanted is to enhance the degree of confidence of intended users in the financial statements. ISA 200 goes on to say that 'this is achieved by the expression of an opinion by the auditor on whether the financial statements are prepared, in all material respects, in accordance with an applicable financial reporting framework' (IAASB, 2010, ISA 200, §3). In other words, if what is wanted is to enhance confidence, then this, in conjunction with the belief that what enhances confidence is giving an opinion, will result in a desire to give such an opinion. This is an example of practical reasoning from one desire to another. Standard setters may then go on to require auditors to give an opinion on the financial statements. Although the nature of the opinion is said to depend upon the applicable financial reporting framework and any applicable law or regulation (IAASB, 2010, ISA 200, §8), in ISA 700 the auditor needs to 'form an opinion on whether the financial statements are prepared, in all material respects, in accordance with the applicable financial reporting framework' (IAASB, 2010, ISA 700, §3). This clarifies the meaning of 'opinion' by explaining what is expressed in the opinion. ISA 700 explains that the opinion is 'based on an evaluation of the conclusions drawn from the audit evidence' (IAASB, 2010, ISA 700, §6). The evidence results in the auditor obtaining reasonable assurance about whether the financial statements as a whole are free from material misstatement. Reasonable assurance is explained as 'a high level of assurance. It is obtained when the auditor has obtained sufficient appropriate audit evidence to reduce audit risk (that is, the risk that the auditor expresses an inappropriate opinion when the financial statements are materially misstated) to an acceptably low level' (IAASB, 2010, ISA 200, §5). If this assurance is obtained, then the auditor can express an opinion 'on whether the financial statements are prepared, in all material respects, in accordance with an applicable financial reporting framework (IAASB, 2010, ISA 200, §11). Presumably, the belief is that the confidence of users will be enhanced if the auditor gives an opinion of this kind based on evidence that gives reasonable assurance that the financial statements are prepared, in all material respects, in accordance with an applicable financial reporting framework. The practical reasoning starts with the desire to enhance confidence. A premise expresses a belief that confidence is enhanced by giving an opinion of the requisite kind. The conclusion is a desire for auditors to give such an opinion. The standard setter will go on to prescribe that auditors give an opinion based on evidence in an auditing standard. This is the requirement in ISA 700 §10. A further belief that the evidence needs to be sufficient and appropriate to enable the auditor to draw reasonable conclusions on which to base the opinion (IAASB, 2010, ISA 500, §4) leads to a desire for such evidence. The belief that the auditor must 'design and perform audit procedures that are appropriate in the circumstances for the purpose of obtaining sufficient appropriate audit evidence', in turn, gives a reason for the requirement, expressed in ISA 500 §6, for such evidence. Desires and beliefs are used in practical reasoning to other desires that result in the prescription of requirements in standards.

It was suggested in chapter 1 that these desires are tested by the kind of forward and backward argument to achieve a 'reflective equilibrium'. If one wants to achieve a certain end and one believes it is to be achieved by certain actions, then one argues forward to a desire for such action. If one does not want to perform such arguments, then one questions the reasons for a desire for such actions in the backward argument. ISA 200 identifies further beliefs about what will enhance confidence. Confidence will be enhanced if 'the auditor's independence from the entity safeguards the auditor's ability to form an audit opinion without being affected by influences that might compromise that opinion. Independence enhances the auditor's ability to act with integrity, to be objective and to maintain an attitude of professional scepticism' (IAASB, 2010, ISA 200, §A16). This does not advertise itself as a belief, but this is what this statement amounts to. This leads to the requirement for independence as stated in the International Ethics Standards Board for Accountants (IESBA)'s *Code of Ethics for Professional Accountants*. ISA 200 states that 'the auditor shall comply with relevant ethical requirements, including those pertaining to independence, relating to financial statement audit engagements' (IAASB, 2010, ISA 200, §14). These ethical requirement are set out in the *Code of Ethics*. Once again a desire to enhance confidence and a belief as to how this is achieved underpin a requirement in the sense that a standard setter would use this belief and desire in practical reasoning to a desire to promulgate a prescription that the auditor has to follow. It is interesting to note that prescriptions for auditors in auditing standards are distinguished from prescriptions for auditors in the *Code of Ethics*.

THE PROFESSIONAL ACCOUNTANT'S *CODE OF ETHICS*

The *Code* is said to establish 'the fundamental principles of professional ethics for professional accountants and provides a conceptual framework that professional accountants shall apply' (IESBA, 2013, §100.2). Given the explanations of the conceptual framework in the previous chapter, a framework of ethics for professional accountants would establish what is wanted in the actions of professional accountants and represents things they ought to desire in their actions. Such desires have a desirability characterisation which forestalls further need for justification. The 'fundamental principles' set out the qualities that accountants should display in their work such as integrity, objectivity, professional competence and due care, confidentiality and professional behaviour (IESBA, 2013, §100.5). The standard on independence states that 'compliance with the fundamental principle of objectivity requires being independent of assurance clients' (IESBA, 2013, §291.3). In effect, this is derived by practical reasoning where from a desire to be objective and a belief that objectivity requires independence, one wants accountants, including auditors, to be independent.

It is an interesting question to ask if the 'fundamental principles' identified in the *Code* are actually *fundamental*. The idea of 'fundamental' is not explained in the *Code*. It was suggested that being fundamental means that what is wanted has a 'desirability characterisation'. There is no need to question why they are wanted. The 'fundamental principles' may have this quality. Would anyone question whether 'integrity' in accountants was desirable? However, it is arguable whether some of the other fundamental principles are desirable, good in themselves. In the auditing context where the objective of auditing is to enhance confidence, objectivity may be good because it is a *means* to enhancing confidence. Users who rely upon the work of auditors to enhance confidence will not have their confidence enhanced if they do not believe that auditors are acting with objectivity. The idea that follows from this is that if objectivity requires independence, then independence is a good because without it there cannot be objectivity, and without this there can be no enhancement of confidence. Enhancing confidence is not a 'fundamental principle' according to IESBA, and yet it arguably underlies something that is, namely objectivity.

This raises the question of whether ethical standards are particularly *ethical*. This depends upon the meaning of 'ethical'. Philosophy can be of assistance here. It has been said that 'the central task of philosophical ethics is to articulate what constitutes ethics or morality' (Craig, 2005, p. 243). This might be interpreted, in light of the general characterisation of philosophy in chapter 1, to be the task of explaining the meaning of the expressions 'ethics', 'ethical' and 'morality'. An investigation of these explanations cannot be gone into here in any detail. An Aristotelian view of ethics is that it 'seeks to discover the good for an individual and a community' (Craig, 2005, p. 243). If the community in question are auditors, then the 'good' for auditors may be that which achieves the objectives of auditing. This may be what is meant by an 'applied ethics', that is, one that considers the ethical requirements of particular occupations (Craig, 2005, p. 243). This suggests that ethical requirements of the kind set out in the *Code of Ethics for Professional Accountants* are not requirements for producing good people per se, as might be signified by a *Code* with 'ethical' in the title, but requirements for producing good accountants and auditors. As such, it might be argued, there is nothing particularly ethical about 'ethical requirements' for accountants and auditors. If this is the case, then a prior investigation which seeks to identify the objectives of the practice, of the kind that conceptual frameworking seeks, is necessary. The 'ethical requirement' for objectivity and independence would then be seen as a requirement for bringing about something else that is wanted, in the case of auditing, enhancing confidence, rather as something that is an end in itself.

The forward and backward argument that is involved in identifying what is wanted in a practice and the forward argument to deriving prescriptions of the kind standard setters promulgate suggests that the same reasoning applies to both. This raises the question of the dividing line between theory and prescription. It is suggested that this is negotiable. It is also suggested that the kind of prescriptions that emerge in this process are also negotiable. In fact, these two decisions are interconnected, and this accounts for their negotiability.

THEORY AND PRESCRIPTION

It was suggested that theory, in the sense understood in this book, is something that is useful in deriving prescriptions for practice. This is easier to see if it is envisaged that practitioners are thinking about what prescriptions they wish to adopt for practice. They might start, as the standard setter starts, with an objective for auditing of enhancing confidence of the user in financial statements. It should be noted that what is wanted is *to do something* that will enhance the confidence of users. The desire is not an idle wish but a desire to do something that will bring about a certain end (Dennis, 2014, p. 8). At this point, given such a desire, practitioners might set a prescription for themselves to '(when auditing) do something that will bring it about that the confidence of users is enhanced'. This does not prescribe in precise terms what auditors have to do, only that when they are auditing they should seek to do something that will bring about this end. Saying that one wants to do something is *equivalent* to prescribing an action for oneself. Practitioners are unlikely to conclude with this kind of general prescription. It is too open ended. Every time practitioners audit, they will have to look around for something that will achieve the desired end. It is more likely that experience suggests that certain actions will bring about this end. Auditor may believe that, in general, giving an opinion on financial statements will enhance confidence in them. In conjunction with the desire to enhance confidence and this belief, auditors may conclude that they want to give an opinion on the financial statements. They might prescribe an action for themselves in the context of an audit such as 'give an opinion on the financial statements' that expresses a desire to give an opinion. Given this prescription the previous prescription to do something to enhance confidence constitutes the reason for wanting to give an opinion. It might be consigned to something else, perhaps a *theory* of the practice of auditing, that is, something that is useful in making a prescription to give an opinion that gives a reason for the latter prescription.

Merely prescribing to oneself something like 'give an opinion' may not be helpful. It is important to clarify the kind of opinion that is needed. Some explanation is needed of the nature of the opinion, what it *means* when it is said that an opinion should be given. This might be explained by saying that when an opinion is prescribed, it is an opinion on whether the financial statements are prepared, in all material respects, in accordance with the applicable financial reporting framework. This definition is useful because it is believed that an opinion of this kind is the kind of opinion that will enhance confidence. In other words, the desire that underpinned the desire to give an opinion also underpins the meaning 'opinion' to be given. As stated in chapter 1, language is naturalistic in the sense that the meaning of expressions in a language needs to be understood in relation to the human interests, needs and practices, in other words, the desires that motivate the practice, in the context in which the expressions operate. Similar explanations of the meaning of 'evidence' and 'reasonable assurance' will be required in drawing conclusions about further desires.

In this description of the thought process that occurs in developing the practice of auditing, there is a move from desires to prescriptions supplemented with explanations of the meaning of expressions used in the prescriptions. At what point has the practitioner moved on from theory to prescription? It looks like the point at which one moves from a desire to do something to achieve an end, prescribing a desire, to the specification of more detail as to what has to be done given a belief about the kind of actions that will bring about an end. It is up to practitioners to determine how far to go in the process of specifying in detail what is to be done. They could rest with a very general desire to do something to achieve an end, or they can consider more specific actions that will achieve this end by considering beliefs about what will achieve the end and by specifying the meaning of terms used in expressing what is to be done.

Does it make any significant difference when, instead of the prescriptions for practice being determined by the practitioner, these prescriptions are determined by a standard setter in an institutional practice? The standard setter needs to start in the same way as the practitioner with an expression of what is wanted from a practice. However, their initial premise is, 'We want something that will enhance confidence . . .', and, given beliefs, they will conclude, 'We want to promulgate a rule to do X'. The assumption made by the standard setter is that if he or she promulgates the rule it will be followed and that following the rule will result in actions that bring about the desired end. As with the practitioner scenario, it is up to the standard setter to decide where to end the process of prescription. The standard setter could stop with a prescription for practitioners to do something to achieve an end and leave it up to practitioners to consider on each occasion when they follow the prescription to consider what they believe will bring about the end. Standard setters could themselves consider what more specific actions they believe will bring about the end and reason to a desire to promulgate rules requiring such actions of practitioners. They could supplement these prescriptions with explanations of the meaning of terms used in the prescriptions, in the same way that practitioners who wanted to give an opinion or derive evidence that gave them reasonable assurance about the opinion might go on to consider the meaning of 'opinion', 'evidence' and 'reasonable assurance'. These explanations of meaning can be used to derive further prescriptions. If standard setters want auditors to give an opinion, and the meaning of 'opinion' is that it is something that expresses whether the financial statements are prepared, in all material respects, in accordance with the applicable financial reporting framework, then they may want auditors to state whether the financial statements are prepared in the relevant way. This may lead to further explanations of the meaning of 'material'. There may also be a further examination, given the meaning of terms such as 'evidence', of what specific actions have to be undertaken to bring it about that the auditor has evidence of the required kind. This may result in further prescriptions of these specific actions. How far the standard setter goes determines the kinds of rules that appear in standards (Dennis, 2014, ch. 4). The problem with prescriptions of the kind 'Do something that will bring about an end' is that this provides little guidance to the practitioner as to what, specifically, they have to do. Standards of this kind might be described as 'principles-only' standards. They are 'overly broad standards' and 'often do not provide a sufficient structure to frame the judgment that must be made' by preparers and auditors (SEC, 2003, p. 6). The kind of 'judgment' that is needed for such standards is judgement in determining beliefs about what actions will achieve the desired end.

If standard setters go further and prescribe more specific actions, the kind of standards that result can vary. If they believe that a specific action will bring about what is desired in all circumstances, then it is an easy matter to derive a desire for such an action and to prescribe it. But what if any particular action will not achieve the end on all occasions? Does the standard setter still prescribe it but allow an override? Does the standard setter include exceptions to exclude those instances where performing the action will not achieve the desired end? How many exceptions are allowed to be included in a standard? Where the expressions used in specifying the action are vague and can be interpreted differently, does the standard setter include implementation guidance in the standard to specify the meaning of the expressions that practitioners have to adopt in following the rule, or does he or she leave it to the judgement of the practitioner to interpret the rule, perhaps guided by the desire or objective of the standard that may, in consequence, need to be included in the standard? How much implementation guidance is allowed? Answering these questions determines the kind of standard prescribed. It will come as no surprise to recognise that the answers to such questions result in characteristics of standards that have been described using the terms 'principles-only', 'principles-based' and 'rules-based'. The SEC's idea of a 'principles-only' standard has already been explained. They also take 'principles-based' standards as standards with few, if any, 'exceptions or internal inconsistencies' that provide an 'appropriate amount of implementation guidance' (SEC, 2003, p. 12). Such standards have been said to allow for the exercise of judgement (ICAS, 2006, p.1) including, presumably, judgement of the kinds referred to here.

There are clearly choices that need to be made by the standard setter who must decide on the best kind of prescription given these considerations. No matter what kind of standard the standard setters ends up with, they begin their deliberations with something that is desired, that is, with the kind of objectives set out in the conceptual framework. Standard setting is 'principles-based' in the sense that standards are based on principles of this kind as set out in a conceptual framework. This is one of the meanings of 'principles-based standards'. Such standards are 'consistent with, and derived from, a coherent conceptual framework' (SEC, 2003, p. 12). However, there are two concepts of principles-based standards (Dennis, 2008, p. 265). The other is explained by the criteria identified in the previous paragraph. The need to decide on the kind of standards depends on decisions that are taken by the standard setter about how far to take the reasoning from the desires in the conceptual framework to decisions about the kind of prescriptions derived from them.

The prescriptions developed by the practitioner are precisely those that are set out or implied by what is stated in ISA 200. As suggested, this standard is a substitute for a conceptual framework for auditing rather than an auditing standard *per se*. ISA 200 appears to include desires, prescriptions and explanations of the meaning in what counts as a theory of auditing. The continuum in which theory becomes prescription seems to be the continuum at which standards migrate from principles-only to principles-based to rules-based ones. The point at which theory stops and standards begin is determined by the standard setter. It might be described as the point at which thinking about the reasons used to make prescriptions stops and making prescriptions about what to do begins. The problem is that with 'principles-based' standards the reasons for prescriptions are meant to be used by professionals in exercising judgement about how to follow the prescriptions. There is no rigid distinction between what is of use in prescribing standards and what is of use in following standards that now include not just the rule but the reasons for the rule. It is not surprising that there is a lack of clarity as to whether ISA 200 is to be understood as part of a theory of auditing or is an auditing standard since theory comes into the standard through the need to exercise *judgement*. Given the conceptual connection between wanting to do something that achieves an end and prescribing an end to be achieved, a statement of prescriptions can be understood as the expression of a desire. A theory of auditing that does the latter can also be seen as something that does the former. If an ISA like ISA 200 states prescriptions of this kind, then it can be said to express theory.

SUMMARY

Exploring what is wanted from auditing in the kind of theorising undertaken in this book is exploring the objectives of auditing. The objectives of auditing stated in ISA 200 are identified. One form of expectation gap arises because of disagreements on what is wanted from auditing. Agreeing on objectives is a matter of agreeing on something wanted that has a desirability characterisation which forestalls further questioning of reasons for promulgating rules. The objective of auditing in ISA 200 is to enhance the degree of confidence of intended users in the financial statements. It does not, at first glance, appear to have a desirability characterisation. However, considering the economic and social context of accounting and auditing helps to understand why this is something desired in itself. The results of this kind of exploration are sometimes referred to as the postulates of auditing. The nature of postulates is considered. It is suggested that ethical standards should be understood as the result of further consideration of what is wanted from auditing and are not particularly ethical in nature. The use of objectives is related back to practical reasoning to decisions to adopt rules in standards.

REFERENCES

AAA (1966) *A Statement of Basic Accounting Theory*. Evanston, Ill.: AAA.

Anscombe, G.E.M. (1957) *Intention*. Oxford: Basil Blackwell.

Baker, G. & Hacker, P. (1980) *Wittgenstein Meaning and Understanding*. Oxford: Blackwell.

Chambers, R. (1964) 'The Moonitz and Sprouse studies on postulates and principles', *Proceedings, Second Conference of the Australian Association of University Teachers*, pp. 34–54, reprinted in S. Zeff (1982) *The Accounting Postulates and Principles Controversy of the 1960's*. New York & London: Garland Publishing.

Chambers, R. (1966) 'The Development of Accounting Theory' in R.J. Chambers, L. Goldberg and R.L. Mathews (eds.) *The Accounting Frontier*. London: F.W. Cheshire.

Craig, E., ed. (2005) *The Shorter Routledge Encyclopedia of Philosophy*. New York: Routledge.

Dennis, I. (2006) *A Philosophical Investigation into the Conceptual Framework for Accounting*. PhD Thesis, London School of Economics, University of London. Accessible at: http://ethos.bl.uk/OrderDetails.do?did=1&uin=uk. bl.ethos.433646 [Accessed 13 January 2015].

Dennis, I. (2008) 'A conceptual enquiry into the concept of a "principles-based" accounting standard', *British Accounting Review*, Vol. 40 (3), pp. 260–271.

Dennis, I. (2010) ' "Clarity" begins at home: An examination of the conceptual underpinnings of the IAASB's Clarity Project', *International Journal of Auditing*, Vol. 14 (3), pp. 294–319.

Dennis, I. (2014) *The Nature of Accounting Regulation*. New York: Routledge.

Flint, D. (1988) *Philosophy and Principles of Auditing*. Basingstoke: Macmillan Education.

Gray, I. & Manson, S. (2011) *The Audit Process*. 5th edn. London: South-Western Cengage Learning.

Hayes, R., Dassen, R., Schilder, A. & Wallage, P. (2005) *Principles of Auditing: An Introduction to International Standards on Auditing*. Harlow, Essex, UK: Pearson Education.

IAASB (2010) *ISA 200 Overall Objectives of the Independent Auditor and the Conduct of an Audit in Accordance with International Standards*. New York: International Federation of Accountants.

ICAS (2006) *Principles Not Rules: A Question of Judgment*. Edinburgh: ICAS.

IESBA (2013) *Code of Ethics for Professional Accountants*. New York: International Federation of Accountants.

Lee, T. (1993) *Corporate Audit Theory*. London: Chapman and Hall.

Mautz, R.K. & Sharaf, H.A. (1961) *The Philosophy of Auditing*. Sarasota, Fla.: American Accounting Association.

Moonitz, M. (1961) 'The Basic Postulates of Accounting', *Accounting Research Study No. 1*, New York: AICPA, reprinted in S. Zeff (1982) *The Accounting Postulates and Principles Controversy of the 1960's*. New York and London: Garland Publishing.

Moonitz, M. (1963) 'Why do we need "Postulates" and "Principles"?' *Journal of Accountancy*, Vol. 116, pp. 42–46.

Paton, W.A. (1922) *Accounting Theory*. New York: The Ronald Press Company.

Porter, B. (2003) *Principles of External Auditing*. 2nd edn. West Sussex: John Wiley & Sons.

Power, M. (1997) *The Audit Society: Rituals of Verification*. Oxford: Oxford University Press.

SEC (2003) *Study Report Pursuant to Section 108(d) of the Sarbanes-Oxley Act of 2002, SEC*. Accessible at: http://www.sec.gov/news/studies/principlesbasedstand. htm [Accessed 14 November 2011].

Sikka, P., Puxty, A., Willmott, H. & Cooper, C. (1998) 'The impossibility of eliminating the expectations gap: Some theory and evidence', *Critical Perspectives in Accounting*, Vol. 9, pp. 299–330.

Zeff, S. (1972) *Forging Accounting Principles in Five Countries: A History and an Analysis of Trends Accounting Lectures 1971*. Champaign, Ill.: Stipes Publishing.

Zeff, S.A. (1999) 'The evolution of the conceptual framework for business enterprises in the United States', *Accounting Historians Journal*, Vol. 26 (2), pp. 89–131.

3   The Audit Opinion

It was suggested in chapter 2 that what is wanted from auditing is something that will enhance confidence in the financial statements. The belief implied in ISA 200 is that confidence will be enhanced by giving an opinion on the financial statements. A conclusion from this desire and this belief using practical reasoning is that what is wanted from auditing is to give such an opinion. ISA 200 explains that confidence will be enhanced by 'the expression of an opinion by the auditor on whether the financial statements are prepared, in all material respects, in accordance with an applicable financial reporting framework' (IAASB, 2010, ISA 200, §3). The belief is that an opinion *of this kind* will enhance confidence. It gives the meaning of 'opinion'. ISA 200 also says that the 'opinion is on whether the financial statements are presented fairly, in all material respects, or give a true and fair view in accordance with the framework' (IAASB, 2010, ISA 200, §3). The 'basis' for the auditor's opinion is that the auditor needs to obtain 'reasonable assurance about whether the financial statements as a whole are free from material misstatement, whether due to fraud or error' (IAASB, 2010, ISA 200, §5).

There appear to be three explanations of the meaning of 'opinion' in ISA 200. The opinion is on whether the financial statements are prepared, in all material respects, in accordance with an applicable financial reporting framework; on whether the financial statements are presented fairly, in all material respects, or give a true and fair view in accordance with the framework; and on whether the financial statements as a whole are free from material misstatement, whether due to fraud or error. The last explanation does not appear to be a definition of the kind of opinion required. It gives the 'basis' for the opinion. However, explaining what is meant by an expression is a matter of being able to explain what has to be the case if such an expression is used. This is the idea that lies behind the 'verification principle' in philosophy. Applied to auditing, explaining what has to be the case in order for the opinion of the required kind to be given, the 'basis' of the opinion, is to explain what is *meant* by the opinion of the required kind. If it is believed that an opinion will enhance confidence, then it is necessary to be clear about the meaning of the words used to express the opinion, and this requires that one is clear about what has to be the case if this opinion is to be given.

Given the importance of understanding the meaning of the opinion, it comes as a shock to note that not only is the kind of opinion required explained in different ways but also that the meaning of the expressions used in explaining the opinion are uncertain. In particular, the meaning of 'true and fair view' is not clear, and 'no definition was, or ever legally has been, offered of "true and fair view"' (Alexander and Jermakowicz, 2006, p. 139). This is not to say that no *explanation* of the term has been given. Auditing textbooks explain what it meant by this phrase even if they do not give what amounts to a 'definition'. Explanations of 'true and fair view' should explain what has to be the case if such an opinion can be given. This determines a certain kind of evidence needed to give the opinion. Toba recognizes that such an explanation is needed but acknowledges that auditors 'have been working earnestly on this problem, but without decisive success' (Toba, 1975, p. 14). What is the meaning of 'true and fair' or 'presents fairly' in the opinion, and do they mean the same thing?

THE MEANING OF 'TRUE AND FAIR' AND 'PRESENTS FAIRLY'

Asking about the meaning of 'true and fair' or 'presents fairly' requires a conceptual enquiry. There is a large literature that considers the meaning of these expressions by reviewing how they are used in law, by standard setters and by regulators. Alexander (1999) reviews the meanings of these phrases as they are used in various financial reporting regimes such as those in the UK, in Europe, in Australia, in the U.S. and internationally. This is a *descriptive conceptual enquiry*. However, he starts his enquiry by thinking about why such concepts are wanted or thought to be important. This is trying to understand the interests and needs that the concept is meant to further and constitutes an *evaluative conceptual enquiry*. Alexander does not overtly acknowledge a 'naturalistic' view of language, but what he does say suggests that the concepts of 'true and fair' and 'presents fairly' can be understood as arising out of an interest or need to develop and to identify criteria 'which can be used to determine the content of, and as a yardstick to assess the adequacy of, published financial statements' (Alexander, 1999, p. 240). This begs the question of what it is for something to be 'adequate'. A quick review of dictionary definitions suggests that something is adequate if it meets needs or purposes. In effect, this means that something, in this context financial statements, is adequate or, as it is sometimes expressed, 'good enough', if it fulfils what is wanted from it. 'Criteria of adequacy' of financial statements indicates what is wanted from financial statements if they are 'good enough' for their purposes, that is, if they meet the desires for which they are produced.

Three different 'criteria of adequacy' for financial statements are identified by Alexander. He calls them 'approaches to the problem of stating a
benchmark or criterion against which the adequacy of any particular financial reporting environment, or any specific set of financial statements, can be
determined' (Alexander, 1999, p. 240). The reference to a 'financial reporting environment' and to 'any specific set of financial statements' suggests
that two different things are being determined as adequate. The 'financial
reporting environment' might refer to the adequacy of accounting standards
or standard setting processes. 'Any specific set of financial statements' refers
to the product of following. Clearly the two are connected. The adequacy
of standards might be judged by the adequacy of financial statements produced by following them. This is the point made by Nobes, who comments
that Alexander's analysis 'would be improved by distinguishing between . . .
choice by preparers and choice . . . by regulators' (Nobes, 2000, p. 307).
'Criteria of adequacy' may be used by both parties to guide decisions. This
is important because not all of the 'different approaches' to stating criteria
are capable of being used by standard setters.

Alexander refers something he calls the Type A approach as identifying 'a generally expressed all pervasive fundamental concept'. The Type B
approach involves 'a set of rules, conventions or ways of thinking which are
to be consistently applied to situations both familiar and unfamiliar'. The
Type C approach requires 'the detailed provision of specific methods for
the treatment of all expected problems and situations.' (Alexander, 1999,
p. 240). If 'criteria of adequacy' is understood as expressing what is wanted
from financial statements, then Type A can be re-expressed as a desire for
financial statements that fulfil a generally expressed all pervasive fundamental concept. Alexander identifies the 'true and fair' concept, as it is used in
the UK, as an archetypal example of this kind of criterion (Alexander, 1999,
p. 240). Type B expresses a desire for financial statements that fulfil or follow a set of rules, conventions or ways of thinking which are to be consistently applied to situations both familiar and unfamiliar. An example of this
is the approach of the conceptual framework (Alexander, 1999, p. 240).
Type C can be re-expressed as a desire for financial statements that follow
the detailed provision of specific methods for the treatment of all expected
problems and situations. This is the kind of system that is characterised as
'rules-based' in the sense defined by the SEC as an approach that attempts
to 'specify the appropriate accounting treatment for virtually every imagin-
able scenario' (SEC, 2003, p. 13). This is a system that is often said to exist
in the U.S.

These 'criteria of adequacy' may be used by preparers of financial statements to assess the adequacy of financial statements. Auditors can also use
these criteria in the same way. However, not all of these 'criteria of adequacy'
can be used by standard setters. They want to determine whether standards
they a thinking of promulgating are adequate by considering whether, if they
are followed by preparers, they meet these criteria. Although it is possible

to use Type A or Type B criteria for this purpose, that is, it is possible to ask whether promulgating standards will, if followed, result in financial statements that meet an all pervasive concept or fulfil or follow a set of rules or conventions, it is not possible to use Type C. Asking whether standards will follow the detailed provision of specific methods is pointless since the point of the criteria is precisely to determine what those specific methods are to be. Type C does not provide any criteria for assessing those methods.

Alexander recognises the difference between 'criteria of adequacy' for adequate accounting standards and 'criteria of adequacy' for financial statements. He says that asking the question of the criteria for financial statements is 'logically prior' to the question of the criteria for adequate accounting standards (Alexander, 1999, p. 239). The idea is presumably that adequate accounting standards are those that produce adequate financial statements, so the criteria of adequacy of the latter must be understood before the 'criteria of adequacy' for the former can be determined. Adequate standard setting is something that produces adequate standards which is something that produces adequate financial statements. This throws doubt on the use of Type C criteria for assessing the adequacy of financial statements. Whether or not following the detailed provision of specific methods set out in accounting standards is adequate depends upon whether or not the accounting standards themselves are adequate. This, in turn, depends upon whether they produce adequate financial statements. The same criteria are used to determine the adequacy of both standards and financial statements.

Walton identifies 'three themes' in the literature on the meaning of 'true and fair view'. One 'theme' is that this is an 'independent concept' that is 'independent of accounting regulation'. It is a 'higher objective or ideal towards which accounting is evolving' and which 'should guide standard setting or decisions in specific cases'. Another 'theme' is that 'true and fair view' is a 'legal residual clause' which is the kind of thing included in a legal document that covers 'the intention behind, or the spirit of, the document'. A third theme is to see a 'true and fair view' as 'standing for generally accepted accounting principles' but that it 'does not represent a coherent, rationally consistent set of principles' and is not used 'as a guiding principle by the light of which rules are developed' (Walton, 1991, quoted in Evans, 2003, p. 213). These 'themes' are similar to Alexander's idea of an 'approach' to the problem of stating benchmarks or criteria. They both indicate certain ways of determining what constitutes financial statements that are 'good' or useful and the related question of what constitutes 'good' or useful standards or standard setting processes.

Walton's 'themes' bear some resemblance to Alexander's 'criteria of adequacy', but they are not the same. The idea of an 'independent concept' is similar to Alexander's Type A criterion. It is interesting to see that it can guide standard setting, which makes it sound like a 'principle' in a conceptual framework, that is, a Type B criterion. The fact that it can guide 'decisions in specific cases' suggests that it might be used by preparers in the absence of standards or, perhaps, in decisions to override a standard as the 'true and fair view' concept does in the UK. A 'legal residual clause' sounds like something that expresses the reasons behind the prescription in a legal document. As such it has similarities with the 'principles' in the conceptual framework, that is, a Type B criterion, if these are understood as expressions of desires for financial reporting that guide the standard setter in making standard setting decisions. Two 'themes' or 'approaches' to the 'true and fair' concept, each with three different ways of explaining the term, emerge from this discussion. This trinity is observed also by McGee writing from the legal point of view. He says that 'essentially, there are three possible views about the content of the true and fair view requirement. One is that it simply requires the accounting to have been done according to all the prescribed rules, the second is that there must be adherence to generally accepted accounting principles, which are seen as something more general and of a higher order than the accounting standards. The third view holds that the requirement is superimposed on the basic procedures and formats laid down by the legislation' (McGee, 1991, pp. 877–878). The first concept is similar to Alexander's Type C, the second to his Type B and the third to his Type A.

This brief descriptive conceptual enquiry into the concept of 'true and fair' illustrates the divergence in understanding the concept that is recognised by Toba and may account for the failure to provide a 'legal definition' of 'true and fair'. It suggests that there may be three *different* concepts, three important points of view about, or ways of explaining, the concept of 'true and fair'. The evaluative stage in a conceptual enquiry into this concept involves identifying the needs or desires that lie behind the concept developed. Examining this critically may provide some basis for adjudicating between the different meanings associated with the concept with a view to identifying one that is preferable, the outcome of a prescriptive conceptual enquiry.

AN EVALUATIVE CONCEPTUAL ENQUIRY INTO THE THREE CONCEPTS OF 'TRUE AND FAIR'?

'Criteria of adequacy' of financial statements express what is wanted from financial statements. This is the kind of thing expressed in theories of accounting like the conceptual framework. What is wanted in developing the concepts of 'true and fair' and 'presents fairly' is to identify what is wanted from financial statements. Just as the conceptual framework can assist standard setters in making decisions about setting and also has a role in assisting preparers and auditors in interpreting accounting standards and, in what is particularly relevant in the context of truth and fairness, may help them make decisions as to whether or not to override a standard on a particular occasion, so the 'criteria of adequacy' can do the same thing. To grasp that these 'criteria of adequacy' express desires is the first step in understanding.

The concept of a 'true and fair view' (TFV) was first introduced, as a requirement for company accounts, into English law in the Companies Act 1947. This developed via the Fourth Directive into the Companies Act 1985, as amended, to the requirement that 'the balance sheet shall give a true and fair view of the state of affairs of the company as at the end of the financial year, and the profit and loss account shall give a true and fair view of the profit or loss of the company for the financial year' (S 226(2)). The concept of 'true and fair' was introduced as an adjective of 'view' that identifies a particular kind of 'view' that financial statements, the balance sheet and profit and loss account, should present. It is meant to guide preparers in producing financial statements that exemplify a view of this kind. ISA 700 states that the auditor should give an opinion in one of two forms, which are said to be equivalent, namely that 'the financial statements present fairly, in all material respects . . .' or 'the financial statements give a true and fair view . . .' (IAASB, 2010, ISA 700, §35). Auditors are required to determine whether preparers have given a view of the required kind in their opinion. In order to meet these requirements, both preparers and auditors have to understand the concept of 'true and fair', that is, the meaning of the expression 'true and fair'.

The absence of a definition of this phrase appears strange given its importance. In fact, many concepts we use are not susceptible to definition, at least in the sense often intended by the use of the term 'definition'. What is often is meant by this term is something that gives necessary and sufficient conditions for something coming under a concept or expression. Wittgenstein recognizes that not all of the expressions we use in language are capable of definitions of this kind. The idea that 'definition be a kind of analysis, that it give necessary and sufficient conditions for the application of an expression, was the product of philosophers' pipe-dreams' (Baker and Hacker, 1985, p. 37). There are different kinds of definitions which are not all of this 'ideal' kind. A definition gives an explanation of the meaning of an expression, and there are different kinds of explanation, for example, by genus and differentia, ostensive definition, by samples or examples, contextual paraphrase (Baker and Hacker, 1985, p. 37–38). This point has not filtered through to philosophical reflections on accounting. When it is said that an accounting term, like 'true and fair' for example, has not been defined, what is meant is that no definition in terms of necessary and sufficient conditions, no 'proper' definition, has been given.

There are two extreme responses to the supposed dilemma that a 'proper' definition of the expression 'true and fair' has not been given. The first is to try and supply a definition that sets out the necessary and sufficient conditions for the use of the expression. The second is to accept that it is not definable, at least in the 'proper' sense, and not to bother too much about it.

It is argued here that both of these extreme responses are mistaken. There is a third way that tries to offer at least some explanation of what the expression 'true and fair' means without pretending that it is a definition of the 'proper' kind.

THE FIRST KIND OF RESPONSE

An example of the first extreme response is to define 'true and fair' by supplying necessary and sufficient conditions. One example might be 'financial statements give a true and fair view if and only if they comply with accounting standards . . .' where '. . .' can be filled by something along the lines 'promulgated by the IASB' or 'promulgated by the FASB'. Where the latter is the case in the U.S. context the concept is expressed using the words 'present fairly' rather than 'true and fair view'. Compliance with generally accepted accounting principles (GAAP) is a necessary condition of presenting fairly. Zeff has remarked that ' "Present fairly" is defined by reference to conformity with GAAP' (Zeff, 1993, p. 404). The FASB Accounting Standards Codification is the single source of authoritative nongovernmental U.S. GAAP. As Alexander observes, 'in practice the US criterion for the adequacy of a set of financial statements is the detailed promulgated GAAP of the FASB statements, a Type C criterion' (Alexander, 1999. p. 249). This has been referred to as a 'GAAP based' interpretation of 'true and fair view' (Rutherford, 1985, p. 492). Its meaning is 'to be determined within the accounting arena itself and not derived from legal sources or ordinary meanings' (Rutherford, 1985, p. 484). The advantage of defining 'presents fairly' as compliance with GAAP, as a necessary condition, is that the 'meaning is relatively certain' (McGee, 1991, p. 879). The condition in the definition also appears to be a sufficient condition in that 'at least as far as any particular company, and any particular auditor, are concerned, Type C GAAP, and more particularly the Standards are normally the *only* consideration when determining the adequacy of a set of financial statements' (Alexander, 1999, p. 249). There is no *judgement* involved in determining whether financial statements give a fair presentation. Preparers and auditors have only to determine whether or not they have complied with GAAP, although determining this may involve judgement. However, if this is determined, then by *deduction* financial statements can be said to 'present fairly'. Given this definition there is no possibility that compliance with GAAP could not result in financial statements that present fairly. There could not be any grounds for overriding GAAP in order to present fairly because, by definition, to fail to comply with GAAP means that financial statements do not present fairly. What appears to be wanted from a concept such as 'presents fairly' is a concept that is explained by giving necessary and sufficient conditions that can be used deductively and without judgement in applying it.

If the criterion of adequacy for financial statements is compliance with GAAP, this leaves open how to determine criteria for the adequacy of GAAP. This is obvious since it is not possible to use compliance with GAAP as a criterion of the adequacy of GAAP. 'GAAP is adequate if and only it complies with GAAP' is not a criterion of adequacy. The grounds for adequacy of standards and standard setting are divorced from the grounds for adequacy of financial statements. This has the rather strange implication that what makes accounting standards, and the process of setting them, adequate is not that they result in adequate financial statements. There is some other criterion of adequacy. This is strange because, as noted earlier, the idea of a criterion of adequacy is of something that fulfils the needs or purposes for which it was established. The purposes or needs of financial statements are the kinds of thing expressed in the objectives statements in a conceptual framework for financial reporting. This framework is supposed to guide standard setters in making standard setting decisions. If their standards are followed, this is supposed to result in financial statements that meet the objectives, that is, in financial statements that are adequate. This suggests that the criteria of adequacy of standards and standard setting must be related to the criteria of adequacy of financial statements. This relationship is broken if the criteria of adequacy of financial statements is compliance with GAAP.

The puzzlement that results from breaking this relationship was expressed in a quotation by Tweedie reported in *Accountancy*, August 1997. ' "Are you prepared to sign off accounts that you know are wrong?" Sir David [Tweedie] asked the US. "They said yes because that's what the rules say, and we were just rolling around on the floor at this stage—it's bizarre what the US does." ' (quoted in Alexander, 1999, p. 249). Where 'right' is understood as 'in accordance with the rules' and 'wrong' is understood as 'not in accord with the rules', it is not possible to say that financial statements that are in accord with the rules are wrong. Clearly Tweedie understands 'wrong' in some other sense. No wonder there is misunderstanding and the U.S. position seems 'bizarre'. If 'wrong' means something like 'inadequate', then Tweedie is implying that it is possible that financial statements that are 'adequate' in the sense of complying with standards are not adequate in some other sense. The 'criterion of adequacy' for financial statements is not understood as 'compliance with GAAP'.

It is understandable that the U.S. might have defined 'adequate' when applied to financial statements as 'complying with GAAP'. Few would deny that compliance with GAAP will *generally* result in financial statements that 'present fairly' or give a 'true and fair view'. The IASB suggest that 'the application of IFRSs [International Financial Reporting Standards], with additional disclosure when necessary, is presumed to result in financial statements that achieve a fair presentation' (IASB, 2011, IAS 1, §15) and that 'in virtually all circumstances, an entity achieves a fair presentation by compliance with applicable IFRSs' (IASB, 2011, IAS 1, §17). What is being asserted is something like 'if you follow IFRSs then it will be the case that you give a fair presentation'. The two statements are 'extensionally equivalent' in the sense that when one is true then the other is true. When 'I follow IFRS' is true then 'I present fairly' is normally true. This is another example of the move from observed concomitants of a phenomenon to using this to define the phenomena of the kind Wittgenstein suggested. Arguably, this is exactly what has happened in the U.S. 'Presents fairly' is observed as a 'concomitant' of 'follows GAAP' and now is used to define it. 'Extensional equivalence' had become 'intensional equivalence', that is, 'presents fairly' is *defined* as 'follows GAAP'. What Tweedie, and what might be called the UK School, denies is that 'presents fairly' or 'true and fair view' *means* 'being in accordance with GAAP'. It is not surprising that 'presents fairly' and 'follows GAAP' are extensionally equivalent if, in promulgating standards, standard setters wish those who follow the standards to produce financial statements that 'present fairly' or give a 'true and fair view'. However, if these are not equivalent in meaning, there is always the possibility that a company can follow GAAP but not present fairly or give a 'true and fair view'. This possibility is acknowledged by Tweedie.

This raises the question of what to do about it. If the possibility is not acknowledged, then there is no need to do anything about it. If it is acknowledged, then there are a number of ways of dealing with the problem. If this happens only in a few cases, then perhaps it does not matter. This may work in the U.S. Alexander quotes Zeff as saying, in private correspondence, 'as a matter of fact, acting at the suggestion of the 1978 Cohen Commission on Auditors' Responsibilities, the US Auditing Standards Board actually proposed in 1980 that the term "fairness" be deleted from the opinion paragraph of the audit report! "Fairness" is not in US legislation; it is no more than an amorphous standard of quality invoked by the AICPA' (Alexander, 1999, p. 248). In other words, there is no legislation that requires financial statements to 'present fairly'. This solution would not appear to work in the UK, where there is a requirement in the Companies Act to give a 'true and fair view'.

Another solution to the problem is to change the standard to stop this from happening by excluding the circumstances where it happens from those covered by the standard. In other words, an exception is made in the standard. As an alternative standards that include rules or prescriptions may be conceived as 'rules of thumb'. This means that they are followed except when following the rule will not meet the ends or objectives of the rule. If they do not meet these ends, then the rule can be overridden. One way of understanding this is to say that following the rule will not meet the 'criteria of adequacy' or, as it might also be said, will not 'present fairly' or give a 'true and fair view'. It is not often appreciated that rules can be understood as 'rules of thumb' rather than rules on the 'practice' conception (Rawls, 1955). 'Rules of thumb' are adopted because it is believed that they will achieve certain objectives if followed. On particular occasions where following the rule will not achieve the objectives, the rule may be overridden (Rawls, 1955, p. 161). On the 'practice' conception, rules are to be followed on all occasions and involve 'the abdication of full liberty to act on utilitarian and prudential grounds' (Rawls, 1955, p. 162). With 'rules of thumb' those following the rule need to undertake practical reasoning to decide whether or not they want to meet the requirements on particular occasions. This is not allowed with rules conceived on the 'practice' conception.

The response that is made to the problem that following a standard may not meet the objectives or 'criteria of adequacy' for financial statements on all occasions depends upon the conception of the kind of rules that are promulgated in accounting standards. The U.S. system conceives rules on the 'practice' conception with no effective override. As Zeff has commented, 'While it is true that rule 203 of the AICPA Code of Professional Conduct provides that there may be circumstances in which the auditor could believe that adherence to promulgated GAAP would make the financial statement misleading, experienced US auditors tell me they cannot recall ever seeing "rule 203 exceptions" especially in the financial statements of companies subject to the Securities and Exchange Commission, which would comprehend almost all publicly traded companies' (reported in Alexander, 1999, p. 248). The UK appears to conceive rules in standards as 'rules of thumb'. The availability of an override of the kind available in the UK may be part of what is meant by a 'principles-based' system of accounting standards (Dennis, 2014, ch. 4). For this kind of system to work, the preparer and auditor need to consider the 'criteria of adequacy' for financial statements in deciding whether or not to override the rule in a standard. In this sense, 'criteria of adequacy' are to be used by the preparer in making decisions of this kind and by the auditor in deciding on his or her opinion about the financial statements prepared. Providing these criteria is the aim of the second kind of response.

THE SECOND KIND OF RESPONSE

Recognising that some criteria other than compliance with standards or GAAP is required as to determine the adequacy of financial statements sometimes leads commentators to look on 'true and fair' as being a 'standard of a higher order' (Flint, 1980, quoted in Porter et al., 2008, p. 526). Sometimes it is something that underpins something else, as in Alexander's 'fundamental concept' or as Walton's 'independent concept'. The concept is either 'over' or 'under' standards or standard setting but not on the same level. The difficulty with conceiving of the concept in this way is that it needs to be understood; hence, 'a satisfactory working definition of "true and fair view" is therefore a matter of considerable practical importance to those working in this area' (McGee, 1991, p. 876). That this has not been given, at least in law, is acknowledged in the literature.

There are various accounts of why this is the case. It has been suggested that 'in selecting the phrase "true and fair view" . . . the Legislature in effect conferred a legislative function on the accountancy profession' (Ryan, 1974, p. 14, quoted in Porter et al., 2008, p. 526). The legislature requires preparers to give a 'true and fair view' and auditors to confirm that this has been done, but what this means is left to the professionals to sort out. This seems a little odd. Legislators do not tell people to 'do X' and then leave it to someone else to say what it is they have to do. They normally have some idea about what 'X' is or they could not be sure they want people to do it. Hoffman and Arden, in an opinion given to the Accounting Standards Committee, expressed the view that 'the phrase "true and fair view" was one which could readily be understood as a matter of simple English, and therefore did not require further definition' (McGee, 1991, pp. 878–879). This has been supported by the view that 'virtually nobody has difficulty using *true* or *fair* in everyday discourse' (Clarke, 2006, p. 131) and 'few in a business setting had much trouble with . . . for about 130 years and informally for much longer'. However, 'from about 1965 accountants, regulators, analysts and the like discovered they didn't understand what the term meant' (Clarke, 2006, p. 129). What this really means is not that they could not give an explanation but that there is no 'definition' in the ideal sense. In a legal opinion given by Hoffman and Arden, it is claimed that the 'true and fair view' is 'an abstraction or philosophical concept expressed in simple English' (Hoffman and Arden, 1983, p. 155). If so, 'it does not require further definition' (McGee, 1991, p. 878–879).

The idea of a 'philosophical concept' needs to be explained. In one school of modern philosophy, where philosophy is conceptual enquiry, there are no *specifically* philosophical concepts. Instead philosophy studies the concepts used in various languages, including the language of accounting. Perhaps all that is meant is that with such concepts there is no ideal definition in terms of necessary and sufficient conditions. Philosophical concepts are those that may be explained in other ways, possibly the kind of ways in which our concepts in 'simple English' are explained. If this is what is meant, then understanding such concepts requires that one looks at how these expressions are used and explained (Dennis, 2006, ch. 2). This is the idea behind 'custom and consensus agreement' (Alexander, 1999. p. 242). The problem is that there is 'considerable controversy among accountants as to the meaning of the phrase'. This suggests that 'the difficulties of application are so great as to raise the question whether there is any definable and generally agreed central content at all' (McGee, 1991, p. 879). Alexander explains that 'customary practice, whether regulated or arising from habit, is governed and influenced, but not determined in detail, by concepts of a more fundamental nature' (Alexander, 1999, p. 242). The problem with this is that the nature of these 'concepts of a more fundamental nature' is not explained. The result is that 'a fundamental concept is defined by custom and consensus, which in turn are guided by fundamental concepts'. The reasoning is thus circular (Evans, 2003, p. 314).

Circularity can be avoided by simply saying that 'true and fair' means what people who use the expression mean by it. A problem arises if there is no agreement in explanations of the term and, possibly, a lack of agreement on its application to particular circumstances. Clarke suggests this is not a problem. Tweedie's suggestion that accountants know that accounts are 'wrong', that is, do not give a 'true and fair view', suggests that applying the term may not be a problem. The problem is that they do not seem able to explain why they apply it. 'I just do', rather like 'I know it is wrong when I see it', does not appear adequate and may not fare well in certain jurisdictions and courts of law. Accountants may not wish to be left high and dry and unable to support their judgement. The concept appears to be *vague*. Evans suggests that there are two issues here, one about meaning and one about 'how the meaning is to be applied in practice' (Evans, 2003, p. 314). In fact, these are both part of the *same* issue. To get clear about the meaning is to get clear about explanations of meaning and to clarify how the expression is to be applied in practice. In the case with 'true and fair' either the explanations do not agree or there is no agreement in applying the expression, or both may be the case. One way out of this dilemma is to try to agree on an explanation that supports its application to circumstances. The first kind of response to define the term as 'compliance with standards' as one way out of resolving the issue but appears inadequate. Another way out is to adopt the third approach, or theme, identified in the literature, that is, to make it a Type B concept or a concept that stands for 'generally accepted accounting principles' but 'does not represent a coherent, rationally consistent set of principles'. This is the kind of thing set out in a conceptual framework for accounting.

A THIRD WAY?

Alexander's Type B approach to 'criteria of adequacy' is illustrated by the conceptual framework approach to the problem of stating such criteria (Alexander, 1999, p. 240). It was suggested that Type B can be thought of as expressing a desire to prepare financial statements that fulfil or follow a set of 'rules, conventions or ways of thinking' which are applied to financial reporting situations. These might be thought of as 'principles' of financial reporting though, as noted in chapter 1, the nature of principles is not clear. They are sometimes understood as expressing desires and sometimes as rules that determine what is reported. As conceptual frameworks guide standard setters in choosing detailed rules to prescribe, they are used to derive rules. Principles in such frameworks are like Walton's 'independent concept', which guides standard setters, either by indicating what is wanted in setting standards, in which case they are similar to his 'legal residual clause' which indicates the 'the intention behind, or the spirit of, the document', namely what is wanted from the rule, or they are general rules used to derive specific rules.

Alexander does not think this approach and this kind of framework can provide the ultimate criterion of adequacy for financial statements. They are not 'coherent structures in an internal consistency sense' (Alexander, 1999, p. 240). This applies to both kinds of 'principles'. If they are interpreted as expressing what is wanted from financial statements, the question arises as to whether or not it is necessary for all of the criteria selected in the conceptual framework, that is relevance, reliability, comparability and understandability, to be met. If so this will not be possible since there are conflicts between them. In particular, relevance and reliability sometimes cannot both be met. Another interpretation of these criteria is that they are no more than a euphemism for the 'true and fair view/fair presentation concept' (Alexander, 1999, p. 249). There is inconsistency when interpreted as expressing general rules as sometimes they conflict. An example of such a conflict can be seen in trying to follow the general rule of the matching convention and trying also to follow the prudence convention.

The problem with these arguments is in understanding what is meant by 'internal consistency' in this context. We know what 'inconsistency' means when this is related to statements that are capable of truth or falsity. Two statements are inconsistent if one says 'X is φ' and another says 'X is not φ'. This interpretation is not relevant since statements expressing the qualitative characteristics of useful information are not statements that are true or false. They express what is wanted and do not express statements that are capable of truth or falsity. If there are two valid deductions which have incompatible conclusions, in the sense that both cannot be true, then the premises must also be incompatible (Salmon, 1992, p. 26). Statements expressing qualitative characteristics and those expressing rules are not statements that are true or false. They are used to derive a desire to promulgate standards. If one derives incompatible desires for action, then it might be possible to treat the premises, the desires or rules from which the conclusion is derived, as being inconsistent because the actions are inconsistent in the sense that one cannot do both. So if you want to provide relevant information and believe that information X is relevant, you may conclude that you want to provide information X. If you also want to provide reliable information and believe that information X is not reliable, you might conclude that you do not want to provide information X. You have inconsistent conclusions and so might say that the desires are inconsistent. This is, presumably, the thought behind Alexander's idea that there is inconsistency in the criteria in the conceptual framework. Similarly, you may want to follow the matching principle and therefore want to carry forward a cost against income on the grounds that it is an application of this convention. If you also want to follow the prudence convention and believe you should write off the same cost against income in the current period, then you may want to write off the cost now. There is an inconsistency here for one cannot do both. This is the thought behind the view that these conventions are inconsistent.

Neither of these interpretations of inconsistency necessarily applies to 'principles' of the kind expressed in the conceptual framework. Statements of the desire to meet qualitative characteristics are not, straightforwardly, inconsistent. Wanting relevant information is not inconsistent with wanting reliable information. The idea that if one deduces inconsistent conclusions then the premises are inconsistent only applies if one uses statements expressing qualitative characteristics to *deduce* conclusions about actions. It was suggested in chapter 1 that the conceptual framework is not used in deductive reasoning. They could only be used in this way if what is wanted is universally wanted. It was suggested that the idea that these desires are always wanted is unrealistic. Instead, they should be viewed as something that is *generally* wanted, and these desires are used in *non-deductive practical reasoning*. If one generally wants relevant information and also generally wants reliable information, the fact that one reasons to inconsistent conclusions does not mean that one has to give up one or the other of the characteristics as inconsistent. One generally wants both and still generally wants them even if, on occasion, one cannot fulfil both.

A similar argument can be made about the kind of general rule expressed by the conventions of accounting. If one accepts a rule that states that one must *always* do something *whenever* the circumstances for following the rule arise, then one can deduce, given that the circumstances arise, that one has to do something in accord with the rule. If one reasons deductively in this way and derives inconsistent conclusions about what is to be done, then one of the rules must be given up. However, this is to interpret rules as on the 'practice' conception where accepting a rule means following it on all occasions. It was suggested that rules could be conceived as 'rules of thumb', something that is generally wanted but not wanted on *every* occasion when the rule applies. If there is a clash of such rules, in the sense that one reasons to actions that are inconsistent, this does not mean that one has to give up one of the rules. One does not reason to actions deductively but, again, by practical reasoning. If one decides not to follow a rule on an occasion because there is another rule that requires one to do something that cannot be done if one follows the first rule, this does not mean that one has to give up generally wanting to do what the other rule requires. One can still want to follow the matching principle generally, as a 'rule of thumb', even if one also wants to follow the prudent convention generally, as a 'rule of thumb', and can want both generally even if, on occasion, both cannot be followed.

This shows that rejecting Type B rules as providing 'criteria of adequacy' on the grounds of inconsistency follows from a misunderstanding of the nature of the 'principles' expressed in a conceptual framework or in a system of conventions and a misunderstanding of the kind of reasoning that uses such 'principles' in making decisions about standard setting or decisions about what one wants to do. With deductive reasoning the conclusion follows from the premises *necessarily*. If one accepts the premises one *has* to accept the conclusion. With practical reasoning this is not the case. If one wants to provide relevant information and a certain kind of information is relevant one does not *have* to conclude that one wants to provide such information. One might conclude that one does not want to provide such information because one wants something else, say reliable information, and the information in question is not reliable. This brings out another contrast with deductive reasoning. Deduction is 'erosion-proof' in the sense that 'if new premises are added to a valid deductive argument . . . the argument remains valid' (Salmon, 1992, p. 11). Adding new premises that one wants something else, reliable information, and that one believes that certain information is not reliable means that the conclusion is no longer valid. The argument is not 'erosion-proof'. The argument does not involve deductive reasoning but practical reasoning. The latter does not exemplify the characteristics of deductive reasoning.

In practical reasoning because the conclusion does not follow necessarily from the premises and because conclusions can be undermined by the addition of further premises, accepting the conclusion involves the exercise of *judgement*. One 'goes beyond the premises' in drawing the conclusion. Practical reasoning is 'ampliative' (Salmon, 1992, p. 11). Exercising judgement is drawing conclusions in a non-deductive form of reasoning. It is not exercised in deductive reasoning where you *have* to accept the conclusion if you accept the premises and where the conclusion cannot be undermined by the addition of premises and where the content of the conclusion is implicit in the premises. This will be illustrated further when the exercise of judgement in auditing is examined later in the book.

Alexander's rejects qualitative characteristics as 'a euphemism for the true and fair view/fair presentation concept' because 'they do not provide a clear-cut criterion' (Alexander, 1999, p. 249). He acknowledges such characteristics might be 'helpful as a checklist of background ideas in a situation where one is groping towards a solution to some unusual situation which one needs to present fairly' (Alexander, 1999, p. 249). However, given their nature and their use in practical reasoning to standard setting decisions, this 'euphemism' for 'true and fair' might actually provide an explanation of the meaning of 'true and fair'. In effect, these characteristics provide 'criteria of adequacy' for financial statements in the same way that the conceptual framework, which expresses what is wanted from financial statements, provides such criteria. This provides the starting point for a prescriptive conceptual enquiry into 'true and fair'.

A PRESCRIPTIVE CONCEPTUAL ENQUIRY: EXPLAINING 'TRUE AND FAIR' IN TERMS OF CONCEPTUAL FRAMEWORK PRINCIPLES

It was suggested earlier that 'criteria of adequacy' of financial statements should be understood as expressing what is wanted from financial statements, the kind of thing expressed in conceptual frameworks and accounting theories. In their conceptual framework the ASB acknowledge that 'the concept of a true and fair view lies at the heart of financial reporting in the UK' (ASB, 1999, §10). This suggests that understanding 'true and fair' is understanding the same kind of thing that the conceptual framework seeks to understand. The ASB explain that they did not bring the 'true and fair view' into the conceptual framework although it has 'the true and fair view concept at its foundation'. They explain that 'financial statements will not give a true and fair view unless the information they contain is sufficient in quantity and quality to satisfy the reasonable expectations of the readers to who they are addressed' (ASB, 1999, §12). Relevance and reliability are prime indicators of the quality of financial information. This suggests that giving a 'true and fair view' *means*, inter alia, giving relevant and reliable information. The qualitative characteristic of reliability has been supplanted in the revised IASB conceptual framework by the characteristic of *faithful representation*. In the IASB *Discussion Paper* setting out preliminary views on the improved conceptual framework it is stated that 'faithful representation' and 'reliability' are two terms that mean essentially the same thing (IASB, 2006, BC2.29). This will be accepted here. The term 'reliability' will be used in preference. The conceptual framework thus contributes to the development of the concept of 'true and fair' but does not define it.

One reason the ASB say this is that they believe that this concept is defined as 'compliance with standards' (ASB, 1999, §13). In other words, they appear to see it as a Type C concept. It is rather odd to say that the conceptual framework 'develops' the concept but does not define it. After all, how does one develop a concept except through contributing to its meaning by offering an explanation of it? The reason is probably the preconception about the nature of definition. Given necessary and sufficient conditions for its use would constrain what the ASB calls a 'dynamic' concept (ASB, 1999, §11). If these preconceptions are rejected, then it is quite possible to see the conceptual framework as explaining the concept of true and fair by setting out the 'criteria of adequacy' that both are aiming to set out. In developing the conceptual framework one is developing the true and fair concept. This may lie behind the thought that the concept lies at the heart of financial reporting. This development involves seeing this concept as a Type B concept. It is no surprise that the conceptual framework provides insight into the meaning of 'true and fair' given that both attempt to state what is wanted in financial reporting.

If this is how the true and fair concept is to be understood, then it is possible to see how it has developed from the time it was first introduced into the Companies Act. The idea of 'criteria of adequacy' for financial statements, what was wanted in financial statements or the objective and characteristics of useful information in financial statements, was something that was grasped by professional accountants and was a matter of custom and practice. It was probable that the legislature recognised this and included reference to it under the concept of true and fair but left it to the professionals by, in effect, conferring on them a legislative function. In other words, it was left to them to explain what was involved in a true and fair view, to explain the meaning of the expression 'true and fair'. The kind of theory or framework used by professionals changed from the time the concept was first introduced to the present day (Dennis, 2014, p. 27). This was the move from conventions to the desires in the decisions-usefulness approach. Accounting theory in vogue before the onset of conceptual framework projects explained 'appropriate' accounting practices as 'those that adhered to desirable accounting conventions such as conservatism, consistency, historical cost and matching' (Young, 2006, p. 582). Such theories set out general rules that were to be followed from which more specific and detailed rules could be developed which governed practice. A 'true and fair view' would, presumably, be given by financial statements that followed the general rules or the specific rules derived from them. These were rejected in favour of the identification of desires in the conceptual framework. This move from conventions to the conceptual framework illustrates the 'dynamic' concept of true and fair.

The actual meaning of 'true and fair' in the literature is sometimes examined when audit evidence is explained. This is rather confusing. What is given as evidence of truth and fairness is better understood as something that is implied by the meaning of 'true and fair'. This is understandable given the verification principle. Although this states that the meaning of a proposition is determined by its method of verification this might be restated as the principle that determining what evidence is required for a proposition is a method of determining the meaning of the proposition. This is acceptable as long as 'evidence' is understood as something connected by meaning with the proposition and not something that is connected empirically. This will be examined further in chapter 4 where explanations of 'evidence' in the auditing literature are considered. It is suggested in this chapter that the meaning of 'true and fair' is best understood by adopting the approach of seeing this as a Type B concept. What is wanted in adopting this concept is something that is useful in meeting the desires in the conceptual framework.

THE MEANING OF 'TRUE AND FAIR'

Asking about meaning tends to produce in us a 'mental cramp' in that 'we feel that we can't point to anything in reply . . . and yet ought to point to something'. It is 'one of the great sources of philosophical bewilderment: a substantive makes us look for a thing that corresponds to it' (Wittgenstein, 1958, p. 1). The antidote to this poison is to realise that when one asks the question 'What is the meaning of . . . ?' one is asking for an *explanation* of the meaning of the expression. When one asks 'What is the meaning of "true and fair"?' one is asking 'How would one explain the expression "true and fair"?' There are different kinds of explanation of meaning, and many expressions we use do not have explanations in terms of necessary and sufficient conditions. Given the development of the conceptual framework as something that gives the 'criteria of adequacy' of financial statements, one way of explaining 'true and fair view' is to say that to give a 'true and fair view' is to prepare financial statements that 'provide financial information about the reporting entity that is useful to existing and potential investors, lenders and other creditors in making decisions about providing resources to the entity' (IASB, 2010, §OB2) that is relevant and reliable/faithfully represents and comparable, verifiable, timely and understandable (IASB, 2010, QC4). In other words, financial statements give a 'true and fair view' if they meet the objectives of financial statements and exhibit the qualitative characteristics of useful information as set out in the conceptual framework. This is a Type B approach.

Although this provides some explanation of the meaning of 'true and fair', it is at rather a high level. To 'operationalise' it one has to know what kind of information is included in financial statements and how the objectives and qualitative characteristics are applied to this kind of information. Some indication of this is also given in the conceptual framework. Financial statements give information about the elements of financial statements such as assets, liabilities, equity and income and expenses (IASB, 2010, §4.2). What is relevant and reliable information, or information that faithfully represents, about these elements? ISA 315 explains that the information is presented in the form of assertions. In relation to assets and liabilities these are assertions about the existence of assets, rights and obligations, completeness and valuation and allocation (IAASB, 2010, ISA 315, §111). There are other assertions relating to the other elements set out in this ISA. These assertions comprise information that needs to be relevant and reliable/faithfully represents in order to meet the needs of users and also that fulfils the other characteristics of useful information. The information is provided by following the rules set out in accounting standards, and if the standards are promulgated by standard setters who want to provide information for users that has these qualitative characteristics then, if standard setters have done their job, following the rules should result in information of the required kind. It is this thought that underlies the idea that giving a 'true and fair' view is a matter of complying with standards. The problem is that there might be circumstances where the objective of financial statements and fulfilling the characteristics are not met by following these standards. In such a case it may be necessary to override the standards in order to give a 'true and fair view', that is, produce financial statements that meet the 'criteria of adequacy' expressed in the conceptual framework. In other words, there may be room for a 'true and fair' override. If 'true and fair' is to be understood in terms of achieving the objectives and qualitative characteristics of useful information, does this signify the death of the term?

THE DEATH OF 'TRUE AND FAIR'?

A descriptive conceptual enquiry into the concept of 'true and fair' and of a 'true and fair view' suggests that the concept is vague. The evaluative conceptual enquiry suggests that the underlying need or desire that this concept is meant to fulfil is to provide a 'criteria of adequacy' for financial statements. The prescriptive conceptual enquiry went on to suggest that clarity would be given to the concept if the 'criteria of adequacy' that this concept is meant to express was understood as the criteria expressed in a conceptual framework for financial reporting. To give a 'true and fair view' is to present financial statements that meet the objectives of financial reporting and have the qualitative characteristics set out in the conceptual framework. These criteria express general desires, rather than a set of universal desires, for financial statements to fulfil and constitute a Type B approach to such criterial. Understanding them as general rules rather than universal rules overcomes Alexander's arguments against their use as 'criteria of adequacy' of financial statements. The concept of 'true and fair', understood in this way, can be used in reasoning by standard setters to standard setting decisions as well as by preparers and auditors who need to ensure that these desires are met by financial statements they prepare or audit. If standard setters have done their job well, and if preparers follow the rules in the standards, then it is likely that the financial statements prepared in accordance with the rules will fulfil these 'criteria of adequacy'. However, it is overly sanguine to think that following the rules will always meet these criteria. This blocks the explanation of 'true and fair' in terms of compliance with standards. This may be the approach taken in the U.S. with 'presents fairly', but it is argued that it is inadequate for a 'true and fair view' understood as 'criteria of adequacy'. If, in the particular circumstances, by following the rules the financial statements do not fulfil these criteria, then they should be overridden. Auditors need to consider whether the judgements of preparers are correct and determine whether an override of standards is acceptable.

If these arguments are correct, then there is no reason why the term 'true and fair view' might not be replaced by some other way of expressing what is meant to be conveyed by this term. Instead of saying the financial statements 'give a true and fair view', what is conveyed might be more clearly expressed by something along the lines of saying that the financial statements meet the criteria of adequacy set out in the conceptual framework for financial reporting. This could form the basis of a new opinion to be given by auditors. Explained in this way it is clear that 'true and fair' is not the same concept as 'presents fairly', at least if it is understood as appears to be the case in the U.S. as 'complies with GAAP'. The latter is a Type C concept in Alexander's typology. It could also form the basis of a new kind of opinion in the U.S. The opinion would be along the lines of these financial statements comply with GAAP. The question that would naturally arise from an opinion of this kind is whether financial statements that comply with GAAP do actually meet the 'criteria of adequacy' of financial statements. If not, then the motivation for developing the concept of 'presents fairly' is not to develop a concept that expresses 'criteria of adequacy'. Given a different motivation for the concept of 'presents fairly' from the motivation for developing 'true and fair', it is no wonder that the meaning of these concepts is not the same. The IASB attempt to equate these concepts in the interest of convergence is mistaken. They need to choose between concepts and not pretend that they are the same.

As a 'euphemism' or shorthand for something else, the terms 'true and fair' and 'true and fair view' or 'presents fairly' might be useful in being able to given an opinion on financial statements that is short and pithy. However, it is only useful if what it is shorthand for is clear. At the moment this is not the case. This leaves it unclear what is being conveyed by the opinion and does not make it clear to auditors exactly what they have to do in order to give such an opinion. If giving an opinion that includes the term 'presents fairly' is required, and this only means that it has to be determined whether or not standards are followed, then this requires auditing procedures that are rather different than would be required by giving an opinion that financial statements give a 'true and fair view' where this is understood as saying that 'criteria of adequacy', in the sense that requires to be explained, have been met. The nature of the opinion needs to be understood if auditors are to understand what they are required to do in order to issue an opinion of the required kind.

Understanding what is meant by the opinion ought to be used to guide auditing standard setters in setting out requirements for auditors to meet in order to enable them to meet the objectives of auditing and to give an appropriate opinion on the financial statements. Without a clear grasp of the meaning of the opinion, it is unclear how auditing standard setters can do their job. The suspicion is that such standard setters may determine what auditors need to do guided by only a vague idea about the meaning of the opinion. The meaning might then be reconstructed as something that justifies the requirements that are determined rather using an understanding of the opinion to justify the requirements. Arguably, this is what has happened in giving the meaning of 'true and fair' in terms of 'compliance with standards'. If a theory of auditing is to be used to guide standard setters in setting standards, then this is the wrong way around. Theory should not be developed to justify practice determined on other grounds. Theory ought to determine practice by setting out what is wanted from practice. Examining what is meant by 'true and fair' in this chapter is a contribution to the latter kind of theory of auditing.

SUMMARY

Given a desire to enhance credibility as the objective of auditing, the belief that this is achieved by giving an opinion about the financial statements is explored. The meanings of the expressions 'present fairly' and 'give a true and fair view' are examined. It is suggested that they are intended to capture the idea of criteria of adequacy of financial statements. Different approaches to determining these criteria are considered. The approach that suggests that financial statements are adequate if they follow the rules of GAAP is rejected on the grounds that it makes sense to ask whether financial statements that follow GAAP are, indeed, adequate. This is not possible if being adequate simply means following GAAP. The approach that the criteria express an all pervasive fundamental concept is found wanting given the vagueness of the expressions. The approach that explains adequacy as something that follow rules, conventions or ways of thinking of the kind expressed in conceptual frameworks is supported. Arguments against this interpretation of the expressions are based on misconceptions about the nature of the principles in conceptual frameworks. It is suggested that 'giving a true and fair view' is a matter of financial statements meeting the criteria of useful information in that they are relevant and reliable. What is relevant and reliable information depends upon the kind of information provided in financial statements. It is suggested that talking about truth and fairness could be replaced by talking about relevance and reliability and the audit opinion changed to reflect this.

REFERENCES

Alexander, D. (1999), 'A benchmark for the adequacy of published financial statements', *Accounting and Business Research*, Vol. 29 (3), pp. 239–253.
Alexander, D. & Jermakowicz, E. (2006) 'A true and fair view of the principles/rules debate', *Abacus*, Vol. 42 (2), pp. 132–164.
ASB (1999) *Statement of Principles for Financial Reporting*. London: ASB.
Baker, G. & Hacker, P. (1985) *Wittgenstein Rules, Grammar and Necessity*. Oxford: Blackwell.
Clarke, F. (2006) 'Forum: Analysis and evidence on the principles vs. rules debate. Introduction: true and fair—*anachronism* or *quality criterion* par excellence?' *Abacus*, Vol. 42 (2).
Dennis, I. (2006) *A Philosophical Investigation into the Conceptual Framework for Accounting*. PhD Thesis, London School of Economics, University of London. Accessible at: http://ethos.bl.uk/OrderDetails.do?did=1&uin=uk. bl.ethos.433646 [Accessed 13 January 2015].
Dennis, I. (2014) *The Nature of Accounting Regulation*. New York: Routledge.
Evans, L. (2003) 'The true and fair view and the "fair presentation" override of IAS 1', *Accounting and Business Research*, Vol. 33 (4), pp. 311–325.
Hoffman, L. & Arden, M. (1983) 'Legal opinion on "true and fair"', *Accountancy*, November, pp. 154–156.
IAASB (2010) *ISA 200 Overall Objectives of the Independent Auditor and the Conduct of an Audit in Accordance with International Standards*. New York: International Federation of Accountants.
IASB (2006) *Discussion Paper Preliminary Views on an Improved Conceptual Framework for Financial Reporting: The Objective of Financial Reporting and Qualitative Characteristics of Decision-useful Financial Reporting Information*. London: IASB.
IASB (2010) *The Conceptual Framework for Financial Reporting*. London: IASB.
IASB (2011) *IAS 1 Presentation of Financial Statements*. London: IASB.
McGee, A. (1991) 'The "true and fair view" debate: A study in the legal regulation of accounting', *Modern Law Review*, Vol. 54 (6), pp. 874–888.

Nobes, C. (2000) 'Is true and fair of over-riding importance?: A comment on Alexander's benchmark', *Accounting and Business Research*, Vol. 30 (4), pp. 307–312.

Porter, B., Simon, J. & Hatherley, D. (2008) *Principles of External Auditing*. 3rd edn. West Sussex, UK: Wiley.

Rawls, J. (1955) 'Two concepts of rules', *Philosophical Review*, Vol. 64, reprinted in P. Foot (ed.) (1967) *Theories of Ethics* in the *Oxford Readings in Philosophy* series. Oxford: Oxford University Press.

Rutherford, B. (1985) 'The true and fair view doctrine: A search for explication', *Journal of Business Finance & Accounting*, Vol. 12 (4), pp. 483–494.

Salmon, W. (1992) 'Scientific Explanation' in *Introduction to the Philosophy of Science*. Indianapolis, Ind./Cambridge: Hackett Publishing Company.

SEC (2003) *Study Report Pursuant to Section 108(d) of the Sarbanes-Oxley Act of 2002, SEC*. Accessible at: http://www.sec.gov/news/studies/principlesbasedstand. htm [Accessed 14 November 2011].

Toba, Y. (1975) 'A general theory of evidence as the conceptual foundation in auditing theory', *Accounting Review*, Vol. 50 (2), pp. 7–24.

Wittgenstein, L. (1958) *The Blue and Brown Books*. Oxford: Basil Blackwell.

Young, J. (2006) 'Making up users', *Accounting Organizations and Society*, Vol. 31 (6), pp. 579–600.

Zeff, S. (1993) 'The politics of accounting standards', *Economia Aziendale*, August, pp. 123–142.

4   Audit Evidence

The development of an auditing theory started with the identification of what was wanted from the practice of auditing, that is, with the objectives of auditing. A premise about what is wanted is used in practical reasoning to further desires for auditing given certain beliefs about what kind of practice will fulfil the desire. It is believed that users of financial statements wish to be able to rely upon financial statements to make certain decisions. Auditing is a practice that has the objective of giving *credibility* to the financial statements so that the financial statements can be relied upon. From the desire to assist users in their wish to rely on financial statements a further desire for auditing, namely to give credibility to those statements, is derived by practical reasoning. It is believed that this can be achieved by auditors giving an opinion on the financial statements. The nature of the opinion was considered in the previous chapter. Another desire is derived. What is wanted from auditing is that auditors give an opinion on the financial statements as the means of giving credibility to them. However, in order for the opinion to give credibility it is believed that auditors must be able to *justify* the opinion given and that this requires they have *evidence* to support their opinion. This leads to a desire that auditors search for this evidence as part of their audit work. The nature of evidence and what is involved in the search for evidence is considered in this chapter.

THE IMPORTANCE OF EVIDENCE

There is general agreement amongst auditors, academics and regulators that the search for evidence is central to the activity of auditing. ISA 500 states that 'most of the auditor's work in forming the auditor's opinion consists of obtaining and evaluating audit evidence' (IAASB, 2010, ISA 500, §A2). This requires the auditor to obtain reasonable assurance that the financial statements are free from material misstatement by obtaining sufficient appropriate audit evidence on which to base the auditor's opinion (IAASB, 2010, ISA 200). Although there is a vast literature on judgement and decision-making using laboratory experiment, survey and field study approaches relating to evidential situations in auditing (Nelson and Tan, 2005), there have been few attempts to 'conceptualize on the nature and role of audit evidence' (Lee, 1993, p. 187). As Lee observes in relation to institutional bodies such as the American Institute of Certified Public Accountants and the UK's Auditing Practices Committee, they 'create a situation in which evidence and evidential material are not only not clearly distinguished, but are also described in terms which are either undefined (as in the UK) or defined in a recursive manner (as in the US)' (Lee, 1993, p. 172). The lack of, at least a certain kind of, definition is perhaps symptomatic of a more general lack interest in 'conceptualization' in an activity such as auditing that is, as noted in chapter 1, perceived as inherently practical. As explained in that chapter, conceptual enquiry involves understanding the concepts used in talking about auditing and constitutes a form of philosophical enquiry. This chapter conceptualizes about the nature and role of audit evidence and uses the insights derived to throw light on the nature of professional judgement and scepticism. In other words, it seeks to understand the meaning of 'evidence', 'professional judgement' and 'scepticism'. It argues that these two important activities in the auditing context cannot be understood without adequate conceptualization of the nature of audit evidence. A contribution is made to the current discussion about the importance of judgement and scepticism that is evident in the International Auditing and Assurance Standards Board's ISAs, the European Commission's (EC) Green Paper, *Audit Policy: Lessons from the Crisis* (EC, 2010) and in the UK Auditing Practices Board's *Briefing Paper* (APB, 2012). A descriptive conceptual enquiry into the concept of evidence will now be undertaken. It starts with considering statements about evidence in the IAASB's auditing standards.

THE IAASB'S CONCEPTION OF EVIDENCE

ISA 200 defines 'audit evidence' as 'information used by the auditor in arriving at the conclusions on which the auditor's opinion is based' (IAASB, 2010, ISA 200, §13(b)). The evidence enables the auditor to give an opinion on the financial statements. In order to give the opinion the auditor must obtain reasonable assurance about whether the financial statements as a whole are free from material misstatement. The enables the opinion to be given 'on whether the financial statements are prepared, in all material respects, in accordance with an applicable financial reporting framework. In the case of most general purpose frameworks, that opinion is on whether the financial statements are presented fairly, in all material respects, or give a true and fair view in accordance with the framework' (IAASB, 2010, ISA 200, §3). Management produce financial statements in accordance with an applicable financial reporting framework and in doing so make assertions regarding 'the recognition, measurement, presentation and disclosure of the various elements of financial statements and related disclosures' (IAASB,

2010, ISA 315, §A110). Evidence 'comprises both information that supports and corroborates management's assertions, and any information that contradicts such assertions' (IAASB, 2010, ISA 500, A1). 'Reasonable assurance' that the financial statements are free from material misstatement is obtained when the auditor has 'sufficient appropriate audit evidence' that reduces audit risk, that is, the risk that the auditor expresses an inappropriate audit opinion when the financial statements are materially misstated (IAASB, 2010, Glossary of Terms, p. 14), to an acceptably low level and thereby enables the auditor to draw reasonable conclusions. Sufficiency is 'the measure of the quantity of audit evidence' (IAASB, 2010, ISA 500, A5) and 'appropriateness is the measure of the quality of audit evidence; that is, its relevance and its reliability in providing support for the conclusions on which the auditor's opinion is based' (IAASB, 2010, ISA 500, A5). Evidence is said to be cumulative in nature and primarily obtained from accounting records, audit procedures and the work of a management's expert and may include information from previous audits or the firm's quality control procedures (IAASB, 2010, ISA 500, §A1). Audit procedures to obtain evidence include 'inspection, observation, confirmation, recalculation, reperformance, and analytical procedures, often in some combination, in addition to inquiry' (IAASB, 2010, ISA 500, §A2). Audit evidence is obtained by risk assessment procedures as well as tests of controls and substantive procedures (IAASB, 2010, ISA 500, §A10). ISA 500 gives guidance about the reliability of different kinds of evidence. It suggests, for example, that reliability is increased when evidence is obtained from independent sources outside the entity. Evidence generated internally is more reliable when the related controls imposed by the entity are effective. Evidence is more reliable if in documentary form rather than obtained orally (IAASB, 2010, ISA 500, §A31). The evidence is persuasive rather than conclusive (IAASB, 2010, ISA 200, §7). Scepticism must be applied in determining whether there are misstatements and in being critical in assessing evidence, and judgement must be exercised in gathering evidence (IAASB, 2010, ISA 200, §7).

One problem with these statements in ISAs is that it is not clear how they emerge from a reasoned argument involving practical reasoning that starts with what is wanted from auditing and ends up with requirements that need to be met by auditors. The first thing that will be considered is the idea that evidence enables the opinion to be given.

EVIDENCE THAT ENABLES THE OPINION TO BE GIVEN

It was suggested that the evidence that enables the opinion to be given should be understood, given the verification principle, as something that is implied by the meaning of 'true and fair'. Toba adopts this approach in his exploration of the idea of audit evidence (Toba, 1975). He recognizes that before one can determine the evidence needed in order to issue an opinion one has to understand the 'nature of the proposition' in the opinion. There needs to be agreement among auditors, clients, and readers of examined financial statements on what "fair presentation" implies' (Toba, 1975, p. 14). He claims that the necessary conditions for giving an opinion on the fairness of financial statements under what he calls a 'test audit' are the 'assertions' that the 'accounting policy of the company under review is made in conformity with Generally Accepted Accounting Principles' and that 'a system of internal control (particular, a system of internal accounting control) is in accordance with reasonable standards established within the company under review' (Toba, 1975, p. 14). He does not claim that these are sufficient conditions and that by establishing these assertions it is possible to *deduce* that the financial statements 'present fairly'. However, he claims that by establishing these conditions it makes the opinion 'more probable'. The reasoning involved is 'heuristic' (Toba, 1975, p. 18). The opinion is the 'ultimate proposition' which is confirmed by evidence. Supporting evidence is something that makes the proposition to be supported more *probable*, that is, $P(X|Y) > P(X)$, where P stands for probability, X is the proposition to be confirmed and Y the statement that is evidence for X. Confirming evidence is supporting evidence plus evidence that makes the proposition to be confirmed more probable that its negation, that is, $P(X|Y) > P(notX|Y)$ (Toba, 1975, p. 15). Gibbs noted that this definition of confirming evidence, in effect, implied that evidence confirms a proposition if the probability of the proposition given the evidence is greater than 0.5. This does not represent the auditor's view of confirming evidence (Gibbs, 1977, p. 751). He suggests that evidence is confirming if the probability of the proposition to be confirmed given the evidence is greater than some 'individual threshold of confidence', represented by K. Thus evidence is confirming if $P(X|Y) > K$.

The definition of 'audit evidence' in ISA 200 states that evidence is information used by the auditor to arrive at conclusions on which the auditor's opinion is based. The reference to the connection between information and conclusions connects audit evidence and reasoning since conclusions are obtained by reasoning. This link is emphasized by Mautz and Sharaf, who state that 'evidence gives us a rational basis for forming judgments' (Mautz and Sharaf, 1961, p. 68). Evidence enables the auditor to derive conclusions from premises using some kind of reasoning. Looking for evidence is thus a process of arriving at statements or premises that are then used to derive conclusions in accordance with some kind of reasoning. To understand evidence it is important to understand the nature of the reasoning involved (Toba, 1975, p. 7). It is important to clarify the kinds of premises and the kinds of conclusions that are derived in accordance with some kind of reasoning.

It is odd to say that establishing what has to be the case for a statement to be uttered, as a matter of meaning, constitutes evidence for the statement. This is like saying that if, as a matter of meaning, 'a bachelor is an unmarried man', then one finds evidence that someone is a bachelor by discovering that he is unmarried. This is a necessary condition of being a bachelor. Alternatively, one might say that one finds evidence that someone is unmarried by establishing that he is a bachelor. This is a sufficient condition of being unmarried. Evidential relations do not seem to depend relations of meaning. The matter is complicated given that the meaning of an expression is not always given by necessary and sufficient conditions. Meaning might be given by something like criteria (see Hacker, 1993, ch. 13). The criterial relationship is a relationship established by the meaning of the expression. This is different from the relationship between what Wittgenstein calls 'symptoms' and another statement. Symptoms provide *inductive evidence* for statements whereas criteria do indicate an empirical correlation. Criteria, unlike symptoms, 'determine the meanings of expressions for which they are criteria' whereas 'inductive evidence for something counts as a symptom' (Hacker, 1993, p. 250). Wittgenstein explains that inductive evidence or symptoms can be undermined by introducing further evidence (Hacker, 1993, pp. 250–251). This 'distinguishes a symptom from a sufficient condition' since 'if p logically implies q, then no matter what other propositions are true, it still implies q' (Hacker, 1993, p. 251). Although the distinction criteria and symptoms appear to be sharp, 'there is commonly, especially in science, a fluctuation between criteria and symptoms' (Hacker, 1993, p. 252). Symptoms are discovered in experience whereas criteria give grounds for asserting something laid down by the meaning of the expression. An important difference between 'inductive evidence' and what might be called 'criterial evidence', or grounds for the use of an expression, is that 'if p is inductive evidence for q, then it makes sense to identify q independently of p' (Hacker, 1993, p. 261).

Given this distinction between criteria and symptoms Toba's 'theory of evidence' focuses on the criteria of giving an opinion rather than about the evidential support given by symptoms. Toba develops a theory about what will be called *criterial* evidence rather than a theory about *inductive* evidence. It is important to distinguish the two as statements about evidence for the one may not apply to statements about evidence of the other. The idea of criterial evidence will be considered further.

CRITERIAL EVIDENCE

Toba suggests that there are two kinds of audits, a 'detailed audit' and a 'test audit'. The audit opinion has a different meaning in these different kinds of audit. A 'detailed audit' involves 'verification . . . of "the correctness" or "the accuracy" of all accounts and transactions' (Toba, 1975, p. 12). Toba explains that in a 'detailed audit' the ultimate proposition G, the opinion, is 'equivalent' to the set of elementary propositions E. G is the case if, and only if, E. E is equivalent to the set $\{e_1, e_2, e_3, \ldots, e_n\}$ where e states something like 'transaction t was correctly processed' or, as it was sometimes stated in the audit report, the books and accounts were 'found correct in every particular' (Toba, 1975, p. 12). E is the set of statements about all of the transactions. The opinion G means something like 'all transactions were correctly processed'. This kind of audit was replaced by a 'test audit' where the audit opinion given is that the financial statements give a 'fair presentation'. Asserting fair presentation in such an audit involves asserting that the accounting policy conforms to GAAP and that the system of internal control in a company is in accordance with reasonable standards. Toba explains that the first proposition is 'a set of elementary propositions which describe specifically the accounting policies adopted by the company'. An example of one of these elementary propositions is 'the inventory is valued at cost, on a first-in, first-out basis'. The second proposition is a set of elementary statements that stated that elements of the system of internal control are reasonable. These might be understood as *criteria* of financial statements giving a fair presentation and are implied by the *meaning* of 'fair presentation'. The evidence is *criterial evidence*.

Much of the subsequent development of the theory of evidence was concerned with evidence in the sense of criterial evidence. Some writers suggested that the Toba 'framework' is not accepted by practicing auditors even with the modification suggested by Kissinger (1977) that departures from GAAP are restricted to immaterial effects or failures of a system of internal controls will not lead to material errors (Stephens, 1983). Even if these two conditions are established, practitioners do not all agree that an unqualified opinion can be given. Stephens suggests that this is because the auditors concerned desired more 'evidential matter' (Stephens, 1983, p. 73). A more accurate way of expressing this would be to say that these auditors do not think 'presents fairly' means conforming to GAAP and that the system of internal control is reasonable. The idea that more 'evidential matter' is needed is really the contention that the meaning of this expression implies something further. It was suggested in chapter 3 that giving a 'true and fair view' does not mean following the rules in GAAP. Giving a 'true and fair view' should be understood as meeting 'criteria of adequacy' of financial statements, the kind of thing expressed in the conceptual framework by the objectives and qualitative characteristics of useful financial information. It is difficult to be dogmatic on this point. The IASB equate giving a 'true and fair view' as equivalent to 'fair presentation', but it is unclear whether this is to be interpreted as the U.S. 'presents fairly', namely, as conforming to GAAP, or as the UK 'true and fair view', a fundamental concept (Evans, 2003).

Another problem in determining whether something is a criterion or not lies in the nature of a criterion itself. In Wittgenstein's philosophy, some criteria constitute sufficient conditions for the use of an expression. If this is so, then if following GAAP is a criterion of presenting fairly, and if the rules are followed, the financial statements must present fairly. However, some criteria do not constitute sufficient conditions. Although the criterion in general means that something comes under the expression this is 'defeasible' in certain circumstances. For example, if someone hammers his or her finger instead of a nail and screams, assuages the injured finger and reacts in other ways, then these are criteria of being in pain. However, where this is done in a play, then taking these reactions as evidence of pain is undermined as the criteria are defeasible (Hacker, 1993, p. 251). Is the same the case with 'presents fairly'? Is the criterion of following the rules of GAAP defeasible in the light of the circumstances? Is the fact that following the rules is not taken as a sufficient condition of the concept of 'true and fair view' because it is not a criterion or is it a criterion which is defeasible? It was argued in chapter 3 that meeting the 'criteria of adequacy' set out in the conceptual framework is what is meant by giving a 'true and fair view'. Following the rules is not a criterion, though there may be extensional equivalence between them in that most of the time when it is the case that a 'true and fair view' is given then it is also the case that the rules are followed. With concepts like these the vagueness can be accounted for by pointing to different criteria for the use of the expression or by a different understanding of what constitutes criteria.

Much of the discussion about evidence in Toba's work and the work that followed its publication was concerned with establishing what counts as criterial evidence for the opinion, or the meaning of the opinion. Kissinger criticises Toba's explanation of meaning by pointing out that a set of accounting policies is not equated with a statement that the accounting policies conform to GAAP. He disputes Toba's account of the meaning of the two propositions that need to be established if the opinion is to be given. This illustrates the importance of giving an acceptable explanation of the meaning of the opinion or of statements used to explain the meaning of the opinion. According to Toba, the opinion is a *general* proposition supported by instances which are expressed by elementary propositions (Toba, 1975, p. 10). If the opinion is a generalisation, then confirming instances of the general proposition are taken to increase the probability of the generalisation. Although an instance of a generalisation does not conclusively establish it, an account of the confirmation of generalisations brings in the idea that these positive instances increase the probability of the generalisation. This is the idea behind Toba's idea that e is supporting evidence for G given that $P(G|e) > P(G)$.

It is important to distinguish the idea that positive instances of a generalisation increase the probability of the generalisation from the idea that criterial evidence for a proposition increases the probability of the proposition. It is difficult to see what probability has to do with criterial evidence. If giving a 'true and fair view' *means* following the rules in GAAP, then finding that the rules in GAAP have been followed is criterial evidence that the financial statements give a 'true and fair view'. It does not increase the probability that the financial statements give a 'true and fair view', though. The two propositions 'the financial statements give a true and fair view' and 'the financial statements follow the rules in GAAP', or the two events or states of affairs, are not *independent* where there is this connection in meaning between them. It is not that, as a matter of fact, whenever the rules of GAAP are followed it happens to be the case that the financial statements give a 'true and fair view'. Following the rules is not a *symptom* of giving such a view. It is not an 'inductive correlation of two distinct, externally related phenomena', for it is not possible for there to be an 'independent identification' of the symptom and what it is a symptom *for* (Hacker, 1993, p. 249). There is an internal connection between the criterion and the thing it is a criterion for, a connection forged by *meaning*. 'Following the rules' and giving a 'true and fair view' are not independent events in that it is possible for the one to happen without the other. The apparatus of mathematical probabilities cannot be applied to events or propositions that are not independent. The idea of probability does not throw any light on criterial evidence. The reason why it appears to do so in the case of evidence to support the opinion is that the meaning of the opinion is taken to be a generalisation that is confirmed by its instances. Probabilities may be relevant to establishing the generalisation which is used to explain the opinion in the sense that establishing some of the instances constitutes a sample that may enable some statement to be made about the population as a whole. However, having established this generalisation, no light is thrown on how the generalisation provides criterial evidence for the opinion.

How does the IAASB understand the meaning of the opinion and of what constitutes criterial evidence for the opinion?

THE IAASB'S CRITERIAL EVIDENCE FOR THE OPINION

It was suggested in chapter 3 that there are different explanations of the meaning of 'opinion' in ISA 200. The idea that the opinion identified is 'on whether the financial statements are presented fairly, in all material respects, or give a true and fair view in accordance with the framework' (IAASB, 2010, ISA 200, §3) suggests that the opinion means something like 'the financial statements follow the rules set out in the financial reporting framework'. This is to adopt the Type C approach to 'criteria of adequacy' of financial statements. The evidence required to give this opinion would be evidence that establishes the criteria that the rules are followed. There is also a requirement for evidence to corroborate or contradict management's assertions in the financial statements. Giving a 'true and fair view' is a matter of having evidence about the assertions. The assertions need to exhibit the characteristics of an 'all pervasive fundamental concept' of Type A or follows 'a set of rules, conventions or ways of thinking' of Type B. The auditor also has to have evidence that the financial statements are free from material misstatement. Materially misstatement might be a matter of not following the rules or of making assertions that are not corroborated or supported. Having evidence of all of these things enables the opinion to be given that the financial statements give a 'true and fair view'. The IAASB's statements about evidence are, at the moment, disconnected. They have not made up their mind on what the opinion means and what constitutes criterial evidence for the opinion.

If the explanation of 'true and fair view' as following GAAP is rejected, then the alternative of considering whether financial statements meet the 'criteria of adequacy', that is, the objectives and qualitative characteristics of useful information, should be explored. It is important to identify what kind of information is included in financial statements and to understand why it means for such information to meet the 'criteria of adequacy'. Information in financial statements, according to the conceptual framework for financial reporting, should provide relevant and reliable information. The IAASB suggest that in order to give an opinion evidence is needed to support and corroborate or contradict management assertions. The idea that information in financial statements amounts to management assertions needs to be considered.

ASSERTIONS IN FINANCIAL STATEMENTS

The focus of the evidential process on the assertions in financial statements has a fairly long history. The importance of obtaining evidence of assertions in order to give an opinion is evident in the work of Mautz and Sharaf (1961). This work strongly influenced subsequent studies on auditing concepts including evidence (Toba, 1975, p. 7). This influence is also evident in the statement in ISA 500 that evidence comprises relating to management's assertions. Mautz and Sharaf explain that financial statements consist of a 'series of assertions' and that 'auditing is concerned with the verification or testing of' these assertions (Mautz and Sharaf, 1961, p. 79). Auditors give an opinion on these assertions and require evidence to enable them to do so. This suggests a two stage process. The first stage is for auditors to get evidence about management's assertions included in the financial statements. The second is for them to give an opinion about these assertions.

Mautz and Sharaf state evidence is relevant to judgements about the truthfulness of the financial statement propositions that the auditor reviews (Mautz and Sharaf, 1961, p. 110). This implies that the assertions in the financial statements are meant to express truths and that the objective of the auditor is to determine whether the assertions are true. The opinion is to the effect that they are true. It is important to get clear about the nature of the assertions in financial statements if the nature of the opinion about them is to be understood. Mautz and Sharaf are not quite as narrow in their conception of the assertions that are judged by auditors in giving an opinion. They recognize assertions about the existence of physical and non-physical things, of past events, of quantitative and qualitative conditions as well as assertions that are mathematical (Mautz and Sharaf, 1961, p. 80). They give as examples the assertion of the existence of cash, receivables and inventories in the balance sheet but also further assertions that these items are 'appropriately disclosed and described and that their classification accords with an acceptable interpretation and application of generally accepted accounting principles' (Mautz and Sharaf, 1961, p. 79). They recognize that the opinion implies that the assertions are not simply statements of fact that are true or false. They refer to assertions about income which involve, as they refer to it, 'value judgements' (Mautz and Sharaf, 1961, p. 82). Included in this category are judgements about bad debts or the collectability of debts. These are called 'assertions of qualitative characteristics' which are either 'definitely stated' or 'implied by the classifications and arrangements we find in the statement' (Mautz and Sharaf, 1961, p. 83). It is not quite clear *exactly* what is asserted in assertions of this kind. It is acknowledged that assertions will require different kinds of evidence, and there is a need to be clear about the kind of assertions made and, hence, about what kind of evidence is required in order to give an opinion about such assertions.

Mautz and Sharaf's idea that the auditor verifies assertions in financial statements appears to be straightforward. Surely financial statements consist of statements and these statements assert something. Take as an example a statement of non-current assets in the statement of financial position:

Property, plant and equipment   £456,253,396

What does this statement assert? This question is really asking about the 'criterial evidence' for this statement, and this is a matter of working out what the statement *means*. Looking at the note to the accounts is useful in identifying what is stated. The notes suggest that assets at cost or valuation amounted to such and such and after deducting depreciation and impairment of such and such amount the balance amounts to the figure in the statement of financial position. In order to verify these statements one has, again, to know what they mean and what 'criterial evidence' would be required to verify them. That the assets cost a certain amount usually means that the company paid a certain amount to acquire the asset in a purchase transaction. It means something slightly different if the asset was not purchased but was constructed. The statement that the asset has a certain value means something different. The value may represent the market price that could be obtained if the asset was sold. It may be that the market actually priced the asset at a certain amount or, where there is no market price, a valuer may have estimated the value by considering what the asset could be sold for if it were to be sold now. The value may be determined by considering what the future cash flows might be from this asset discounted back to present value. These kinds of valuation involve predictions that are not statements of something that is true or false but of something that is reasonable to make given certain assumptions and estimates. The statement about depreciation is also not a statement of something that might be called a matter of fact. The amount of depreciation is a calculation that depends upon the cost of the asset, its residual value and an estimate of the useful life of the asset and of the way in which the asset reflects 'the pattern in which the asset's future economic benefits are expected to be consumed by the entity' (IASB, 2003, IAS16, §60). The statement of depreciation also involves predictions.

The analysis of this statement about the asset of property, plant and equipment shows that it is not entirely an assertion that is capable of truth or falsity. Mautz and Sharaf do recognise this fact even though they talk about judging the truthfulness of propositions. In so far as there are estimates and predictions, these are not assertions that are true or false. It is not true or false that 'the boilerman will come tomorrow'. It may, nonetheless, be reasonable to make this statement if one has good reasons for thinking that he will come. Some statements implied by the statement about the asset are statements that are capable of truth or falsity. For example, it is true or false that the company bought an asset that cost a certain amount. However, financial statements do not consist simply of assertions of this kind. An assertion is a sentence that states something to be true. In some systems of logic an assertion sign is used to signify such statements (Blackburn, 1994, p. 27). It is important to understand the nature of the statements in order to understand what counts as 'verifying' such statements. Assertions are verified by evidence that they are true. If they are not assertions, then verification consists of something else, for example, determining whether or not it is reasonable to make such a statement on grounds other than providing reasons for thinking the statement is true.

There is an interesting shift in Mautz and Sharaf's discussion of assertions. They start off by giving examples of assertions such as the assertion of the existence of certain assets such as 'cash exists', 'receivables exist' and 'inventories exist'. That financial statements make assertions of this kind is reasonable. Take the statement in the financial statement that a particular kind of asset cost £X. One philosopher, Russell, put forward a 'Theory of Descriptions' that analysed propositions that assert a property of something, such as 'The King of France is wise', as implying an assertion that something exists, namely the assertion 'There is a King of France'. If there was no such person, then the assertion that this person is wise is false because the implied assertion that there is such a person is false. Another philosopher, Strawson, disagreed with Russell and maintained that propositions that assert a property of something do not imply a statement that something exists, but *presuppose* it. If there is no such thing, then the proposition is not false but is neither true nor false or fails to make a statement (Wolfram, 1990, pp. 39–43). It is not necessary to go into any more detail about this issue. Whether the nonexistence of something referred to in the financial statements results in the statement being false or in it failing to make a statement does not matter since either way the statement is not true. If the auditor has to verify statements that such statements are true, then they need to establish the existence of the thing referred to. It seems reasonable to accept that financial statement do assert the existence of assets.

Although it is reasonable to think that financial statements make assertions about the existence of assets, it is less easy to think that the financial statements actually assert some of the other things that Mautz and Sharaf say they do. That assets are 'appropriately disclosed and described and that their classification accords with an acceptable interpretation and application of generally accepted accounting principles' is not something that financial statements actually assert. This might be asserted by management or auditors *about* the financial statements, but these are not management assertions that appear in financial statements. Smieliauskas and Smith take up the idea that the auditor has to confirm assertions to support his or her opinion and identify six assertions or 'propositions' that must be confirmed. Their first proposition, P1, is similar to Mautz and Sharaf's assertion. It states that 'all assets, liabilities, and transactions exist at a given date (the balance sheet date) or that all transactions have occurred during the given period'. Another states that 'all transactions and accounts that should be presented in the financial statements are so indicated' (Smieliauskas and Smith, 1990, p. 409). It is suggested that 'standards change over time' and that the set of assertions of the kind identified by AICPA in 1985 relating to existence, completeness, rights and obligations, valuation and presentation, with the addition of a proposition that immaterial errors associated with these other assertions add up to an immaterial error for the set of assertions, are those that must be confirmed by the auditor. These are also the kind of assertions identified by the IAASB in ISA 315. They are assertions are about classes of transactions and events for the period under audit and include assertions about their occurrence, completeness, accuracy, cut-off and classification. There are also assertions relating to account balances at the period end including assertions about existence, rights and obligations, completeness and valuation and allocation. Thirdly, there are assertions about presentation and disclosure that include assertions about occurrence and rights and obligations, completeness, classification and understandability and accuracy and valuation (IAASB, 2010, ISA 315, §A111).

It is a mistake to suggest that these assertions are made *by management* in the financial statements. ISA 315 follows this tradition in stating that 'in representing that the financial statements are in accordance with the applicable financial reporting framework, management implicitly or explicitly makes assertions regarding the recognition, measurement, presentation and disclosure of the various elements of financial statements and related disclosures' (IAASB, 2010, ISA 315, §110). However, such assertions are not stated 'implicitly or explicitly' in the financial statements. It is true that the financial statements include assertions, though not all statements are assertions that are true or false. It is just that these are not the assertions or statements actually made. These assertions actually explain what is meant by 'relevant and reliable' information in an opinion that states whether or not financial statements are relevant and reliable. It was suggested earlier that an opinion that financial statements give a 'true and fair view' should be understood, as a matter of meaning, as an opinion that the financial statements are relevant and reliable. These statements confirm what is meant by 'relevant and reliable', in other words, they are 'criterial evidence' of these terms implied by the meaning of the opinion.

Management are charged with the responsibility of producing financial statements that give a 'true and fair view' and hence express relevant and reliable information. This requirement is stated in the UK Companies Act. However, management are not required to assert that they have done so in the financial statements. Auditors are required to determine whether or not the financial statements give a 'true and fair view' in an audit report. It is misleading to say that auditors have verified management's assertions in financial statements when management have not asserted the things that ISA 315 and writers like Mautz and Sharaf and Smieliauskas and Smith say are asserted. The latter refer to these assertions as 'audit assertions'. This is what they are. They are what is implied by the meaning of the opinion that auditors assert. They too should be understood as 'criterial evidence' for the 'relevance and reliability' implied by the meaning of the audit opinion.

It is odd that if these assertions explain what is meant by 'relevant and reliable' information in financial statements, they are not the same kind of explanation of these terms that appear in the conceptual framework explanations of these terms. Relevant financial information is information 'capable of making a difference in the decisions made by users' (IASB, 2010, QC6). Information that faithfully represents, or is reliable, is information that maximises the qualities of completeness, neutrality and freedom from error. These explanations of relevant and reliability are at rather a high level. In other words, they do not explain in much detail what kind of information is capable of making a difference or has the qualities of reliability. The general assertions identified by ISA 315 and AICPA and the other writers provide more detail. In effect, they result from practical reasoning that starts with the desires expressed in the conceptual framework, relevance and reliability as explained therein, and via beliefs about what kind of information is capable of making a difference in maximising the qualities of completeness, neutrality and freedom from error, and arrives at desires for information in financial statements that states the existence, rights and obligations, completeness and valuation and allocation of account balances and the desire for information about classes of transactions and events. What is useful in the explanations of relevance and reliability in ISA 315 and AICPA and others is that they consider what kind of information is included in financial statements, that is, about transactions and account balances, and what it is for these kinds of information to be relevant and reliable. This is understandable when it is realised that these explanations are largely given from the perspective of the practicing accountant. They are not concerned with the more abstract explanations of relevance and reliability in the conceptual framework but with, practically, what constitutes these qualities in the kind of information actually asserted in financial statements. It is a shame that the conceptual framework does not go more down this route in explaining the qualitative characteristics of useful information. It would mean more to practicing accountants and auditors if it did.

What is particularly unhelpful about the explanations in the conceptual framework is that they do not appear to appreciate that what constitutes relevant and reliable information, what these qualities mean, may vary with the kind of information that is being considered. Information in financial statements that asserts matters of fact is relevant and reliable in a different way than information that expresses predictions. The quality of reliability relating to statements of matters of fact may be, as Mautz and Sharaf explain, that such statement be true. The quality of reliability that relates to predictions is not that such statements are true, but that they are reasonable in the circumstances, that is, based on reasonable assumptions and acceptable generalisations based on past experience. Auditors have to determine whether the statements in financial statements are relevant and reliable in order to give an opinion. This requires that they understand what these terms mean when applied to the kind of assertions that are made in financial statements. ISA 315 helps the auditor to understand this and provides a number of questions that need to be answered if the statements in financial statement have the 'criteria of adequacy' or relevance and reliability.

Taking the example of assertions about property, plant and equipment, are these assertions relevant and reliable? The statement that assets have a certain cost or valuation implies an assertion that a certain amount was paid to acquire assets or that they have a certain market value or that they could be sold for a certain amount. The assertion about what was paid is a factual statement that is capable of truth or falsity. The statement that an asset could be sold for a certain amount is a predictive statement. What needs to be established to determine the relevance and reliability of such statements may differ given they are different kinds of statement. The other statements in the financial statement, such as those relating to depreciation, also need to be identified, and what needs to be established for them to have the requisite qualities must be determined. Obviously, the statement in financial statements is not about one particular asset but about a group of assets. To determine whether the statement about a group of assets is relevant and reliable, it is necessary to determine whether statements about the particular assets have this quality. What constitutes evidence of these factual statements or predictive statements? Why do these procedures count as evidence of the assertions about these assets? What explanations of evidence of this kind have been given in the literature?

EXPLANATIONS OF EVIDENCE

Mautz and Sharaf distinguish different types of evidence. This includes 'natural evidence' based on observations but also 'rational argumentation' that follows 'logically from observed facts' (Mautz and Sharaf, 1961, p. 69). Evidence of this kind relates to establishing the truth or falsity of factual propositions or statements. This is an empirical matter, and empirical assertions, like those in science, 'must ultimately face the test of observation' (Earman and Salmon, 1992, p. 43). Taking the example of property, plant and equipment, auditors may be able to observe specific items at the end of the year in order to verify their existence. Not all knowledge in science is based on observations, though. Quite a lot of scientific knowledge 'depends upon inference as well as observation' (Earman and Salmon, 1992, p. 44). Auditors cannot always make observations that either directly or indirectly confirm assertions of existence. This is clear where the events happened in the past. As an example take transactions like sales. The sale took place in the *past*, and the auditor verifies the sale not by looking at the occurrence of the sale but by looking at sales invoices *now* in order to verify the past event of the sale. Justifying an assertion about something that is not observable now is a matter of inferring it from other statements that *are* based on observations.

Finding evidence to support 'conclusions' about some of the statements in financial statements is understood as finding something that allows such statements to be derived using 'rational argumentation' or reasoning. The reference in ISA 200 to the connection between information and conclusions connects audit evidence and reasoning since conclusions are obtained by reasoning. Evidence enables the auditor to derive conclusions from premises using some kind of reasoning. An example is the evidence of a sale provided by a sales invoice. From the statement that one observes a sales invoice the conclusion that a sale took place is derived by some kind of reasoning. The importance of reasoning in understanding the idea of evidence is acknowledged in the legal literature. Modern systems of evidence in law involve 'the process of drawing rational inferences' (Murphy, 2009, p. 4). Reasoning of some kind is involved in the search for evidence. The concern of the literature on evidence in the legal context is on 'the use of evidence as material in the reconstruction of past events' (Murphy, 2009, p. 2). In other words, evidence is used to derive conclusions about what happened in the past. 'Evidence' has been defined in this literature as 'any material which has the potential to change the state of a fact-finder's belief with respect to any factual proposition which is to be decided and which is in dispute' (Murphy, 2009, p. 2). In an audit the auditor has to arrive at factual statements about past events. As noted, this is not the only kind of conclusion that has to be arrived at. The auditor must also arrive at conclusions that are predictions about what *will* happen. An example of this is determining useful life of an asset in depreciation calculations. The search for evidence supports statements about what happened in the past and what will happen in the future. Both kinds of statements are made in what is stated in financial statements. Evidence of the reliability and relevance of both kinds of statement is required in order to give an opinion. Different kinds of evidence are needed to support or confirm predictions as are needed for past events. Many of the assertions in financial statements are statements of matters of fact. These will be examined. It must be remembered, though, that these are not the only kind of statements that the auditor has to confirm.

An assumption is made in the law, that also needs to be made in auditing, that in using evidence 'it is possible in principle to attain present knowledge of past events; and that the accumulation of evidence and derivation of rational inferences from that evidence is a correct method of achieving such knowledge' (Murphy, 2009, p. 4). The connection between evidence and reasoning is also clear in the philosophical literature. It has been said that 'a rational man is one who makes a proper use of reason: and this implies, among other things, that he correctly estimates the strength of evidence. In many instances, the result will be that he is able to vindicate his assertions by adducing other propositions which support them. But what is it for one proposition to support another? In the most favourable case, the premises of an argument entail its conclusion, so that if they are true the conclusion also must be true. It would seem, however, that not all our reasoning takes the form of deductive inference. In many cases . . . we appear to run beyond our evidence: that is, we appear not to have a logical guarantee that even if our premises are true, they convey their truth to the conclusion. But then what sort of inference are we making, and how can it be justified?' (Ayer, 1972, p. 3). The same question needs to be asked in auditing: what kinds of inferences are drawn in finding evidence, and what are the conclusions that are derived in evidential reasoning? The suggestion made by Ayer is that we are not talking about *deductive* inference but some other kind of inference. The aforementioned examples of evidence suggest that the reasoning involved is not deductive. If the auditor observes some sales invoices and concludes a sale took place this is not a deductive inference.

In this example of an evidential situation in auditing there are two events or states of affairs. The first is an event or state of affairs of observation that is described in a statement or proposition. This constitutes evidence for another event or state of affairs that constitutes a statement or proposition that is to be proven by the evidence. Evidence of this kind is distinct from 'criterial evidence'. The evidence event is a 'symptom' or provides *inductive* evidence for another event. There is an *empirical correlation* between the two. These events are *independent* of each other in the sense that the one can occur without the other occurring. This is not the case with 'criterial evidence' where there is a connection in meaning between the description of the one event and the description of the other and the criterial evidence is not independent of the other event. For example, being relevant and reliable is a criterion of giving a 'true and fair view', and then one cannot say that financial statements give a 'true and fair view' without implying that they are relevant and reliable. The event or state of affairs of giving a 'true and fair view' is not independent of the event or state of affairs of being relevant and reliable. In auditing situations the event of observing a sales invoice is independent of the event of a sale. A sale could have happened without the observation of the invoice, and one could observe an invoice without a sale having occurred. There may be a correlation between both events such that the occurrence of the one is a symptom of the other. When sales are made invoices are often observed, and when invoices are observed sales have often been made. If an auditor reasons from a premise expressing an observation to a conclusion expressing that an event occurred, this is a case of *inductive* reasoning. In this context 'inductive' is understood as 'the term most widely used for any process of reasoning that takes us from empirical premises to empirical conclusions supported by the premises, but not deductively entailed by them' (Blackburn, 1994, p. 192). It is important to understand the differences between this kind of inference and deductive inference.

DEDUCTIVE AND INDUCTIVE REASONING

Deductive reasoning is drawing conclusions from premises in accordance with rules set out in a system of formal logic. Some of the characteristics of deductive reasoning were set out in chapter 1 and chapter 3. With such reasoning if one accepts the premises, then no further choice or decision is required in drawing a conclusion from the premises. This might be summed up by saying that it is non-ampliative and that no *judgement* is required in drawing conclusions by deductive reasoning. Inductive reasoning, like practical reasoning, has a number of characteristics which contrast with those of deductive reasoning. The conclusion goes beyond the content of the premises. In other words, it is *ampliative*. With inductive reasoning, the premises may be true but the conclusion false. Nonetheless, 'the premise can make it reasonable to believe the conclusion, even though it does not guarantee that the conclusion is true' (Craig, 2005, pp. 442–443). This is an important characteristic from the auditing perspective. Mautz and Sharaf observe that 'compelling evidence is available to support only a limited number of financial statement propositions and that a great many other propositions, probably the great majority, are such that the mind of the auditor is not compelled but rather only persuaded of the reliability of the assertion at issue' (Mautz and Sharaf, 1961, p. 84). The addition of new premises can invalidate the argument. This kind of argument is not 'erosion-proof'. The argument can be *more or less strong* in that 'in some inductions the premises support the conclusions more strongly than in others' (Salmon, 1992, p. 11).

In both the reasoning from sample to population and from a statement of one event to a conclusion of another one, the reasoning involved has the qualities of inductive rather than deductive reasoning. Mautz and Sharaf observe that 'audit evidence will influence the auditor in degrees which vary all the way from being compelling to being little more than persuasive.' (Mautz and Sharaf, 1961, p. 78). They quote Keynes who explains that 'part of our knowledge we obtain direct; and part by argument'. There are 'different degrees in which the results so obtained are conclusive or inconclusive . . . many . . . arguments are rational and claim some weight without pretending to be certain . . . most of the arguments, upon which we habitually based our rational belief, are admitted to be inconclusive in a greater or lesser degree'. They agree with Keynes that in drawing conclusions in evidential situations 'the study of probability is required' (Keynes, 1948, p. 3, quoted in Mautz and Sharaf, 1961, pp. 72–73). However, they note that auditing is mostly concerned with 'rational probability' rather than with 'statistical measures of probability'. They say that 'the quality of rationality cannot be reduced to a mathematical formula, at least not at our present state of development' (Mautz and Sharaf, 1961, p. 73). The idea that evidential reasoning involves probabilities was a seminal idea in the auditing literature. Its influence has not always been conducive to clarifying the nature of evidence, though.

PROBABILITY AND AUDIT EVIDENCE

We have already examined Toba's idea that that something counts as supporting evidence if it increases the probability of a proposition. Toba also has the idea, later modified by Kissinger, that something is confirming evidence if it renders the probability of the proposition greater than a certain value K, to be determined by the auditor. This idea was not found to be useful in relation to 'criterial evidence'. It may be more useful for understanding inductive evidence. Murphy's idea that evidence is material that has the potential to change the state of a fact-finder's belief with respect to any factual proposition which is to be decided might be interpreted in terms of probability. Evidence is something that changes 'the degree of conviction with which an individual believes in one proposition' (Earman and Salmon, 1992, p. 81). This might be expressed by saying that evidence is something that changes the probability of a proposition to be proven, where probability is understood as a degree of conviction. Supporting evidence would then be something that increases the fact-finder's conviction with which he or she believes a proposition. Confirming evidence would be something that increases that conviction beyond a certain value K. Auditors look for confirming evidence to increase their conviction in the statements in financial statements. This seems an intuitively attractive idea. Auditors need evidence to confirm their belief that statements are relevant and reliable, that is, present fairly or give a 'true and fair view', in order to give an opinion on them. The evidence does not give certainty to the statements but does give them a degree of probability. Evidence establishes the degree of conviction in them. Much hangs, however, on what 'probability' actually *means* in this context. Understanding 'probability' as a degree of conviction is to give it a 'subjective interpretation' (Earman and Salmon, 1992, p. 81). The question arises as to whether this is an 'admissible interpretation' of the mathematical concept of probability. This is an interpretation that satisfies the basic rules or axioms of the mathematical calculus of probability (Earman and Salmon, 1992, p. 74). If this is the case, then it also satisfies the derived rules of the calculus including Bayes's rule. The importance of this is that Bayes's rule can be used to aggregate the probabilities of multiple items of evidence to arrive at the overall probability of the statement to be confirmed. There is a large literature on aggregating evidence using a Bayesian model (see Dutta and Srivastava, 1993). This is important for auditors who have to find multiple items of evidence to confirm statements and need to derive overall probabilities of statements from these items.

The problem with interpreting 'probabilities' as degrees of conviction is that it does not satisfy the rules or axioms of the mathematical calculus. There is plenty of empirical research that shows this to be the case (Earman and Salmon, 1992, p. 81). There is also research in the auditing literature that concludes that auditors do not use Bayesian methods for evidence aggregation (Mock et al., 1997). Auditors who have degrees of conviction that do not satisfy the mathematical calculus of probability are 'incoherent'. A suggestion might be made that people who are incoherent should adopt '*coherent sets of degrees of conviction*' by conforming to the rules of the probability calculus, that is, adopt '*personal probabilities*' (Earman and Salmon, 1992, p. 82). These probabilities, by definition, amount to an 'admissible interpretation' of the mathematical calculus of probabilities. This is a normative prescription rather than a description of what is done. It says auditors *should* do rather than what they actually do.

The major problem with this prescription is that it is not clear how auditors are meant to do what is suggested. The problem is that 'with a couple of trivial exceptions, the mathematical calculus of probability does not by itself furnish us with any values of probabilities . . . You plug in some probability values, turn the crank, and others come out' (Earman and Salmon, 1992, p. 84). But how does the auditor arrive at the values of probabilities in the first place? Although these systems provide a method of aggregating the values of evidence, they 'do not provide any method for evaluating the probative values of the individual times of evidence. Rather, they require that these values are judged subjectively by the auditor' (Gronewold, 2006, p. 374). 'Probative value' refers to the 'auditor's perception of the evidence's value' (Gronewold, 2006, p. 348), which can be understood as the 'degree of conviction' with which the auditor believes in the proposition. Bayes's rule can be expressed as $P(p|E) = (P(p) \times P(E|p)/P(E))$, that is, the probability of p, the proposition to be proven, given the evidence (E) is equal to the prior probability of p multiplied by the probability of the evidence given p

divided by the prior probability of the evidence. How does one calculate the prior probabilities if not subjectively, and what happens if these 'degrees of conviction' are not reasonable? It has been suggested that we need stronger restrictions on these probabilities (Earman and Salmon, 1992, p. 84). Moreover, the rule requires that the probability of the evidence given the proposition be calculated. What happens if 'innumerable propositions can be invented, which, if true could, correctly explain how the evidence E can arise' (Smieliauskas and Smith, 1990, p. 417)? How can we correctly determine the probability of the evidence given a particular proposition if there are any number of different ways of accounting for the evidence that do not involve the proposition to be proven?

The problem here is in determining what it means to talk of the probability of the evidence given the event expressed by p. Where there is a causal link between the event that is expressed by the proposition to be proven p, for example, a sale being made, and the event of finding evidence, say the observation of an invoice or an entry in the ledger, that is, the proposition that expresses the evidence e, this causal relationship may have probabilistic aspects. The event of the sale is part of the cause of the event of finding the evidence. Given the event of the sale, there is a certain probability of the event of the evidence. The probability of the evidence given the event expressed by p might be interpreted as the *causal tendency* of the event to produce the evidence. However, there is a problem with interpreting this probability as a causal tendency or *propensity* (Earman and Salmon, 1992, p. 80). The trouble is that 'the propensity interpretation is not an admissible interpretation of the probability calculus' because 'causes precede their effects and causes produce their effects, even if the causal relationship has probabilistic aspects'. Although it is possible to speak meaningfully of the causal tendency of a cause to produce its effect, 'effects do not produce their causes. It does not make sense to talk about the causal tendency of the effect to have been produced by one cause or another' (Earman and Salmon, 1992, pp. 84–85). However, the rules of the mathematical calculus do allow the calculation of an 'inverse probability', that a given effect was produced by a particular cause, by rearranging the equation in the Bayes's rule. This does not make sense if probabilities are interpreted as causal tendencies or propensities.

If the rules of the mathematical calculus are to be used for aggregating the values of individual items of evidence, then the probability of evidence given the event p to be proven has to be interpreted in some other way. This looks difficult if there are any number of different ways of accounting for the evidence. Where there are innumerable propositions that can be invented to explain how the evidence can arise, 'it is important to develop a convincing explanation of the relationship between the evidence and the proposition' (Smieliauskas and Smith, 1990, p. 417). The idea of a causal connection between the proposition and the evidence, or at least between the events expressed by them, would appear to be 'a convincing explanation'.

However, this precludes the interpretation of probabilities as mathematical. Something counts as evidence if there is a causal connection between the event expressed by p and the event expressed by the evidence proposition e. That there is such a connection is not *sufficient* for evidence to count as confirming evidence of a proposition, though. There may be other propositions that express something that has a causal connection with the evidence. In other words, there are different ways of accounting for the evidence which do not involve the event expressed by the proposition p to be proven. The auditor cannot say that, because the event described by the proposition p *could* have a causal connection with the evidence e, the event occurred and the proposition p that expresses the event is confirmed because e happened. On the other hand, without such a causal connection, an event described by evidential propositions cannot be confirming evidence of the event to be proven described by p. It is a necessary condition of the event to be confirmed that it be part of the causal mechanism of the event that constitutes evidence.

The idea of the necessity of a causal connection is implicit in the idea, expressed in the legal literature, that there must be a *story* connecting the event to be proved and the event expressed by the evidential statement. Another strand in the legal literature is the idea that one event, the event that constitutes the finding of evidence, is connected with another event, the event to be confirmed by evidence, by generalisations used in evidential reasoning. These two strands will now be considered.

STORIES AND GENERALISATIONS IN LAW

Inductive evidence about past events establishes an inductive correlation between two distinct, externally related phenomena. The event of a sale and the event of observing of a sales invoice in the auditing example are two independent or distinct events. One can occur without the occurrence of the other. One cannot deduce from the fact that one has observed a sales invoice that a sale has taken place, and one cannot deduce from the fact that a sale has taken place that one can observe a sales invoice. It is possible to establish an inductive correlation between these two events, though. If one occurs, then the other occurs. What has to be established is how to reason from a statement of fact that constitutes evidential material, e, to a statement of fact about what happened, p. What is needed is to establish a correlation between the occurrence of the evidential event and the occurrence of the event that is to be confirmed by the evidence.

An example from the law can be used to illustrate the point. A proposition that suspect A killed victim B, P, needs to be proven, and evidence is required to prove this proposition. The victim was stabbed to death. It may have been established that A has been found with the victim's blood on his hands. This constitutes evidence that A killed B but only if there is some generalisation to the effect that often, or perhaps almost always, when someone stabs another person that person's blood is found on the killer's hands. The fact that B's blood is found on A's hand might result in a conclusion being drawn that A killed B. No one would argue that the conclusion *has* to be drawn from the generalisation and the fact of the blood being found. The conclusion does not follow deductively. However, there may be an inductive argument that draws this conclusion from the premises.

The use of generalisations in evidential reasoning is acknowledged in the legal literature. Generalisations are 'underlying and often unspoken' (Murphy, 2009, p. 5). 'Mainstream evidence theory gives a central place to the role of generalizations in "rational" fact determination. Every inferential step from particular evidence to a particular conclusion . . . requires justification by reference to at least one background generalization . . . they are necessary as providing the only available basis for constructing rational arguments' (Twining, 2006, p. 334). The inductive reasoning in the example illustrates the two conditions that must be met if something is to count as evidence, namely that 'the evidential proposition has to pass for being true and the connection between the propositions has to pass for being truth preserving' (Ayer, 1972, pp. 86). The former is clearly the case if the proposition that A has B's blood on his hands is true. The connection is truth preserving if the inductive argument is sound.

Generalisations are said, in the legal literature, to be 'drawn from the accumulated experience of society about the causes and courses of events' and are acceptable 'to the extent that they correspond to common human experience' (Murphy, 2009, p. 6). These may be expressed in *differing strengths*. The generalisation in this judicial example might be expressed as 'when someone stabs another person then that person's blood is nearly always/frequently/sometimes found on the killer's hands'. The generalisation could also be expressed in probabilities, for example, 'when someone stabs another person there is an 83% chance that this other person's blood is found on the person's hand', but it may be unrealistic to think that such probabilities could be established. The conclusion that A killed B will be more *strongly* drawn if the generalisations are expressed as 'nearly always' rather than as 'frequently' or 'sometimes'. That use of generalisations in evidential reasoning is not always appreciated 'because generalisations remain an unspoken part of the reasoning process, their influence cannot always be seen directly' (Murphy, 2009, p. 6). The persuasiveness or reliability of the conclusion, what might be termed its probative force or value, depends upon the strength of the generalizations used in evidential inductive reasoning. This is problematic for 'it is widely recognized that such generalizations may be more or less indeterminate, unarticulated, vague, or precise. They may be backed by scientific evidence, "general knowledge", sheer speculation, or prejudice. They are often overtly or covertly value laden. They are said to be rooted in what passes for common sense or knowledge in a given society (or sub-group) at a given time' (Twining, 2006, p. 335). Generalizations are, however, *dangerous* because they 'tend to provide invalid, illegitimate, or false reasons for accepting conclusions based on inference' (Twining, 2006, p. 335). Finding that certain kinds of evidence are correlated with certain kinds of events happening in general does not guarantee that in particular instances an event happened when evidence of a certain kind is observed. What is missing in this account of evidence?

It is important to realise that the generalisations are developed in certain circumstances. It may be observed that in a number of circumstances where there has been a stabbing and someone has been killed the murderer has had blood on their hands. A correlation may be established between the fact of the blood and the event of murder. The problem is that this correlation is sound only when there is a *story* connecting the stabbing to the fact of having blood on hands. What needs to be established is some *causal connection* between the event of the killing and the event of blood on the hands. There must be a *causal story* linking the event to be confirmed and the evidence. It is only where there is such a story that the generalisation linking the blood to the killing is reliable. This brings in the other strand of thinking in the legal theory of evidence, namely that 'stories and story-telling are central to fact determination . . . juries determine "the truth" about alleged past events mainly by constructing and comparing stories rather than critically evaluating arguments from evidence' (Twining, 2006, p. 336). In the legal example the story is that there was a killing, and as a causal result of this event the killer has blood on their hands. Without this causal story connecting the blood on the hands to the act of killing, the fact that there is blood will not count as evidence of the killing.

Further facts might emerge that undermine the causal story. Perhaps it is established that the suspect was not in the same city as the victim at the time of the murder. Perhaps it is established that the suspect visited the morgue and touched the victim's body thus resulting in the suspect having blood on his hands. This suggests that a different story can now be told that establishes that the suspect could not have been the killer and that also accounts for the evidence that was found. This new evidence does not undermine the generalisation. It may still be the case that, in certain circumstances, the generalisation applies. However, the new evidence establishes that the circumstances are different, and the generalisation does not apply. Generalisations are established in certain circumstances and may only be relevant when those circumstances occur. The generalisation is not undermined but is shown to be *irrelevant* where the circumstances do not exist. It is dangerous to draw conclusions using such generalisations if the circumstances do not exist. This shows that the original reasoning from generalisations and facts is not to be 'erosion-proof'. What is required for something to count as evidence of the truth of a proposition to be confirmed is that there must be some causal connection between the event to be confirmed and the evidence of that event.

The story establishes the propensity or causal tendency of certain events to produce other events that may be taken as evidence. This explains why something counts as evidence and 'why the evidence was chosen out of all the potential universe of evidence available' (Smieliauskas and Smith, 1990, p. 420). If a particular event, the event that is to be confirmed, has a causal tendency to produce another event, the evidence event, then a generalisation connecting the evidence event with the event to be confirmed may be established. This generalisation can be used to derive a conclusion that the event to be confirmed is likely to have happened given the occurrence of the evidence event given the *correlation* between such events and the evidential events. However, these correlations are dangerous for the reason from an effect to a cause. Without a *causal story* that connects the event to be confirmed with the evidence event, the generalisation correlation may be irrelevant.

Stories are also dangerous, though. They are used to fill in gaps or help to explain the motivation for actions, but they can also be used 'to violate or evade conventional legal norms about relevant, reliability, completeness, prejudicial effect, etc . . . and is widely regarded as appealing to intuition and emotion and as a vehicle for "irrational means of persuasion"' (Twining, 2006, p. 336). It is observed that 'generalisations are, by definition, general; stories are particular', and 'there is an intimate interaction between the general and the particular in all arguments about questions of fact' (Twining, 2006, p. 338). Different stories can be told in particular cases to explain why the evidence occurs. In the legal example another story can be told given the further fact that the suspect visited the morgue. What jurors are looking for is the *best explanation* of the available evidence by considering the most relevant story amongst the possible stories that could be told. This is the story that best accounts for all of the known evidence. The best explanation is the one with 'maximal specificity'. The idea behind the requirement for 'maximal specificity' in inductive arguments is that in constructing these arguments 'we must include all relevant knowledge we have that would have been available, in principle' (Salmon, 1992, p. 26). In the judicial example, although a story can be told whereby the suspect had blood on his hands because he killed B, there is another story that brings in the fact that the suspect was not in the city at the time of the killing and provides another account of why the victim's blood was on the suspect's hands. The best explanation of the known evidential facts, the one with 'maximal specificity', is not that A killed B. Other generalisations are relevant, and the original one becomes irrelevant. The introduction of new premises undermines the conclusion. The original argument is not 'erosion-proof'. All available knowledge was not taken into account (Salmon, 1992, pp. 25–26). These insights can be used to throw light on the idea of evidence of factual statements in auditing.

STORIES AND GENERALISATIONS IN AUDITING

In auditing the propositions expressing factual statements that need to be verified are those expressed in the financial statements. Looking at the statement about sales, the sales figure in the financial statements represents a summary of a number of sales transactions that have occurred which are added together from entries reporting individual sales in the ledger. The auditor needs evidence that these individual transactions occurred. What evidence is required can be determined in different ways. It is possible to rely on generalisations that state that it is generally the case that when entries are made in sales ledgers then there will be invoices that show the amount of the sale that was made. Further generalisations might be relevant, for example that where invoices have been raised, with some likelihood, the transaction of a sale has occurred. Finding the requisite invoices might constitute evidence that the sale was made. The reasoning includes a generalisation such as 'It is quite likely that where invoices are raised a sales transaction has occurred'. Given a factual statement 'Here is a sales invoice', a conclusion 'A sales transaction has occurred' may be derived.

Although the generalisation may be true, this is only the case in certain circumstances. What is needed is a causal story that links the observation of the invoice with the occurrence of the sale. The event of the sale *causes* a sales invoice to be raised, and this partially *causes* an entry to be made in the ledger. The event of raising an invoice and of making an entry in the ledger are causes, or at least part of the cause, of the observation of the invoice and the entry in the ledger. The auditor observes the invoice and the entry and concludes that the sale has happened. The problem is that there might be other stories that account for the evidential facts. If management has incentives to inflate sales, then they might produce an invoice and record a sale in the accounting records without there having been a sale. If so, then the observations do not count as evidence that a sale took place. The new fact about management incentives suggests a new story that accounts for the observations and changes the auditor's understanding of the circumstances. A more relevant explanation of the evidence of invoice observation might be given. There are now two causal stories. They both propose causal relations between the occurrence of one event or state of affairs, either management wanting to inflate sales or a sale having occurred, with another, the observation of an invoice or accounting record. The auditor has to choose between stories. Other facts can be introduced which substantially change the causal story relevant to the statements in the financial statements. Audit failures often point to evidential facts that should have been found which undermine the acceptability of statements in the financial statements. An example might be where all of the evidence appears to confirm that a sale has happened but for further hidden facts, for example, the existence of a side letter which suggests that the sales transaction is nullified in certain circumstances. This undermines the statement that a genuine sales transaction took place. Relying on generalisations linking the evidence and the event to be confirmed may lead to the wrong conclusion being drawn. The auditor has to determine the *best explanation of the evidential events*.

How does the auditor do this? The auditor may look for further facts that are part of the causal story being told. If an invoice is raised and results from the event of a sale, then the invoice should be settled or, at least, the customer should agree that the amount is payable. The auditor may look for new facts that suggest a payment has been made by looking at bank statements or suggest that the customer agrees that the amount is payable by sending and receiving back debtor confirmation. The new facts constitute evidence because they have the potential to change the state of a fact-finder's belief about a factual proposition. If the payment is made or the amount confirmed by the debtor, then this suggests that the story that includes the fact that a sale has been made is a better explanation of the evidential facts than the story that proceeds from management incentives. One story is shown to be more relevant than the other in that it accounts for the new evidence that has been found. The new facts alter the perception of what is the best explanation of the evidence. They introduce more *specificity* into the explanation given that takes into account 'all relevant knowledge'. This fulfils the objective of aiming at *maximal specificity* in the search for evidence.

The problem is that there may be innumerable causal stories or causal explanations of the known evidence that involve other events than the one to be confirmed. This is why Smieliauskas and Smith require that a 'convincing explanation' be developed between the observation that is supposed to be evidence and the event to be confirmed. Their definition of confirming evidence is that the probability of p given e is greater than a certain level K and that 'the probability is high that there is an explanatory connection between the proposition p and evidence e' (Smieliauskas and Smith, 1990, p. 417). It is not clear whether this is enough. There may be a number of explanations that have a high probability, even a probability in excess of K. It is suggested that what is needed is to establish that p is the *best explanation* of the evidence e in the circumstances. The evidence e must include *all of the evidence* in the circumstances in order for it to be convincing and constitute the best explanation. Evidence does not come individually but in *stories*. The IAASB's statement that evidence is 'cumulative' does not mean that different items of evidence can be aggregated using conditional probabilities. Additional evidence alters the fact-finder's belief by changing the story that can be told to account for all of the known evidence.

This account of the meaning of 'evidence' is expressed in very general terms. It does not consider, with respect to particular statements that need to be confirmed in the financial statements, exactly what has to be done by the auditor. Clearly, it provides only the beginning of understanding what must be done. Being an example of normative theorising, it is something that assists in the activity of promulgating rules that determine the practice of finding evidence in auditing. It does not prescribe the rules that determine what must be done. The detail about what must be done is given in the prescriptions of auditing standards. The standard setter should start with what is wanted from the activity of searching for evidence and the explanations of the relevant concepts used in stating what is wanted. The standard setter then needs to determine beliefs about what rules will result in achieving these desires.

The statements made about audit risk should be understood from the perspective of the results of theorising. Identifying the risk of misstatement also identifies the evidence that needs to be considered to ensure that misstatements have not occurred, that the risk has not materialised. This is considered in ISA 315. Risk assessment procedures are 'audit procedures performed to obtain an understanding of the entity and its environment, including the entity's internal control' (IAASB, 2010, ISA 315, §4). Inherent risk identifies factors that suggest causal factors, such as incentives to misstate financial statements, that are relevant to understanding possible causal stories that account for evidential material. Assessing control risk requires an understanding of the causal story that explains how from transactions and events that are supposed to have happened the evidential material is raised and entries, upon which financial statements are based, are made. Both of these risk assessment procedures are relevant to understanding the *causal story* by which transactions are recorded and reported in financial statements and what evidential material the auditor must search for. The story of how the statements in the financial statements are derived from the transactions that occur is supplied by management. This is why ISA 315 requires that 'the auditor shall obtain an understanding of the information system' and 'the related accounting records, supporting information and specific accounts in the financial statements that are used to initiate, record, process and report transactions; this includes the correction of incorrect information and how information is transferred to the general ledger' (IAASB, 2010, ISA 315, §18). The auditor needs to determine whether or not he or she accepts management's explanation of how the evidence arises, that is, the auditor needs to determine whether to accept management's story of the causal genesis of the evidence. The auditor then goes on to obtain such evidence by inspecting and observing the documents and records and indications that controls have been exercised. How much evidence of this kind is required depends upon the auditor's assessment of the detection risk.

This account of evidence relates only to evidence that certain events or transactions reported in the financial statements actually occurred. This is not the only kind of statements that appear in the financial statements.

OTHER KINDS OF EVIDENCE

Determining what other kinds of evidence are needed depends upon understanding the nature of the statements in the financial statements. This involves understanding their meaning or, in the term used earlier, understanding the criterial evidence required. In examining the nature of evidence in the preceding sections, the statements were taken to be statements of fact. To determine the reliability of such statements, which is required if the auditor is to give an opinion that the financial statements give a 'true and fair view', evidence was required to determine that the statements of fact are true. Some of the statements in financial statements are not statements reporting matters of fact. They involve, instead, predictions or estimates. The criterial evidence for such statements is different than for statements of fact. The reliability of these other statements is not a matter of determining that these statements are true but that they are *warranted* or *acceptable* given other statements that are established and count as evidence for these other statements.

A full consideration of the nature of estimates and predictions is outside the scope of these books. However, a few remarks will indicate the kind of evidence that the auditor may need to consider in verifying estimates or predictions involved in the statements included in financial statements. In science predictions are based on the same kind of premises that are used in explanations. According to the 'explanation-prediction symmetry thesis . . . any acceptable explanation of the particular fact is an argument, deductive or inductive, that could have been used to predict the fact in question if the facts stated in the explanans had been available prior to its occurrence' (Salmon, 1992, p. 25). The 'explanans' of the argument involves generalisations of the law-like kind, such as Boyle's Law, which states 'at constant temperature, the pressure of gas is inversely proportional to its volume', or of the statistical variety, such as 'Almost all cases of streptococcus infection clear up quickly after the administration of penicillin'. It also involves certain 'antecedent' or 'initial' conditions, such as 'the initial volume of the gas is 1 cubic ft.', 'the initial pressure is 1 atm.' and 'the pressure is increased to 2 atm.' or 'X has a streptococcus infection' and 'X received treatment with penicillin'. From these premises a conclusion can be drawn which might be in the form of a prediction 'the volume will decrease to 1/2 cubic volume' or 'X will recover completely'. The 'explanation-prediction symmetry thesis' suggests that it might also be in the form of an explanation of the kind 'the volume decreased to 1/2 cubic volume' or 'X recovered completely' because of the law/generalisation and initial conditions.

Predictions of the amount expected to be realised from the sale of the inventories might be based on generalisations and initial conditions. The auditor needs to understand the argument that has led management to predict the net realisable value of inventories. Acquiring evidence of the prediction would involve determining whether the premises in the argument are reasonable. Is the assumption of a law-like statement or generalisation reasonable, and are the statements of fact in the initial conditions true? Obviously, predictions of amounts realised from sale may not be based on the kind of scientific generalisations in these examples, but more 'informal' predictions will be based on some assumptions about what generally happens along with factual statements. Evidence is something that establishes that the assumptions are reasonable and that the facts are true. What can be said about evidence in general given these explanations?

WHAT IS AUDIT EVIDENCE?

The IAASB definition of audit evidence as 'information used by the auditor in arriving at the conclusions on which the auditor's opinion is based' requires an understanding of the nature of the opinion and, hence, of what needs to be established before the opinion can be given. As suggested, this could be described as the 'criterial evidence' for the opinion and requires an understanding of the meaning of the opinion. The idea that the opinion states that the statements in financial statements are relevant and reliable requires an appreciation of the kind of statements that are actually made in financial statements. It was suggested that some of these statements are statements of fact and some are statements that express estimates and predictions. The kind of evidence of the reliability of these statements depends on the kind of statements in financial statements the auditor is considering. Evidence relating to factual statements is something that would enable the auditor to conclude that the statement is true. Evidence relating to predictions is something that enables the auditor to conclude that the predictions are reliable. Instead of trying to define 'evidence', it might be more perspicacious to explain what is meant by a search for evidence. Evidence could then be explained as what is searched for in a search for evidence. The search for evidence for factual statements includes the following procedures:

i) Identify the 'criterial evidence' for the statement of fact in the financial statements, that is, what the statement means and what event it states has happened;

ii) Identify a causal story from the event to be confirmed which is reported in the financial statements to the evidential events that result causally from the event to be confirmed;

iii) Observe the evidential events;

iv) Consider whether other evidential events exist which might suggest another causal story of the evidence found and which undermine acceptance of the statements in the financial statements and give rise to different generalisations from the evidential events (the search for explanations with 'maximal specificity') to other events that are causally related to the evidential events;

v) Conclude as to the best explanation of the evidence.

If all of these things have been confirmed and considered, then the auditor has evidence that the factual statements in the financial statements are reliable. This will enable the auditor to give an opinion on the reliability of such statements.

The search for evidence of predictions includes the following procedures:

i) Identify the 'criterial evidence' for the statement of predictions in the financial statements, that is, what the statement means and what event it states will happen;

ii) Identify the generalisations that are used in predictions and confirming their reasonableness, i.e. acceptability for making predictions given experience that confirms them;

iii) Identify the truth of the initial conditions that are used in making the prediction;

iv) Agree the derivation of the prediction from the generalisation and initial conditions.

This kind of analysis of the search for evidence is not evident in the ISAs of the IAASB. This might suggest a failure on the part of the IAASB to adequately explain the nature of audit evidence. One reason why standard setters do not think it necessary to explain the nature of the 'information' required in evidential situations or the nature of the reasoning involved is that they may assume that this is already familiar to auditors in their professional life and, also, is clear to everyone in everyday life. After all, individuals continually evaluate and assess evidence for assertions that they wish to corroborate or contradict in everyday life. This is an assumption that is also made in criminal trials where ordinary people, those who are invited to constitute juries, are thought to be capable of understanding and assessing evidence. In particular, they are deemed capable of determining whether there is sufficient and appropriate evidence to corroborate or contradict the assertions made by prosecutors given reasonable guidance by judges about when evidence is sufficient and appropriate. They do not need explanations about what counts as evidence and how it is related to the assertions made. Similarly, in the area of auditing practicing accountants are deemed to understand the nature of audit evidence and why something counts as evidence of assertions made in financial statements. ISAs do not need to explain this. Indeed, the explanations that are given in ISAs would not explain what evidence is to someone who did not already know this.

A grasp of the nature of evidence and evidential reasoning is nonetheless useful in suggesting guidance about auditing procedures. An example of this is the requirement to 'plan and perform an audit with professional scepticism' (IAASB, 2010, ISA 200, §15). The nature of scepticism can only be understood with a clear grasp of the nature of evidence.

SCEPTICISM

Scepticism is defined in ISA 200 as 'an attitude that includes a questioning mind, being alert to conditions which may indicate possible misstatement due to error or fraud, and a critical assessment of audit evidence' (IAASB, 2010, ISA 200, §13 (l)). The auditor is required to recognize that circumstances may exist that cause the financial statements to be materially misstated' (IAASB, 2010, ISA 200, §15). In a *Discussion Paper* on auditor scepticism the UK Auditing Practices Board suggest that a distinction can be drawn between a 'neutral position (where the auditor does not assume either that the financial statements are misstated or that management is dishonest)' and a 'more questioning approach that is sometimes referred to as "presumptive doubt" '. They suggest that the latter attitude is reflected in the updated ISAs (APB, 2010, §4–5). Some of the responses in Comment Letters relating to the *Discussion Paper* object to the view of scepticism as involving 'presumptive doubt' explained in this way. The Institute of Chartered Accountants in England and Wales (ICAEW) suggest that this kind of doubt is more that of a *'cynic'* or a *'pessimist*, who assumes the worst' (ICAEW, 2010, p. 2). A similar objection is made by ICAS, who distinguish between ' "aggressive sceptics" ' as those who would apply "presumptive doubt" ' and 'the ideal auditor' who is 'a "measured sceptic" who acts appropriately according to the evidence' (ICAS, 2010, p. 3). Baker Tilly states that 'presumptive doubt' involves the suggestion that there is an assumption of material misstatement rather than just 'being alert to conditions that may indicate possible misstatement' (Baker Tilly, 2010, p. 2).

One problem with understanding scepticism as involving an attitude like 'presumptive doubt' is that is that it is an *unthinking* attitude. This is not the idea of scepticism as it appears in, for example, philosophical scepticism. In philosophy scepticism is related to *reasoning*. The philosopher A. J. Ayer suggests that 'it is clear that when, as is commonly the case, a statement is accredited on the basis of certain others, their support of it must be genuine; the passage from evidence to conclusion must be legitimate. And it is at this point that the sceptic attacks. He produces arguments to show that the steps which we presume to be legitimate are not so at all . . . most of our claims to knowledge are thereby put in question' (Ayer, 1956, p. 71). The philosophical sceptic questions the *inferences* from one statement to another. In other words, the sceptic attacks the *reasoning* involved with such inferences. In philosophy, scepticism is sometimes associated with a wholesale rejection of a particular kind of reasoning. One example is the rejection of inductive reasoning because there is no justification for reasoning from what has happened in the past to what will happen in the future without assuming what is to be justified, namely that the future will be like the past. Often inductive reasoning is rejected by sceptics simply because it is not deductive reasoning and does not follow the rules of such reasoning. This kind of 'global' scepticism where a kind of reasoning is rejected is not the kind of scepticism intended when auditors are required to be sceptical. What is required is for the auditor to consider whether the evidence adduced to support a conclusion is reliably associated with the conclusion. Scepticism questions the way the standards of proof are applied to examples of inductive reasoning but does not question the use of inductive reasoning in drawing conclusions as such.

Being sceptical in the auditing context is a matter of questioning the *reasons* that are put forward for accepting assertions upon which the audit opinion is based. It is only if those reasons are insufficient that the acceptability of the statement is itself questioned. Statements should not be accepted if there are *insufficient grounds* for accepting them. Being sceptical is a matter of adopting *an attitude towards the reasoning that supports statements*. The *APB Discussion Paper* refers to behaviours expected of sceptics that include undertaking an 'expanded information search', 'increased contradiction detection' and 'increased alternative generation' (APB, 2010, p. 20). These behaviours can be understood in relation to the search for evidence that has been examined earlier. The auditor needs to draw conclusions about the statements in the financial statements. This involves looking for evidence to support those statements. The kind of conclusions that the auditor needs to make about those statements is either that they are true, in the case of assertions, or that they are warranted, in the case of predictions. An application of scepticism in drawing conclusions about matters of fact involves the auditor identifying a story that results in certain evidence. The auditor is given the story by management and needs to confirm that the evidence is actually available. Scepticism requires that the auditor does not believe management's story without evidence to confirm the evidential events. Even if evidence is acquired to confirm the evidential events identified in the story, the auditor needs to determine whether or not there is another story, not involving the event that is to be confirmed, that better explains the evidential events. The auditor needs to look out for other evidential events that are not expected given the story that management present but that might be expected if some other story that explains the evidential events is presented. This is the requirement for 'maximal specificity'. The auditor must then consider what is the *best explanation* for *all* of the known evidential facts and whether or not this involves the truth of the statement in the financial statements. The best explanation is the most *likely* explanation given all of the relevant knowledge available. The auditor must consider the strength of the conclusion about the statements in the financial statements given the strength of the most likely explanation.

The IAASB explains the process of the search for evidence in ISA 500. The auditor must design audit procedures that fulfil the purpose of 'obtaining sufficient appropriate audit evidence' (IAASB, 2010, ISA 500, §6) which 'supports and corroborates management's assertions' (IAASB, 2010, ISA 500, §A1). This is evidence that provides 'reasonable assurance about whether the financial statements as a whole are free from material misstatement' and which reduces 'audit risk (that is, the risk that the auditor expresses an inappropriate opinion when the financial statements are materially misstated) to an acceptably low level'. 'Reasonable assurance' is 'a high level of assurance' but not 'an absolute level of assurance, because there are inherent limitations of an audit which result in most of the audit evidence on which the auditor draws conclusions and bases the auditor's opinion being persuasive rather than conclusive' (IAASB, 2010, ISA 200, §5). ISA 500 gives some indication of the evidence that is likely to give reasonable assurance and, hence, should assist in understanding what this expression means. Reasonable assurance is obtained when the auditor has obtained 'sufficient appropriate audit evidence'. It states that 'sufficiency is the measure of the quantity of audit evidence' (IAASB, 2010, ISA 500, A5) and that 'appropriateness is the measure of the quality of audit evidence; that is, its relevance and its reliability in providing support for the conclusions on which the auditor's opinion is based' (IAASB, 2010, ISA 500, A5). It is acknowledged that 'whether sufficient appropriate audit evidence has been obtained to reduce audit risk to an acceptably low level, and thereby enable the auditor to draw reasonable conclusions on which to base the auditor's opinion, is a matter of professional judgment' (IAASB, 2010, ISA 500, §A6).

The problem with these explanations in ISA 500 is that they do not proceed from a firm grasp of the nature of the reasoning involved in the search for evidence. Sufficiency is meant to be a measure of quantity, but this is ambiguous. It could mean something about the sample size that is necessary for drawing conclusions about the population as a whole. It can also mean that a number of different observations need to be made in order to derive a statement about the occurrence of the event to be confirmed. This was seen in the earlier auditing example. The evidence that the sales figure is derived from accounting records and that the entries in the records are supported by observed invoices was not strong enough evidence because other explanations of why the invoice could be observed can be given. Other evidence may strengthen the conclusion that the event to be confirmed occurred if this event is part of the causal story that explains not only the original evidence but also this other evidence. For example, if a payment of the invoice is made or a debtors' circularization shows that the customer agrees to the debt, then the occurrence of the event of the sale may constitute the best explanation of all of the relevant facts. Further evidence from observing controls in the accounting system may strengthen the causal story. The additional evidence might be described as meeting the need for a greater quantity of evidence. Quantity should be explained in terms of the adequacy of the explanation in the causal story which conditions the strength of the conclusions about management assertions drawn. Some decision is required about the strength of the conclusion about the events to be confirmed given the explanation of the evidence considered.

It is important to grasp that the reasoning that the auditor undertakes to derive conclusions about the statements of fact in financial statements in a sceptical manner is not deductive. The auditor does not deduce that management's story about how the fact to be confirmed and the evidential facts that are caused by it is confirmed by the existence of the evidential facts. Although the existence of the evidential facts is a necessary condition of the story being true, it is not a sufficient condition of its truth. Determining what is the best explanation of the relevant evidential facts is not something that can be deduced from reviewing alternative stories given the known evidential facts. The best explanation is the most likely explanation but not the only possible explanation. It is always possible that there may be additional facts and other stories that offer a better explanation. The explanation of the search for evidence and the nature of evidence that it suggests does explain the kind of behaviour that counts as sceptical identified by the APB. The auditor should undertake an 'expanded information search' to identify other evidential facts that may alter what counts as the best explanation in the circumstances. These additional fact may result in 'increased contradiction detection' in so far as they cannot be accommodated in a causal story that includes the event to be confirmed. The example of the side letter shows how additional evidence suggests a different causal story of the evidence which does not involve an event of the sale. The idea of 'increased alternative generation' can be explained as the idea of identifying causal stories that account for the known evidence other than the explanation that includes the event to be confirmed. The approach to scepticism, in so far as it involved reasoning that is not deductive, requires the exercise of judgement. If the auditor reasoned deductively, then there would be no room for the exercise of judgement. In deductive reasoning the conclusion follows from the premises necessarily. There is no scope for any kind of decision in drawing such conclusions. This is not the case with inductive reasoning. The conclusion does not follow necessarily, and drawing a conclusion involves determining the strength of the conclusion given the premises. Judgement must be exercised in drawing the conclusions in such reasoning. Taking a sceptical approach in auditing involves the exercise of judgement.

Scepticism can be exercised in the search for evidence of predictions as well. An application of scepticism in drawing conclusions about predictions involves the auditor starting with the meaning of the statement to be proven in financial statements. The generalisations that allow the prediction to be derived are examined, and the inductive evidence of their acceptability given past experience is assessed. The evidence of the initial conditions is also assessed. Being sceptical is to be understood as a particular way of exercising judgement in inductive reasoning by questioning the generalisations and the conclusions that constitute the predictions derived from them inductively. This is a matter of being critical of the premises and reasoning used in accepting predictions.

One of the important skills required of auditors who are to exercise scepticism is that they should grasp the nature of the reasons and reasoning that underlies the acceptance of statements and of the ways in which such reasoning can be undermined. This has implications for recruitment and training of auditors. Successful auditors are likely to be those who can grasp the nature of the kind of reasoning to conclusions required in auditing situations. Training in scepticism should focus on getting auditors to understand the nature of inductive reasoning. Training material in firms, audit firm policies and the requirements set out in auditing standards should indicate the importance of gauging the strength of arguments, the ways in which arguments can be undermined and the requirement for 'maximal specificity' in inductive arguments. Auditing standards contain guidance that recognizes the importance of the strength of evidence and the need to consider whether additional evidence undermines a conclusion previously derived from evidence obtained and insist on the need for the exercise of judgement and scepticism in searching for evidence. What is missing from the guidance given by standard setters and in the academic literature on the search for evidence in auditing is any indication of how the nature of the reasoning involved in evidential situations explains and justifies the practices and guidance that is included in auditing standards. This, in turn, results in a failure to adequately explain the nature of the judgement that needs to be exercised in evidential situations and the nature of scepticism that is meant to be adopted in such situations. If one asks why different kinds of generalisation may give different levels of assurance or why it is important to search for facts and generalisations that may undermine conclusions previously derived, little in the way of explanation can be derived from the existing academic literature or the briefing papers of standard setters. This results in a failure to adequately grasp what is meant by the term 'evidence' and also undermines understanding of what the terms 'judgement' and 'scepticism' mean when it is stated that auditors must exercise judgement and scepticism in evidential situations.

SUMMARY

In order for the opinion to give credibility to the financial statements, it must be believed that auditors can justify their opinion. This requires them to have evidence to support it. The opinion is based on such evidence. Criterial evidence, that is, what needs to be established given the meaning of the opinion, is distinguished from inductive evidence that establishes an empirical connection between evidence events and the events that are to be confirmed. The events to be confirmed are those that are asserted in the financial statements. This leads to the idea that evidence relates to these assertions. Some assertions are about matters of fact, and some assertions amount to predictions about what will happen. It is suggested that the kind of assertions identified in ISA 315 are not actually asserted in financial statements. These represent explanations of what needs to be established by the auditor if the statements in financial statements are relevant and reliable. They constitute criterial evidence of relevance and reliability. The nature of inductive evidence of assertions of matters of fact is explored. It is evidence that established an empirical correlation between independent evidence events and events to be confirmed. The idea that the one event makes the other more probable is examined. The kind of probability involved is not a mathematical probability that satisfies the mathematical calculus of probability but represents degrees of conviction of some other kind. Evidence in auditing is something that arises from the causal propensity of events to be confirmed to produce effects that, if found, constitute evidence of these events. This lies behind the idea in the legal literature that something counts as evidence if there is a causal story linking the event to be confirmed with the event that constitutes evidence. Any generalisations that might link the evidence event with the event to be confirmed depends upon this background causal story. Auditors establish the causal story linking events asserted in financial statements with evidence events. They then search for the evidence events. If found they then must confirm that the event to be confirmed is the best explanation of the evidence events. Other explanations may be better in the light of further evidence that may be found. The auditor needs to look for all of the relevant evidence that exists in the circumstances of the company audited and determine the best explanation of this evidence, that is, they must look for maximal specificity. The objective is to determine whether the event to be confirmed is the best explanation of the evidential events they have identified. The idea of evidence to support predictions is also examined. To adopt a sceptical approach in the search for evidence is a matter of adopting a certain attitude towards the reasoning that supports statements in financial statements. This involves questioning the stories that causally connect the events to be confirmed with the evidential events, looking for additional events that might undermine the story and considering alternative explanations of the evidential events identified. The skill required of auditors who are to exercise scepticism requires a grasp of the reasoning that underlies the acceptance of statements made in financial statements and of the ways in which such reasoning can be undermined.

REFERENCES

APB (2010) 'Auditor Scepticism: Raising the Bar'. Discussion Paper. Accessible at: http://www.frc.org.uk/getattachment/2a1e0146-a92c-4b7e-bf33-305b3b10fcd2/Discussion-Paper-Auditor-Scepticism-Raising-the-Ba.aspx [Accessed 1 August 2012].

APB (2012) 'Professional Scepticism: Establishing a Common Understanding and Reaffirming Its Central Role in Delivering Audit Quality'. Briefing Paper. Accessible at: http://www.frc.org.uk/getattachment/1aecac64-6309-4539-a6d9-690e67c93519/Briefing-Paper-Professional-Scepticism.aspx [Accessed 1 August 2012].

Ayer, A. (1956) *The Problem of Knowledge*. Middlesex, UK: Penguin Books.

Ayer, A. (1972) *Probability and Evidence*. London: Macmillan.

Baker Tilly (2010) 'Comment Letter'. Accessible at: http://www.frc.org.uk/apb/publications/response_scepticism.cfm [Accessed 2 January 2011].

Blackburn, S. (1994) *The Oxford Dictionary of Philosophy*. Oxford: Oxford University Press.

Craig, E., ed. (2005) *The Shorter Routledge Encyclopedia of Philosophy*. New York: Routledge.

Dutta, S. and Srivastava, R. (1993) 'Aggregation of evidence in auditing: A likelihood perspective', *Auditing: A Journal of Practice and Theory*, Vol. 12, Supplement, pp. 137–160.

Earman, J. and Salmon, W. (1992) 'The Confirmation of Scientific Hypotheses' in M. Salmon (ed.) *Introduction to the Philosophy of Science*. Indianapolis, Ind./ Cambridge: Hackett Publishing Company.

EC (2010) *Audit Policy: Lessons from the Crisis*. Green Paper. Brussels, Belgium: European Commission.

Evans, L. (2003) 'The true and fair view and the "fair presentation" override of IAS 1', *Accounting and Business Research*, Vol. 33 (4), pp. 311–325.

Gibbs, T. (1977) 'A general theory of evidence as the conceptual foundation in auditing theory: A comment', *Accounting Review*, July, pp. 751–755.

Gronewold, U. (2006) 'Probative value of audit evidence: A framework and synthesis what do we know 45 years after Mautz/Sharaf?', *Journal of Forensic Accounting*, Vol. 7, pp. 345–394.

Hacker, P. (1993) *Wittgenstein Meaning and Mind Part I Essays*. Oxford: Blackwell.

IAASB (2010) *ISA 200 Overall Objectives of the Independent Auditor and the Conduct of an Audit in Accordance with International Standards*. New York: International Federation of Accountants.

IAASB (2010) *ISA 315 Identifying and Assessing the Risks of Material Misstatement through Understanding the Entity and Its Environment*. New York: International Federation of Accountants.

IAASB (2010) *ISA 500 Audit Evidence*. New York: International Federation of Accountants.

IASB (2003) *IAS 16 Property, Plant and Equipment*. London: IASB.

IASB (2010) *The Conceptual Framework for Financial Reporting*. London: IASB.

ICAEW (2010) 'Comment Letter'. Accessible at: http://www.frc.org.uk/apb/publications/response_scepticism.cfm [Accessed 2 January 2011].

ICAS (2010) 'Comment Letter'. Accessible at: http://www.frc.org.uk/apb/publications/response_scepticism.cfm [Accessed 2 January 2011].

Kissinger, J. (1977) 'A general theory of evidence as the conceptual foundation in auditing theory: Some comments and extensions', *Accounting Review*, April, pp. 322–339.

Lee, T. (1993) *Corporate Audit Theory*. London: Chapman and Hall.

Mautz, R.K. and Sharaf, H.A. (1961) *The Philosophy of Auditing*. Sarasota, Fla.: American Accounting Association.

Mock, T., Wright, A., Washington, M. & Krishnamoorthy, G. (1997) 'Auditors' uncertainty representation and evidence aggregation', *Behavioural Research in Accounting*, Vol. 9, Supplement, pp. 123–147.

Murphy, P. (2009) *Murphy on Evidence*. Oxford: Oxford University Press.

Nelson, M. and Tan, H. (2005) 'Judgement and decision making research in auditing: A task, person, and interpersonal interaction perspective', *Auditing: A Journal of Practice and Theory*, Vol. 24, Supplement, pp. 41–71.

Salmon, W. (1992) 'Scientific Explanation' in M. Salmon (ed.) *Introduction to the Philosophy of Science*. Indianapolis, Ind./Cambridge: Hackett Publishing Company.

Smieliauskas, W. and Smith, L. (1990) 'A theory of evidence based on audit assertions', *Contemporary Accounting Research*, Vol. 6 (2), pp. 407–426.

Stephens, R. (1983) 'An investigation of the descriptiveness of the general theory of evidence and auditing', *Auditing: A Journal of Practice and Theory*, Vol. 3 (1), pp. 55–74.

Toba, Y. (1975) 'A general theory of evidence as the conceptual foundation in auditing theory', *Accounting Review*, Vol. 50 (2), pp. 7–24.

Twining, W. (2006) *Rethinking Evidence*. 2nd edn. Cambridge: Cambridge University Press.

Wolfram, S. (1990) *Philosophical Logic*. New York: Routledge.

5 Materiality

Materiality is an important concept in auditing both in planning the scope of the audit and in determining the extent of audit testing and evaluating the evidential support for an audit opinion (Holstrum and Messier, 1982). Given its importance it is perhaps surprising to hear that the auditor's determination of materiality 'is a matter of professional judgment' (IAASB, 2010, ISA 320, §4). It might be expected that the profession or regulators would say more about the concept of materiality and the judgements required. However, it has been acknowledged that 'no general standards of materiality can be formulated that could hope to take account of all the considerations that enter into experienced human judgment' (FASB, 1980, p. xiii, quoted in Roberts and Dwyer, 1998, p. 574). It is a 'black box' (Bernstein, 1967, p. 90), one part of 'the black box of auditing practice' (Power, 1997, p. 40). Exercising judgement might be a 'mysterious process, undefinable and inexplicable', but surely something can be said about it if a 'proliferation of loose standards and practices' is to be avoided (Bernstein, 1967, p. 91). It has recently been referred to as 'accounting's best kept secret' (Brennan and Gray, 2005). This chapter attempts to open the lid of the 'black box' and explore this 'secret' by conducting a conceptual enquiry into the concept of materiality and of the judgement involved.

THE IMPORTANCE OF JUDGEMENTS ABOUT MATERIALITY TO THE AUDITOR

The importance of materiality in auditing is clear from ISA 200 given that the objective of the auditor is to determine that the financial statements are free from material misstatement. If there are misstatements, then the auditor must determine whether 'uncorrected misstatements are material, individually or in aggregate' (IAASB, 2010, ISA 450, §11). If the auditor discovers material misstatement, then financial statements need to be altered or the auditor must 'express clearly an appropriately modified opinion on the financial statements' (IAASB, 2010, ISA 705, §4). The auditor must use judgement in determining when a misstatement is material. This auditor must understand of the meaning of 'material' in relation to misstatements. A descriptive conceptual enquiry into 'material misstatement' will be undertaken.

A DESCRIPTIVE CONCEPTUAL ENQUIRY INTO 'MATERIAL MISSTATEMENT'

A 'misstatement' is defined in ISA 450 as 'a difference between the amount, classification, presentation, or disclosure of a reported financial statement item and the amount, classification, presentation, or disclosure that is required for the item to be in accordance with the applicable financial reporting framework'. This definition will be accepted, and the descriptive conceptual enquiry will be on the meaning of the expression 'material'. A FASB *Discussion Memorandum* states that 'the concept of materiality is generally understood ultimately to involve determination of the importance of a matter for financial reporting purposes' (FASB, 1975, p. 3, quoted in Messier et al., 2005, p. 155). ISA 320 states that the concept of material is derived from financial reporting frameworks where it is 'generally' explained that 'misstatements, including omissions, are considered to be material if they, individually or in the aggregate, could reasonably be expected to influence the economic decisions of users taken on the basis of the financial statements' (IAASB, 2010, ISA 320, §2).

The IAASB's explanation of materiality appears at first glance to be similar to that in the IASB's *The Conceptual Framework for Financial Reporting*. The latter says that 'information is material if omitting it or misstating it could influence decisions that users make on the basis of the financial information of a specific reporting entity' (IASB, 2010, QC11). There is an important difference, though. The IASB definition talks about misstatements that 'could' influence decisions whereas the IAASB talk about misstatements that 'could reasonably be expected' to influence decisions. Statement of Financial Accounting Concepts 2 (SFAC 2) states that 'the omission or misstatement of an item is material . . . if . . . the magnitude of the item is such that it is probable that the judgment of a reasonable person relying upon the report would have been changed or influenced by the inclusion or correction of an item' (FASB, 1980, §132). The idea that the misstatement 'would' probably affect users is preferable to the idea that it 'could'. The latter suggests only that it is *logically possible* that user decisions might be affected. Do auditors need for the auditor to worry about possibilities, or should they only be concerned with probabilities? American standard setters were worried that the IASB's word 'could', without the addition of 'reasonably', might result in a low threshold of materiality (Messier et al., 2005, p. 155). Auditors should only be concerned with the reactions of 'reasonable persons'. Irrational users who might be concerned about certain kinds of misstatement should not be considered. The IAASB's use of 'reasonably be expected' might be their way of expressing the same idea as the FASB.

How does the auditor determine whether a misstatement could 'reasonably be expected' to influence the economic decisions of users? This sounds like an empirical matter, but it is not usually possible to directly observe that a misstatement *does* affect users. This is obvious from the fact that determining whether a misstatement is material either prevents it being made or alerts users to the misstatement by highlighting it in the audit report so that it does not affect them. The auditor is required to determine whether, *counter to the facts*, if the misstatement was made, it *would* affect user decisions. The auditor has to be able to justify such a *counterfactual statement*.

COUNTERFACTUAL STATEMENTS

Counterfactual statements are of the form ' "if p were to happen q would happen", or "if p were to have happened q would have happened" where the supposition p is contrary to the known fact that not-p' (Blackburn, 1994, p. 86). The counterfactual statement in materiality judgements is 'if a misstatement of a certain kind were to happen users would have changed the decisions they make using the financial statements'. This is counter to the facts since the misstatement is either not made or is neutralized. It is not necessary to go into the logic of counterfactual statements. It is important to realise that even though counterfactuals are not based on observations about what happens, they still depend upon scientific knowledge. A counterfactual depends on *inference from generalisations*. They are often derived from laws of nature. In the area of financial reporting, the generalisations would be to the effect that when misstatements of a certain kind are discovered by users, the users change their decisions. Auditors could reasonably expect that a particular misstatement would affect users if, contrary to facts, it was made and discovered by users, because they infer this from laws or generalisations that state that users change their decisions if they discover misstatements of this kind. To reasonably expect something is to have a *belief*, albeit a belief not about what has happened but about what *would* happen, if something else was to occur. What kind of reasoning from generalisations to counterfactuals are we talking about here, and what kind of generalisations are involved?

REASONING FROM GENERALISATIONS
TO COUNTERFACTUALS

The generalisations might be universals like laws along the lines 'all misstatements of kind X influence the decisions of users'. Given that misstatement is of kind X, a conclusion can be *deduced* that if a misstatement of kind X were to happen then users would change their decisions. The word 'would' indicates a counterfactual. The belief in the counterfactual conclusion is *reasonable* given the universal generalisation and the statement that the misstatement is of a certain kind. As the conclusion follows deductive it follows *necessarily*. There is no choice in accepting the conclusion given the acceptance of the premises and *no exercise of judgement* in determining that a misstatement will affect users. An exercise of judgement arises only if the reasoning is not deductive and does not involve universal generalisations.

The belief that the reasoning is not deductive might lie behind the FASB statement that there are no general standards of materiality. This can be understood as the claim that no universal generalisations about materiality can be formulated. An example of a universal generalisation is 'all misstatements in excess of 5% of reported profits influence the economic decisions of users taken on the basis of the financial statements'. If this is the kind of statement that the FASB has in mind when talking about 'general standards of materiality', then it is fairly clear from the empirical research on actual materiality judgements that there is no agreement on quantitative criteria of this kind (Iskandar and Iselin, 1999, p. 211–212; Messier et al., 2005, p. 157). What other kind of generalisations and reasoning might be involved in deriving counterfactuals about the impact of misstatements on users?

OTHER KINDS OF REASONING TO COUNTERFACTUALS

Another kind of reasoning might start with a premise that is a *statistical* generalization such as 'it is likely that misstatements of kind X influence the decisions of users' or 'it is probable that misstatements of kind X influence the decisions of users'. From this and a premise 'this is a misstatement of kind X' it is possible to *deduce* a counterfactual 'it is probable/likely that if a misstatement of kind X were to happen happened users would change their decisions'. The conclusion is not that the misstatement *would have* influenced decisions, only that it is probable or likely that they would do so.

This raises an important issue. The IAASB definition of material misstatements as those that could reasonably be expected to influence decisions might be interpreted as saying that a misstatement is material if it is likely/probable that it would influence decisions of users, in effect, the FASB definition of 'material'. Are they equivalent, though? To see that they are not equivalent, an example of a materiality judgement in auditing will be considered. The generalisation 'misstatements in excess of 5% of reported profits are likely to influence the economic decisions of users taken on the basis of the financial statements' would appear, from empirical research, reasonable to a number of professional auditors although there may be a lack of agreement on the percentage (Brennan and Gray, 2005; Messier et al., 2005). The problem is that although a statement that a particular misstatement is likely to influence users could be derived from the generalisation plus a statement that the particular misstatement was in excess of 5% profits, it may not be reasonable to expect that it would affect users *in certain circumstances*. Profits may be abnormally low. Another generalisation may be relevant in such a case. For example, if it is also the case that 'misstatements less than 0.5% of turnover are unlikely to influence the economic decisions of users', then if the particular misstatement is less than 0.5% of turnover, the conclusion will be drawn that it will not influence users. If the definition of 'material' is 'being likely to influence the decisions of users' and the definition of 'immaterial' (= 'not material)' is 'being not likely to influence the decision of users', then the same misstatement is both material and not material. Although the misstatement is likely to influence decisions, given the other generalisation and conclusion, it would not be reasonable to conclude that it 'could reasonably be expected to influence the economic decisions of users'.

The problem is the same kind of problem that arose in connection with audit evidence. Generalisations apply in certain circumstances but not in others. If evidence is introduced that changes the circumstances, then the generalization may no longer be relevant. The problem is that the generalisations are of the 'inductive-statistical' kind. An example from the philosophical literature illustrates the problem.

INDUCTIVE-STATISTICAL REASONING

Assume that there is a true generalisation that 'almost all cases of streptococcus infection clear up quickly after the administration of penicillin'. Given a true factual premise that 'Jane Jones had a streptococcus infection' and 'Jane Jones received treatment with penicillin', a conclusion could be derived that 'Jane Jones recovered quickly'. Another generalisation might be introduced, though. It is also true that 'almost no cases of penicillin-resistant streptococcus infection clear up quickly after the administration of penicillin'. From premises 'Jane Jones had a penicillin-resistant streptococcus infection' and 'Jane Jones received treatment with penicillin', the conclusion might be drawn that 'Jane Jones did not recover quickly'. The conclusions contradict each other. Would it, in the circumstances, be 'reasonable to expect' that Jane Jones would recover? If the conclusions were deduced from the premises, then, given the incompatible conclusions, at least one of the premises would have to be incompatible. Interestingly, in this example *all* of the premises in both arguments could be true, but the conclusions are incompatible. This could not happen with deductive reasoning, for with such reasoning the addition of new premises does not undermine a conclusion previously drawn (Salmon, 1992, p. 26). This suggests that the kind of reasoning involved with this kind of generalisation is not deductive.

In both cases the conclusions would be reasonable, given the premises, but it would not be reasonable to draw conclusions that are contradictory. The solution to this problem is to introduce the requirement into reasoning of the 'inductive-statistical' kind the idea of 'maximal specificity' introduced in chapter 4. Applied to statistical generalisations, it is the requirement to include all relevant knowledge. If it is known that the infection is of a certain kind and if this knowledge is relevant in the situation, then one of the generalisations becomes irrelevant. Another is introduced that is more relevant to the current situation. Only if *all of the relevant information* is identified and if *only the generalisations relevant to the situation are considered* would it be reasonable to draw a conclusion about what would be the case.

Applied to the auditing situation where one is trying to determine whether it is reasonable to expect that users will be influenced by a misstatement, it is necessary to look for the generalisation that is *most relevant* given the known facts. The generalisation in the first argument that it is likely that misstatements that affect profit by more than 5% influence the economic decisions of users no longer appears relevant in circumstances where profits are less than 10% of turnover. Another generalisation is that most misstatements that affect profit by more than 5% where profits are less than 10% of turnover are *not* likely to influence the economic decisions of users. The second generalisation has 'maximal specificity', that is, greater relevance given the known facts. The first argument is rejected because another generalisation is more relevant in the circumstances. It is reasonable to expect that a misstatement will not affect users given the more relevant second generalisation.

This suggests that in determining materiality auditors have to make themselves aware of the particular circumstances in which a misstatement is made and identify the most relevant generalisation *in those circumstances*. The auditor must *decide* what is the most relevant generalisation in determining materiality. One way to avoid having to make this kind of decision is to replace the generalisations about what is likely with universal generalisations. For example, the auditing generalisation might be 'misstatements that affect profit by more than 5% influence the economic decisions of users except where profits are less than 10% of turnover'. In conjunction with a statement that a particular misstatement affects profit by more than 5% but where profits are less than 10% of turnover, the conclusion that the misstatement would influence users will not be drawn. The problem in formulating such generalisations is in identifying *all* of the circumstances where an exception to the generalisation is warranted. This may be one interpretation of the FASB statement that 'no general standards of materiality can be formulated that could hope to take account of all the considerations that enter into experienced human judgment'. Once again, the universal generalisations cannot be found that would eliminate choices or decisions and hence judgement.

This analysis suggests that for auditors to conclude that it is reasonable to expect that a misstatement would affect the decisions of users, they need find the statistical generalisations that are the most relevant generalisations in the particular context where materiality judgements need to be made given the criterion of 'maximal specificity'. This requires an exercise of judgement. What are the problems in finding statistical generalisations?

FORMULATING THE GENERALISATIONS THAT UNDERPIN MATERIALITY JUDGEMENTS

The statistical generalisations that are used in determining materiality do not necessarily involve probabilities, at least not 'objective' or mathematical probabilities, but may involve 'subjective probabilities' based on degrees of conviction as explained in chapter 4. Objective probability is relevant where there are experimental facts such as the throwing of a dice and determining the frequency of the results obtained. It does not make sense when it is used in contexts like auditing that are not experimental and involve 'unrepeatable or non-experimental events' (Steele, 1992, p. 38). Subjective probability might involve the assignment of a number to indicate a degree of confidence in it. They can be indicated by language that involves expressions like 'quite probable', 'fairly certain' or 'more likely' of the kind suggested earlier. Subjective probability has been said to be the 'language of judgement' (Steele, 1992, p. 38). These are the kind of generalisations used in deriving counterfactual statements about the impact of misstatements.

This raises the question of where the statistical generalisations that underpin counterfactual statements come from. Holstrum and Messier identify this as a problem in their review of empirical research on materiality. The concept of materiality is tied to the idea of what users would do, but little is known about how financial statement information is used in economic decision-making. One empirical study exemplifies 'the difficulties of implementing a user orientation toward materiality issues in an economic environment where user groups have dissimilar views as to which items are most important' (Holstrum and Messier, 1982, 53). Later studies confirm this (Messier, Martinov-Bennie and Eilifsen, 2005, p. 155). Although being 'material' was defined as something that would affect users' decisions, nothing very definite can be said about what generally affects such decisions. It is 'left up to the individual making the judgment', and 'individual judgments are required to assess materiality in the absence of authoritative criteria or to decide that minimum quantitative criteria are not appropriate in particular situations' (Holstrum and Messier, 1982, p. 48). Stating that it is a matter of judgement is not very helpful in describing how these generalisations are derived.

This is one aspect of the more general problem of basing financial reporting requirements on how users make use of the information in financial statements, that is, in adopting the decision-usefulness approach. Statements about user needs may be based on some theoretical model about what 'rational' users want rather than on empirical research into what *actual* users want. This is implied by the reference to the 'reasonable person' in SFAC 2 noted earlier. Generalisations about user needs are based on statements about how such users *ought* to go about making decisions rather than on actual evidence of how real users use financial statement information to make decisions (Young, 2006). The fallback position is to allow individual auditors to use their judgement in deciding what generalisations are relevant. Why is it left to them to determine these generalisations rather than to standard setters and regulators or the collective judgement of professionals?

At the firm level, materiality guidelines may be developed by professionals within the firm. This is an example of the 'institutional isomorphism' that 'is a constraining process that forces one unit in a population to resemble other units that face the same set of environmental conditions' (DiMaggio and Powell, 1991, p. 66). Within firms a combination of 'coercive isomorphism', through statements in audit manuals and the 'normative pressures' of professional training regimes (DiMaggio and Powell, 1991, pp. 67–74), and 'mimetic processes', whereby professionals influence each other and the experience of professionals is passed down to newer recruits. They may result in agreement on materiality judgements *within* firms, and there may be no requirement for professionals to exercise judgement in applying the materiality guidelines within firms.

This raises the question of how the firms arrive at these materiality guidelines. Auditors may make 'materiality determinations without the consent of users, based on assumptions about user needs' (Roberts and Dwyer, 1998, p. 576). This 'knowledge' may be the product of the 'system of financial auditing knowledge' (Power, 1997, p. 36). Practical routines may be developed '*ad hoc* at the level of practice and, due to environmental demands, gradually percolate upwards and become codified, first at the level of in-house documentation, then sometime more abstractly at the level of professional institutes and regulatory bodies' (Power, 1997, pp. 36–37). However, there may be insufficient agreement on materiality guidelines *between* firms. This is clear from the extensive empirical research on materiality. There is little agreement on the percentage that constituted the materiality threshold particularly between large and small firms (Holstrum and Messier, 1982, p. 59; Messier et al., 2005, p. 158).

Empirical research of this kind does not directly support generalisations about the effect of misstatements on user decisions, but rather identifies what audit firms *believe* will impact user decisions. It is acknowledged that judgement plays a significant role in coming to beliefs of this kind (Messier et al., 2005, p. 163). Research into *why* auditors or audit firms have the beliefs identifies other factors that are present when such decisions are made. For example, an appreciation of the nature of the item or type of transaction, the size of audit firms, whether or not the misstatement would create earnings surprises, professional experience, personal characteristics and audit cultures can all have an effect on judgements about materiality (Messier et al., 2005). Some of these factors may be believed to have an effect on user decisions whereas others appear to be more concerned with other factors not related to empirical facts about how users react to misstatements but more on fear of the consequences of exercising judgement by auditors about the effects of adopting materiality decisions. For example, if auditors are in a litigious environment, this may lead them to adopt higher materiality thresholds. This is not because auditors believe that users would change their decisions but because they believe that users might sue them if they do not press for a correction of a misstatement and they wish to avoid such confrontation. Other considerations might also be at work in determining materiality. There may be 'profit maximisation motives' (Roberts and Dwyer, 1998, p. 576) given that 'materiality is critical in determining the amount of work carried out during an audit' (Brennan and Gray, 2005, p. 10). It may be that 'auditors have incentives to choose high levels of materiality—this reduces the amount of work to be done on the audit and therefore makes the audit less costly/ more profitable' (Brennan and Gray, 2005, p. 26). This is an example of 'the problem of reconciling economic pressures to trim and prune the audit process with programmatic demands for assurance' (Power, 1997, p. 38). Materiality is sometimes used to excuse deliberate misstatements where auditors do not insist on adjustment using materiality guidelines to allow such treatment (Levitt, 1998, p. 6). This research provides evidence about what is *wanted* in identifying misstatements as material.

That these motivations are present may be something of an embarrassment to auditors and may contribute to the desire for 'secrecy' about materiality. Auditors may simply not want to identify the kind of misstatement that would affect user decisions. They want instead to identify a kind of misstatement that, if not detected, would have deleterious consequences. They want a kind of misstatement whose detection does not involve uneconomic costs. The concept of a material misstatement which results from desires like these identifies the 'importance of a matter for financial reporting purposes', but what is of importance is not focused exclusively on misstatements that will affect user decisions. This is alleged by people like Arthur Levitt of the SEC, who refers to 'accounting hocus-pocus' in the use of materiality. He complains that 'in markets where missing an earnings projection by a penny can result in a loss of millions of dollars in market capitalization, I have a hard time accepting that some of these so-called non-events simply don't matter' (Levitt, 1998, p. 5). In other words, he does not believe the generalisations that auditors and preparers use in deriving the counterfactuals about what users would do if a misstatement were made. There are other factors at work, other desires that have directed the development of the concept of materiality. What kind of guidance should be given by standard setters and regulators about the determination of materiality?

WHAT GUIDANCE SHOULD BE GIVEN BY STANDARD SETTERS AND REGULATORS?

The lack of agreement on the generalisations that are used to derive counterfactuals may prevent standard setters from offering a re-definition of 'material misstatement' based on such generalisations. This blocks the move from 'symptoms' to 'criteria' observed by Wittgenstein and noted earlier in the book. It is easier to see how this could happen if there were universal empirical generalisations about the effect that certain misstatements have on user decisions. If it was always the case, empirically, that misstatements of more than 5% of net income affect users' decisions, then 'material' might be re-defined as 'a misstatement that affects income by more than 5%'. A re-definition in these terms would give a sufficient condition of a misstatement being material. There may be more than one sufficient condition. Are these conditions necessary? Whether or not these re-definitions are useful depends upon how they are used. If they are used to move from the identification of a misstatement having such a property to a statement that the misstatement is material, then they may be useful. However, if the requirement is to identify *all* misstatements that are material, as required by ISA 200, then unless all of the sufficient conditions of a misstatement being material are identified, then the auditor will not be able to determine what he or she has to do to identify *all* material misstatements. Another possible interpretation of the FASB claim that there are no general standards of materiality would be that it is not possible to offer a re-definition of this kind because there are no empirical generalisations of this kind from which such a re-definition can be formulated. This may be what is meant by saying that 'audit is rather a craft whose central concepts, such as materiality, resist precise codification' (Power, 1997, p. 36). A 'precise codification' would be a definition in terms of necessary and sufficient conditions.

Another response would be to propose a re-definition *in spite of* the absence of agreed generalisations. This is one way of interpreting Elliott's proposal that 'the materiality judgment process be replaced by a mechanical rule' (referred to in Roberts and Dwyer, 1998, p. 574). 'Material misstatement' could be defined by a mechanical rule of the kind 'if a misstatement affects net income by more than 5% then it is material'. This gives a sufficient condition of a misstatement being material. The definition could also include a necessary condition, namely, 'if misstatement is material, then it affects net income by more than 5%'. A combined definition would be 'a misstatement is material if and only if it affects net income by more than 5%'. The usefulness of such a definition would then have to be debated. Elliott's argument was that 'at least users would know the purported level of financial statement precision' (referred to in Roberts and Dwyer, 1998, p. 574). There may be a demand for definitions of this kind, but there is a 'tension between . . . institutionalized demands for formal structure and practitioner demands for preserving situated judgement and discretion' (Power, 1997, p. 38).

One compromise that might be explored is the possibility that certain characteristics might be taken as *criteria* in Wittgenstein's sense. They may constitute *presumptive evidence* that something comes under an expression, but this evidence is defeasible in the light of countervailing evidence (Hacker, 1990, p. 257). This would set up some *meaning* connection between one event or state of affairs and another. If it is observed that misstatements in excess of 5% of net income *usually*, but not universally, change user decisions, it may be that being a misstatement in excess of 5% of net income could to be taken as a *criterion* of being material. This does not mean that all misstatements with this quality are material but that, as a matter of meaning, they are taken as material, but this is defeasible in the light of other evidence, say evidence that net income is abnormally low. If this happens, then new criteria for a misstatement being material may be devised on the basis of inductive evidence. This is a variation on the suggestion that what is today observed as a concomitant of a phenomenon will tomorrow be used to define it. What this means is that there is a move between an inductive-statistical generalisation to a new meaning connection, that is, one that sets up criteria for applying an express. If materiality generalisations are of this kind, then the concept of materiality may be developed in this way. The FASB search for general standards of materiality may not be a search for necessary and sufficient conditions but for criteria that constitute new grounds, as a matter of meaning, for applying the concept of materiality to misstatements. Adopting this approach allows some 'formal structure' and, at the same time, gives scope for the exercise of 'situated judgement and discretion'.

These different ways of approaching the question of the kind of guidance about materiality that might be provided by standard setters all start from the desire to identify misstatements that will affect user decisions. Is this the only way to approach the development of the concept of materiality and the question of the kind of judgement that must be exercised in applying this concept?

WHENCE MATERIALITY . . .

The discussion of the concept of material misstatement suggests a number of different ways of interpreting what is wanted in developing the concept of materiality. What is perceived as needed are:

i) Universal empirical generalisations about the characteristics of misstatements that will influence user decisions;

ii) Inductive-statistical empirical generalisations about the characteristics of misstatements that will influence user decisions;

iii) Sufficient (and possibly necessary) conditions that can be used to define misstatements that will influence user decisions derived from universal empirical generalisations;

iv) Criteria that can be used to define misstatements that will influence user decisions derived from inductive-statistical empirical generalisations.

If either i) or iii) are possible, then no judgement needs to be exercised in using the generalisations or definitions to identify material misstatements.

This is because the conclusion that a particular misstatement is material follows deductively from either the generalisation or the definition plus a statement that the misstatement has the characteristics that universally affect user decisions, and hence are material, or mean that the misstatement is material. With ii) and iv) *judgement* needs to be exercised. This is because moving from an inductive-statistical empirical generalisation that most misstatements of a certain kind affect user decisions to a conclusion that user decisions are affected by a particular misstatement involves deciding whether or not the generalisation has 'maximal specificity'. Where a definition of 'material misstatement' involves criteria, a decision about whether or not the criteria, in the particular case, are defeasible needs to be made. In both cases there is a *decision* or *choice* in deriving the conclusion that a particular misstatement is material. This means that the reasoning is not deductive and involves an exercise of judgement.

These approaches assume that the concept of materiality should be centred upon the effect of misstatements have on user decisions. The problem that is then created is how to determine the empirical generalisations that underpin the counterfactual. Given the orthodoxy of the user needs/decision-usefulness approach, it is difficult to challenge these moves. One response would be to insist that more research is needed in determining the actual needs of users and how they use information to make decisions. Another response might be to question the assumption that determining user needs is a matter of determining *empirically* what information users need to make decisions and, hence, what they actually think of as important in financial information. Instead it might be suggested that what needs to be determined is some theory about decision-making and what information *ought* to be used to make decisions with some related theory about what information users *ought* to think of as important. A third response is to question whether the idea of the importance of financial information and of misstatements therein should be tied to decision-making by users. Other considerations may be relevant to determining the importance of misstatements.

Another interpretation of the FASB point that there are no general standards of materiality that take into account all the considerations that influence human judgement might be that the desires and beliefs, the 'considerations' that underpin the acceptance of a concept of materiality, are not agreed. It may be left to individual auditors to determine these for themselves. In other words, what is wanted in developing a concept of materiality, what kind of misstatements are taken as important, is left to the judgement of auditors to determine. Deciding what is important may involve choices or decisions. The idea that concepts are developed, that materiality is made up to meet certain desires, is to take what has been called a 'naturalistic' view of language and is implicit in the idea of 'social construction' explained in chapter 1.

Exploring these underlying desires and beliefs is part of an evaluative conceptual enquiry. The question arises as to who is to make judgements of this kind. Should it be practicing auditors who then have to determine their own concept of materiality, or should standard setters do this with consultation of practitioners? Unless it is realized that the concept of materiality is made up in this way, there is likely to be little progress in securing agreement on the concept and on the application of this concept in audit work. The FASB suggestion that the development of the concept of materiality begins with a desire to identify misstatements that matter for financial reporting purposes might be questioned. If this is the starting point, then beliefs about what matters must be considered. Is what matters what affects user decisions? If so, then unless there is adequate knowledge of what kind of misstatement would affect user decisions, a concept like this is *not useful*. There is no point in making up a materiality concept that cannot be used. One response would be to agree that the focus of research should be on developing generalisations about what influences user decisions. Another response is to abandon the desire to identify misstatements that would affect user decisions and to focus instead on misstatements that *ought* to affect user decisions. This would require the development of some theory about how users ought to make decisions and what information they ought to take into account, including information about the kind of misstatements they should be concerned with. This might be described as some 'theory' about decisions that, to quote the FASB, a 'reasonable person relying upon the report' would take.

One consideration that is identified in the conceptual framework is the *cost constraint*. The conceptual framework says that the standard setter should consider this constraint in developing financial reporting standards (IASB, 2010, §QC38). However, such a constraint could also be used by preparers and auditors to determine the importance of misstatements in financial information. They may consider the cost of identifying and correcting misstatements in the financial statements against the benefits to users of making decisions on information that does not contain the misstatement. There are costs to auditors in identifying misstatements and the possibility of reimbursement for that work and the fact that preparers, and ultimately 'users', may have to pay for this work. They may also need to consider the costs they might incur if they do not find a misstatement in terms of potential costs of litigation and the costs of impairment of reputation. Determining the importance of a matter for the purposes of financial reporting is not quite as simple as the explanation of materiality suggests. What it requires is a consideration of what is wanted from such a concept. Empirical research on materiality judgements suggests that there may be different desires at work which underlie their concept of materiality. It is not surprising that different concepts of materiality emerge where there are different desires and different weightings of desires at work in determining the concept that is constructed. Progress in agreeing on a concept of materiality that is constructed is unlikely to be achieved with agreement on the desires and beliefs that underpin its acceptance.

Several 'secrets' about materiality have been identified in this chapter. To what extent is the profession aware of the 'secrets' of how materiality is 'made up'? Recognising that the concept is 'made up' might undermine the profession's claim of professionalism and command of the unique abstract knowledge that justifies the privileges that comes with it (Abbott, 1988, p. 8). That determining materiality is not just a matter of knowledge but involves deciding what is wanted in making up the concept needs to be acknowledged. It is understandable, however, that the profession may wish this 'secret' to remain hidden.

SUMMARY

Material misstatements are usually explained as misstatements that could or could reasonably be expected to influence the decisions of users of financial statements. Given that the importance of considering materiality in connection with misstatements is to detect or prevent them being made, they will not actually affect these decisions. The idea that they could do so depends upon a counterfactual statement that if they were made, then the decisions of users would be affected. These counterfactual statements are based on generalisations about what influences the decisions of users. This raises the question of where these generalisations come from. It is generally accepted that little is known about how financial statement information is used in making decisions. This results in differences between professionals about materiality guidelines and how to determine if a misstatement is material. Although this problem may arise from a lack of empirical investigation into the effect of misstatements on users, it may also result from insufficient agreement on what is wanted from the concept of materiality. Progress in reaching agreement on materiality judgements will only be made if both the desires and beliefs that underpin material guidelines are explored further.

REFERENCES

Abbott, A. (1988) *The System of Professions An Essay on the Division of Expert Labor*. Chicago: University of Chicago Press.

Bernstein, L. (1967) 'The concept of materiality', *Accounting Review*, January, pp. 86–95.

Blackburn, S. (1994) *The Oxford Dictionary of Philosophy*. Oxford: Oxford University Press.

Brennan, N. and Gray, S. (2005) 'The impact of materiality: Accounting's best kept secret', *Asian Academy of Management Journal of Accounting and Finance*, Vol. 1, pp. 1–31.

DiMaggio, P. and Powell, W. (1991) 'The Iron Cage Revisited: Institutional Isomorphism and Collective Rationality in Organization Fields' in P. DiMaggio and W. Powell (eds.) *The New Institutionalism in Organizational Analysis* Chicago: University of Chicago Press.

FASB (1980) *Statement of Financial Accounting Concepts 2*. Stamford, Conn.: FASB.

Hacker, P. (1990) *Wittgenstein Meaning and Mind*. Oxford: Blackwell.

Holstrum, G. and Messier, Jr., W. (1982) 'A review and integration of empirical research on materiality', *Auditing: A Journal of Practice & Theory*, Vol. 2 (1), pp. 45–63.

IAASB (2010) *ISA 320 Materiality in Planning and Performing an Audit*. New York: International Federation of Accountants.

IAASB (2010) *ISA 450 Evaluation of Misstatements Identified during the Audit*. New York: International Federation of Accountants.

IAASB (2010) *ISA 705 Modifications to the Opinion in the Independent Auditor's Report*. New York: International Federation of Accountants.

IASB (2010) *The Conceptual Framework for Financial Reporting*. London: IASB.

Iskandar, T. and Iselin, E. (1999) 'A review of materiality research', *Accounting Forum*, Vol. 23 (3), pp. 209–239.

Levitt, A. (1998) *Remarks by Chairman Arthur Levitt Securities and Exchange Commission*. Accessible at: http://www.sec.gov/news/speech/speecharchive/1998/spch220.txt [Accessed 20 March 2012].

Messier, Jr., W., Martinov-Bennie, N. and Eilifsen, A. (2005) 'A review and integration of empirical research on materiality: Two decades later', *Auditing: A Journal of Practice and Theory*, Vol. 24 (2), pp. 153–187.

Power, M. (1997) *The Audit Society: Rituals of Verification*. Oxford: Oxford University Press.

Roberts, R. and Dwyer, P. (1998) 'An analysis of materiality and reasonable assurance: Professional mystification and paternalism in auditing', *Journal of Business Ethics*, Vol. 17, pp. 569–578.

Salmon, W. (1992) 'Scientific Explanation' in *Introduction to the Philosophy of Science*. Indianapolis, Ind./Cambridge: Hackett Publishing Company.

Steele, A. (1992) *Audit Risk and Audit Evidence: The Bayesian Approach to Statistical Auditing*. London: Academic Press.

Young, J. (2006) 'Making up users', *Accounting Organizations and Society*, Vol. 31 (6), pp. 579–600.

6 Professional Judgement in Auditing

The numerous references to the exercise of judgement in the previous chapters suggests that it plays an important part in the practice of auditing. The IAASB, in the *Preface to the International Standards on Quality Control, Auditing, Review, Other Assurance and Related Services (Preface)*, confirm this when they say that 'the nature of the International Standards requires the professional accountant to exercise professional judgment in applying them' (IAASB, 2010, Preface, §15). ISA 200 explains that 'professional judgement is essential to the proper conduct of an audit. This is because interpretation of relevant ethical requirements and the ISAs and the informed decisions required throughout the audit cannot be made without the application of relevant knowledge and experience to the facts and circumstances' (IAASB, 2010, ISA 200, §A23). This knowledge and experience will assist in 'developing the necessary competencies to achieve reasonable judgements' (IAASB, 2010, ISA 200, §A24). ISA 200 requires that 'the auditor shall exercise professional judgement in planning and performing an audit of financial statements' (IAASB, 2010, ISA 200, §16).

It is yet another manifestation of the failure to conduct adequate conceptual enquiry into the concepts of auditing that, despite the importance of professional judgement to auditors, little attention has been given to explaining the nature of such judgement. Over forty years ago it was suggested that judgement was 'a vital part of any professional's work', but it was not defined in the literature (Bernstein, 1967, p. 90). A search of this literature over twenty years ago revealed that although there were 939 references to judgement, 'none of these references . . . explain what is meant by judgement' (Mason and Gibbins, 1991, p. 21). Some progress has been made in analysing and describing judgement since this time. The Canadian Institute of Chartered Accountants (CICA) has produced reports on judgement in financial reporting (CICA, 1988) and in auditing (CICA, 1995). They offer definitions of 'professional judgement'. A later report, *A Professional Judgement Framework for Financial Reporting* (ICAS, 2012), actually spends *no* time in explaining what is meant by 'professional judgement'. This might be because it is thought that CICA gave the last word on this concept. However, respondents to the IAASB *Proposed Strategy and Work*

Programme for 2012 supported a project to consider the *conceptual aspects* of professional judgement (IAASB, 2011, p. 31). This suggests that there is still a feeling that the nature of such judgement had not been adequately explained.

It has been claimed that without adequate enquiry into this concept the profession may become subject to 'a proliferation of loose standards and practices' (Bernstein, 1967, p. 91). If the standards require auditors to exercise judgement, then they need to understand what it is they are exercising (Mason and Gibbins, 1991, p. 23). Professional judgement is an input to audit quality (IAASB, 2011 p. 22), and a lack of clarity as to what is involved makes it difficult to see how regulators and auditing standard setters are to improve the quality of audits by insisting on its application. An enquiry into the concept of professional judgement would only be unnecessary if practitioners and regulators agree on what it means. This chapter conducts such an enquiry into the nature of professional judgement in auditing to see if this is the case. The underlying objective of constructing a concept of professional judgement will be identified in an evaluative conceptual enquiry by examining various exercises of judgement and by considering its role in decision-making. It will draw on the work on evidence and materiality in previous chapters. A new definition of judgement is put forward in a prescriptive conceptual enquiry. Some implications for the standard setter and the auditing educator are drawn by considering the effect of this new definition.

A DESCRIPTIVE CONCEPTUAL ENQUIRY INTO PROFESSIONAL JUDGEMENT

The CICA study, *Professional Judgment in Financial Reporting*, defines 'judgment' as 'the process of making a choice, a decision, leading to action' (CICA, 1988, p. 4). The same body defines 'professional judgment in auditing' as 'the application of relevant knowledge and experience, within the context provided by auditing and accounting standards and Rules of Professional Conduct, in reaching decisions where a choice must be made between alternative possible courses of action' (CICA, 1995, p. 5). An important difference between the two definitions is that the auditing definition makes reference to the context provided by standards. Auditors may be faced with different types of judgement situations. These include selecting from alternative actions in standards, determining the meaning of a phrase used to express a requirement, as well as following requirements that explicitly state that judgement must be exercised. A similar definition of 'professional judgement' in the auditing context is given in ISA 200. It is defined as 'the application of relevant training, knowledge and experience, within the context provided by auditing, accounting and ethical standards, in making informed decisions about the courses of action that are appropriate in the circumstances of the audit engagement' (IAASB, 2010, ISA 200, §13 (k)).

One problem with definitions of this kind is that they do not make clear what kind of decisions or choices about courses of action are made in exercising professional judgement. The first CICA report talks of judgement as a *process* whereas the second refers to *application* knowledge and experience and also training. ISA 200 also refers to an 'application'. What kind of 'process' is being referred to? What is the nature of an 'application'? Insights into how these expressions are to be understood should be derivable from the academic literature where actual judgements made by auditors are examined, that is, in the judgement and decision-making (JDM) literature.

JDM research 'uses a psychological lens to understand, evaluate, and improve judgements, decisions, or choices in an auditing setting' (Nelson and Tan, 2005, p. 41). There is little explanation of the kinds of judgement and decision-making that is studied in the largely experimental work in this area. A number of review papers do put forward a definition of 'judgement' and 'decision-making'. Bonner (1999) distinguishes judgements from decisions. She explains that 'the term *judgment* typically refers to forming an idea, opinion, or estimate about an object, an event, a state, or another type of phenomenon. Judgments tend to take the form of predictions about the future or an evaluation of a current state of affairs' (Bonner, 1999, p. 385). This initially looks rather odd. The first part of the definition refers to what might be conceived as an activity, that is, 'forming an idea, opinion, or estimate'. This appears akin to a 'process' or 'application' and points to some kind of activity. The second part of the definition explains judgements as 'predictions' of some kind and of 'evaluation of a current state of affairs'. There is a shift from conceiving of judgement as an activity to something that is the *outcome* of this activity. One way to make sense of this shift is to say that a judgement is the outcome of the activity of judging. For example, looking for evidence that a particular sale took place in the financial year is a process of judging, and the result is a judgement about a matter of fact.

Bonner defines a 'decision' as 'making up one's mind about the issue at hand and taking a course of action. Decisions typically follow judgments and involve a choice among various alternatives based on judgments about those alternatives and, possibly, preferences for factors such as risk and money' (Bonner, 1999, p. 385). The idea is that 'judgments reflect one's belief, and decisions may reflect both belief and preferences' (Bonner, 1999, p. 385). If an auditor has preferences, that is, wants to identify misstatements in sales, and forms a 'judgement', a belief that inspecting sales invoices against entries in sales records will identify misstatements, then he or she will decide to act by inspecting sales invoices. It is not clear why there is a choice amongst alternatives here. When an auditor decides to follow the requirements of an auditing standard, there does not appear to be any judgement involved. If the rule says 'look for material misstatements', what the auditor does depends upon his or her understanding of what 'looking for material misstatements' *means*. Is this 'making up one's mind about the issue at hand'? This would not appear to involve determining empirical facts or predictions. Given the CICA definition of professional judgement in auditing and the definition of ISA 200, auditing actions are undertaken in the context of standards which set out requirements. These decisions do not typically involve judgements about matters of fact.

In another review of the literature on auditor judgements and decision experiments, Solomon and Trotman are also confused. They state that 'we use the term judgment to refer to subjective assessments made as a prelude to taking action. Consistently, we use the term decision to mean actions that people take to perform some task or solve some problem.' (Solomon and Trotman, 2003). There is no explanation of what 'subjective assessments' are made before taking an action. Are they assessments of facts? It may be that they are assessments of preferences or what is wanted to be achieved in auditing actions. In what sense are these 'subjective'? What one wants is subjective in the sense that it 'relates to the subject' or 'derives from one's own consciousness' or is 'introspective' (*Chambers Dictionary*). Does being subjective simply mean that the desires and beliefs are 'one's own'? A decision is said to be an action, but deciding to do something is not the same as doing it. One decides what to do and then may do it as a result, but one may not end up doing it even if one decides to do it.

The distinction between judgement and decision-making is not universally accepted. In a practitioner's perspective on auditing judgement, Wedemeyer (2010) explains that 'I will use the term "auditor judgment" to describe any decision or evaluation made by an auditor, which influences or governs the process and outcome of an audit of financial statements' (Wedemeyer, 2010, p. 321). Judgement appears to cover both decisions about what to do and judgements, in Bonner's sense, about matters of fact. An interesting point made by Wedemeyer is that the kind of judgement must have some impact upon what the auditor does. Judgements about matters of fact that have no such impact are presumably not the kind of judgement meant when auditing judgement is referred to.

This brief descriptive enquiry into the concept of professional judgement reveals differences in the explanation of the expression 'judgement' in the auditing context. There is also a failure to explore what is meant by some of the explanations that are given. These explanations are given in language, and to understand them one has to understand the expressions used in the explanation. What is the nature of the 'process' or 'choices' that have to be made, and how they are related to decision-making?

DECISION-MAKING

One way of bringing both consideration of what is wanted and what is believed into decision-making is understand it as practical reasoning. This is reasoning from what is wanted and what is believed to fulfil these desires to a desire to do something. It is implicit in both the CICA/ISA 200 definitions of 'judgement', and in Bonner's work the decision is to perform an *intentional* action. The desire and the belief in practical reasoning are reasons for the action. Decision-making is often portrayed as 'rational choice' (March, 1994, p. 1). Rationality can be defined as 'a particular and very familiar class of procedures for making choices' (March, 1994, p. 2). A 'procedure' should be understood as practical reasoning. Decision-making is *coming to have a desire to act as a result of reasoning*.

Decision-making is thus practical reasoning, and to explore the one is to explore the other. A 'process' or 'application' is a *process of reasoning*, and to understand decision-making is to understand practical reasoning. This is the same as 'means-end' reasoning (Archer, 1993) or 'instrumental' reasoning (Mattessich, 1995). If decision-making is practical reasoning, then Bonner's statement that decisions 'reflect both beliefs and preferences' is understandable. The conclusion of such reasoning is a desire to perform an action. This is equated with a decision which 'leads to an action' in the sense that an action results from wanting to perform it. This reasoning might also be called 'rational calculation' for decisions are 'based on an evaluation of alternatives in terms of their consequences for preferences'. This is a 'logic of consequences'. One determines what one wants, looks around for actions that will fulfil what one desires, and then draws a conclusion that one wants to perform the act that will fulfil them.

It is interesting to observe, in the definitions considered here, a tendency to conjoin, and in some instances conflate, explanations of judgement with explanations of decision-making and decisions. Judgement is exercised in making decisions. Decisions follow from judgements. Judgements are a prelude to taking action. If decision-making and practical reasoning are the same, then judgement is exercised in practical reasoning. A judgement, in this sense, is a conclusion of such reasoning. The equation of the exercise of judgement or judging with reasoning appears initially odd. Some kinds of reasoning do not involve an exercise of judgement. Deductive reasoning does not involve judgement as the conclusion drawn in such reasoning follows from the premises *necessarily*. There is no choice or decision to be made as the content of the conclusion is present in the premises. With practical reasoning this is not the case. It goes beyond the content of the premises. If one accepts the conclusion, then there is some kind of *choice* or *decision*. This involves an *exercise of judgement*. Mattessich notes that 'it is a common misconception to believe that normative inferences obey the same formal laws as conventional logic . . . traditional logic without some supplementation—be it a full-fledged logic of action or only some conversion rules—cannot properly master means-end relations' (Mattessich, 1995, pp. 270–271). Practical reasoning is not deductive reasoning.

March states that the choices of what to do in a 'logic of consequences' depend upon answers to four questions. There is the question of determining the alternatives or what actions are possible, the question of expectations or determining what consequences follow from each alternative, the question of preferences in determining how valuable each of the consequences is to the decision maker and answering the question of how a choice is to be made between alternatives (March, 1994, pp. 2–3). These are the questions that have to be answered in practical reasoning. You have to answer the question of what is wanted, or 'preferences'. You need to consider what alternative actions might fulfil these desires. This involves considering the consequences of these alternative actions. You have to weigh the consequences of each action in terms of the extent to which they meet these desires.

Determining what is likely to happen if certain actions are undertaken involves 'using experience' in *inductive reasoning*. Such reasoning is used in inferring a generalization from particular observations. This is called *inductive generalization*. The generalization may be universal, that is, from observing many swans and noting that all of them are white, you may conclude that all swans are white. You may also observe that a certain proportion of them are white and conclude with a statistical generalization that, say, 90% of swans are white. Another kind of inductive argument, which might be called inductive-statistical argument, starts with generalizations of the statistical kind. From 'most swans are white' and a factual statement such as 'there is a swan in the lake', a conclusion 'the swan in the lake is white' may be derived. One does not *have* to accept this conclusion, for the reasoning is not deductive, but it might be *reasonable* to accept it. Inductive reasoning is involved in a 'logic of consequences'. It answers the question of what alternative actions are possible. It is unlikely that the kind of premises that would be required in order to deduce these alternatives could be accepted. When an actor reasons that certain consequences will follow from prospective actions, it is unlikely that the premises will state that consequences *always* follow from certain actions. It is more likely that the generalizations will state that in nearly all/most/many/some cases a consequence will follow. The assumption that 'consequences are defined by the environment, and that decision makers have perfect knowledge of those alternatives and their consequences', that is, 'pure versions of rational choice', are not credible (March, 1994, p. 4). Not all alternatives are known, and actors do not consider all of the consequences of actions. There is 'limited (or bounded) rationality' (March, 1994, p. 8). This should be understood as recognizing that the reasoning to alternatives is inductive rather than deductive. Accepting conclusions in inductive reasoning involves some kind of choice or decision, as does practical reasoning.

Other exercises of judgement may be required in a 'logic of consequences'. How does one answer the questions of preferences in determining how valuable the consequences of actions are to the decision maker? How is a choice made between alternatives in terms of the value of such consequences? People may want a number of things, and it may be that several actions bring about the same consequences. Where certain actions cannot be undertaken at the same time, a decision or choice has to be made as to which action to undertake. Other consequences may follow from one or other of the actions that either do or do not bring about what is wanted. What if the auditor wants also to keep the costs associated with an action to a minimum? It may be that one of the actions is more cost-effective than the other. In order to make a decision, the auditor needs to consider all of the desires that might be fulfilled by an action. Some weighting of desires may be needed. *All relevant desires* must be considered before deciding on actions, and a decision whether some things wanted are wanted more than others needs to be made. The conclusion of practical reasoning may be *undermined* by introducing another desire into the premises. It is not, like deductive reasoning, 'erosion-proof'.

It is interesting to consider how the preferences for certain desires over others are arrived at. One starts out with a premise that expresses some desire from which the desire to undertake an action is derived by practical reasoning given other premises that state a belief that the action will achieve the desire. One then considers whether there are other premises expressing desires and beliefs that allow the derivation of a desire not to perform the action in question. Given these conflicting conclusions, one chooses whether or not to perform the action. The fact that the action will achieve something desired and something not desired does not force one to abandon either of these desires. One still wants to achieve certain ends and not to achieve the other ends, *in general*. That one has a preference for the one rather than the other is shown by the fact that one concludes one wants to do something that achieves one of the desires. The fact that one gives preference to the one over the other on this occasion does not mean one *always* desires the end achieved.

One of the assumptions of 'rational choice theory' is that 'all decision makers share a common set of (basic) preferences . . . and that all preferences relevant to the choice are known, precise, consistent and stable' (March, 1994, pp. 3–4). The idea is that it is possible to identify what is wanted and that some weighting of these various desires can be given in advance. The overall decision rule is something like 'maximise expected return' from the actions contemplated or 'choose the alternative that maximizes the value of the actions in terms of the score of desires achieved'. The desire to act is supposed to be *deducible* from the general decision rule and statements about the values of particular actions in meeting the desired end. Whether there is a general decision rule that weighs up particular actions in terms of the desires and their values has been questioned. Actual decisions may be made not in terms of maximizing expected values of things desired but in terms of satisfying or 'choosing an alternative that exceeds some criterion or target' (March, 1994, p. 18). If this 'pure version' of rational choice theory is abandoned, then some alternative kind of reasoning to decisions or choices needs to be used. Practical reasoning in a 'logic of consequences' may involve making some choices or decisions in concluding what an actor wants to do.

The CICA definition of 'judgement' implies that the reasoning to actions is of the practical kind. The concept of judgement is constructed to capture the idea that a certain kind of reasoning is involved in decision-making. The conclusion about what to do is drawn from some kind of reasoning. The premises constitute *reasons* for accepting the conclusion. A conclusion about what to do is not accepted purely on a whim or for no reason. Some reasoning is involved. Wittgenstein suggests that the concept of a reason is related to that of *reasoning* (Hacker, 1996, p. 58). One cannot be said to be exercising judgement in making a decision if one has not *reasoned* to a conclusion. The reasoning is non-deductive. This does not mean that 'anything goes' and that *any* conclusion can be derived from premises. Although it may be difficult to formulate the rules associated with alternative kinds of logic (Mattessich, 1995, p. 270), it does not mean that there are *no* rules.

This discussion assumes that decisions about what to do are made using a 'logic of consequences'. Another kind of logic, a 'logic of appropriateness', was identified in chapter 1. Is this kind of logic used by auditors in the decisions they make in the context of an audit rather than a 'logic of consequences'?

A 'LOGIC OF APPROPRIATENESS'

A 'logic of appropriateness' looks at decision-making as 'resulting from rule following'. Individuals and organizations who follow rules do not consider preferences or the consequence of actions (March, 1994, p. 57). Instead they consider three questions: 'What kind of situation is this?', 'What kind of person am I?' or 'What kind of organization is this?' and 'What does a person such as I, or an organization such as this, do in a situation such as this?' (March, 1994, p. 58). Modern accounting and auditing have been characterized as rule-governed practices. In auditing many of the rules that govern auditing practice are set out in auditing standards. It is an 'institutional practice' where auditors follow the rules of a standard setter whose authority the auditor accepts. The reasoning to promulgating a rule is undertaken by the standard setter, not by the practitioner. Where they prescribe rules by considering reasons in a 'logic of consequences', or practical reasoning, it is the standard setter who exercises judgement. One meaning of 'principles-based' standards is that they are standards based on the kind of reasons for standards set out in something like a 'conceptual framework' (Dennis, 2008).

The idea of accounting as a practice of following rules has been examined by Dennis (2014). In the case of a 'logic of appropriateness', the desire that is included in practical reasoning to actions is the desire to *act in accord with a rule*. The rule is the *reason* or part of the reason for acting (Baker and Hacker, 1985, p. 156). This is evident from the fact that those who follow rules invoke rule-formulations and explain what they do by citing rules and using them to justify, evaluate, criticize and correct what they do (Baker and Hacker, 1985, p. 45). If someone wants to follow a rule, then they want to act in accord with the rule. They need to understand what actions are in accord with the rule (Baker and Hacker, 1985, p. 97). They need to understand the meaning of the expressions that are used to express the rule. There would appear to be no decision about what course of action is necessary, and no judgement is apparently to be exercised in deciding what to do. The reason for this is clear. If it is possible to deduce what to do from the desire to follow a rule and a statement about the meaning of the rule, that is, a statement that says that acting in accord with rule A is doing X, then there is no exercise of judgement in drawing a conclusion that one wants to do X.

The possibility of deducing what to do from a desire to follow a rule depends upon the nature of the rule. If the rule is to do X, where it is clear what is involved in doing X, and one wants to follow the rule, then one wants to do X as understood. A simple example would be the rule 'drive on the left-hand side of the road'. Someone wanting to follow the rule would be in little doubt as to what has to be done. Are the rules in ISAs like this? Take the rule 'the auditor is to identify and assess the risks of material misstatement, whether due to fraud or error, at the financial statement and assertion levels, through understanding the entity and its environment, including the entity's internal control, thereby providing a basis for designing and implementing responses to the assessed risks of material misstatement' (IAASB, 2010, ISA 315, §3). Although this is expressed as an 'objective' of the standard, it is, in fact, just a restatement of a requirement (Dennis, 2010, pp. 314–316). If it was clear what following the rule involved, then there would be little need for the extended explanation and implementation guidance that is actually provided in the standard. With standards like this the standard setter still feels it necessary to state that 'the auditor uses professional judgment to determine the extent of the understanding required' and enjoins the auditor to consider 'whether the understanding that has been obtained is sufficient to meet the objective stated in this ISA'. This merely means that the auditor has to consider whether he or she has done enough to meet the requirements of the standard. In effect, the standard setter is saying, 'We cannot set out exactly what you have to do in order to meet the requirements of the rule in every circumstance in which it applies, but we have indicated the kind of thing you need to do, and you must decide exactly what you need to do to follow the rule in specific circumstances'. This is what is implied by the admission that the auditor needs to exercise judgement. It only means that the auditor cannot *deduce* what to do by considering what it means to follow the rule. Instead, auditors need to think about what they want to achieve in an audit and determine what they need to do in the area of risk assessment to achieve this overall aim. What this is really saying is that auditors need to undertake practical reasoning to determine exactly what they want to do given what they want to achieve overall and their beliefs as to what exactly, in the area of risk assessment, they must do to achieve what is wanted. The rule may need to be *interpreted* (FEE, 2007, p. 80).

The need to interpret standards arises because of the obvious point that rules are expressed in language (Dennis, 2014, ch. 5). The idea that language may be imperfect and words vague in that there may be disagreements about the correct use was explored in earlier chapters. Rules, being expressed in language, may be 'interpreted' differently. There might be *one rule-formulation*, one set of words that are used to express the rule, but *two rules*.

Rule-formulations cannot be interpreted in *any* way. What determines whether or not someone has grasped the rule is whether he or she uses these expressions in the *correct* way, and this is governed by the practice of using these expressions. Saying that a rule-formulation is vague is saying that there are disagreements in the practice of using expressions in the rule-formulation. Resolving this problem is a matter of agreeing on what the expressions in the rule-formulation are to *mean* and, hence, what the rule expressed is *to be*. In effect, what is happening is that decisions or choices have to be made about these matters. Deciding on what the rule is to be, given choices between what the words that express the rule are to mean, involves the same kind of reasoning that was involved in deciding to follow the rule in the first place. It involves practical reasoning, or a 'logic of consequences'. Given that this kind of reasoning is not deductive and counts as an exercise of judgement, it is no surprise to see that interpreting rules is said to be an exercise of judgement.

That following a rule might require an exercise of judgement recognizes that rules are not always in the nature of 'algorithms', that is, they are not 'a finite set of instructions for performing a particular task' (FEE, 2007, §254). It is for this reason that the Fédération des Experts Comptables Européens acknowledge that professional judgement is required when 'decision-making is not susceptible to algorithmic resolution' (FEE, 2007, §256). The idea of 'algorithmic resolution' should really be understood as the idea that it is possible to *deduce* a set of instructions about what to do from the rule. Judgement is necessary when deduction is not possible. It arises because the reasoning to what has to be done from the rule is not deductive.

The objective of implementation guidance is to overcome the need to exercise judgement. It explains the meaning of expressions used in the rule-formulation and clarifies what the rule expressed is to be (Dennis, 2010, p. 314). The ideal kind of guidance would eliminate the need to exercise judgement. It would enable those who follow the standard to *deduce* what is to be done from the rule-formulation. As the SEC explains, rules-based standards are designed to 'minimize (and in certain instances to trivialize) the judgmental component of accounting practice through the establishment of complicated, finely articulated rules that attempt to foresee all possible application challenges' (SEC, 2003, p. 15). The problem is that 'it is simply impossible to fully eliminate professional judgment in the application of accounting standards' (SEC, 2003, p. 16). For this reason they claim to support the promulgation of 'principles-based' standards. One way of understanding this is to say that such standards are those that require interpretation, that is, that decisions or choices have to be made about what the expressions in the rule-formulation are to mean, which requires the exercise of reasoning that is not deductive. For this reason 'principles-based' standards are characterized as those that require the exercise of judgement (ICAS, 2006, p.1). This kind of judgement involves determining what the expressions in the rule-formulation are to mean. The rather tortured debate about the nature and authority of explanatory guidance in the contest of the Clarity Project suggests that the IAASB were unclear about the nature of standards and of implementation guidance (Dennis, 2010, pp. 312–314).

Other injunctions to exercise professional judgement in following standards that appear in ISAs can be analysed in terms of the kind of reasoning required. Judgement must be recognised where there is no simple deduction of what to do from the requirements expressed in an ISA. With some standards this may be because there are alternatives in the standards. The standard says that preparers must do either a or b or c, but there is a choice as to what to do, and decisions have to be made as to which of the alternatives are to undertaken. It is not possible to deduce 'do a' or 'do b' or 'do c' from a rule that states 'do a or b or c', for doing any of these things will be in accord with the rule, and nothing in the rule says that one or the other *must* be done. A conclusion as to what to do must be derived, but it will not follow deductively from the rule. Where following a rule requires an assessment of what is wanted and beliefs about what will achieve what is wanted, then practical reasoning is involved. This is not deductive in nature. This confirms the prior insight that the objective of the concept of judgement is to capture decisions that are made using non-deductive reasoning. The evaluative enquiry identifies a similar objective of constructing the concept of judgement, namely to identify decisions that are made using non-deductive reasoning but where the premises involve rules in a 'logic of appropriateness'. There is a need to exercise judgement in following a rule.

Judgement may also be required in deciding whether, on a particular occasion, a rule is to be followed or overridden. Judgement is allowed to be exercised with 'rules of thumb' but not with rules on the 'practice' conception, in the sense explained in chapter 3. This is one of the kinds of judgement identified by the FEE, who state that judgement may be exercised in 'determining alternative audit procedures when a particular relevant requirement is not effective' (FEE, 2007, §274). It involves deciding or making a choice as to whether or not to do what the rule requires. It is not clear whether the IAASB conceive of rules on the 'practice' conception or as 'rules of thumb' (Dennis, 2010, p. 310). ISA 200 does allow a departure from a requirement for a specific procedure (IAASB, 2010, ISA 200, §23), but it was clear during the development of the Clarity Project that the IAASB thought that departure would be rare and that requirements were 'essentially mandatory'. The result is that rules in ISAs appear something of a hybrid between 'rules of thumb' and rules on the 'practice' conception (Dennis, 2010, p. 312). This leaves it somewhat in doubt as to how those who follow the standard are to reason to actions and whether or not judgement as to overriding a rule is to be exercised.

What is clear from the discussion is that even where auditors adopt a 'logic of appropriateness' in following the rules in standards, there may still be scope for the exercise of judgement by auditors in non-deductive reasoning to the auditing actions required by standards. This confirms the suggestion that the exercise of judgement arises where non-deductive reasoning is undertaken. It is by no means clear what kind of judgement the IAASB wishes to allow auditors to exercise in following standards. It is not clear what conception of rules is adopted by the IAASB and whether they can be overridden. They are also unclear as to the nature of explanatory material in standards and whether or not this is meant to preclude or allow the exercise of judgement in interpreting the requirements of standards (Dennis, 2010, pp. 312–314). It is therefore unclear what kind of judgement auditors are allowed to exercise in following rules in standards. The 'Clarity Project' did not clarify these issues.

The exercise of judgement in interpreting rules or in deciding whether or not to override them may have to be exercised by preparers of financial statements who aim to follow the rules set out in accounting standards. In other words, a 'logic of appropriateness' is also used in making decisions about financial reporting, and using such logic may involve an exercise of judgement because such logic is not deductive. This gives rise to the idea that financial reporting may involve exercises of judgement by preparers. Given the requirement of auditors to express an opinion on financial statements, they must consider the reasoning of preparers who have followed the rules in accounting standards. Auditors judge the judgements of preparers. If preparers decide to override the rules in accounting standards by using non-deductive reasoning to conclude whether or not following the rule in the circumstances will fulfil the objective of the standard, then auditors must consider whether they accept the conclusion using similar reasoning. The motive for constructing the concept of judgement, the kind of thing that an evaluative conceptual enquiry explores, is to capture something that arises due to the reasoning involved in decision-making.

Chapter 3 looked at the exercise of judgement as to whether the financial statements 'present fairly' or give a 'true and fair view'. This involves interpreting what these expressions mean. Two further examples of actions that require the exercise of judgement have been examined in chapters 4 and 5. These involve the actions of searching for evidence and actions of assessing whether or not a misstatement is material.

JUDGEMENTS ABOUT THE FINANCIAL STATEMENTS

The auditor is required to obtain 'reasonable assurance' as to whether the financial statements 'present fairly' or give a 'true and fair view' as the basis for expressing an opinion on them. Determining what needs to be established before one can derive the opinion is a matter of determining what *is* the meaning of the opinion. This was referred to as 'criterial evidence' of the opinion. Giving a 'true and fair view' is, as a matter of meaning, meeting the 'criteria of adequacy' set out in the conceptual framework. It *means* giving relevant and reliable information and meeting the other qualitative characteristics of useful information. Relevant information is information that meets the objectives of financial reporting. What kind of information is reliable depends upon the statements in the financial statements. Some are statements of fact and to be reliable is to be true. Some are predictive in nature and to be reliable is to be based on acceptable law-like statements or generalisations statements of fact in the initial conditions that are true. It was suggested that the objectives and qualitative characteristics represent general desires that are to be met by financial reporting information. Given that standard setters undertake practical reason to standard setting decisions using these criteria of adequacy, financial statements that follow accounting standards will usually fulfil these criteria and end up presenting fairly or giving a 'true and fair view'. However, there may be occasions where following the standards will not fulfil these criteria, and there may be a need to interpret the standards in order to fulfil the criteria. Judgement is exercised by preparers in following the standards through practical reasoning from the desires expressed in the objectives and qualitative characteristics chapters of the conceptual framework. In these cases auditors will have to review this practical reasoning and determine whether or not they agree with the conclusions of the preparers. They need to judge the judgements of the preparers in order to judge whether the financial statements meet the 'criteria of adequacy' in order to given an opinion of the required kind.

JUDGEMENTS IN THE SEARCH FOR EVIDENCE

In chapter 4 it was suggested that the search for *inductive* evidence, evidence provided by symptoms, enables the auditor to derive conclusions on which the audit opinion is based. Evidence enables the auditor to derive conclusions from premises in reasoning that is not deductive but *inductive*. The auditor is trying to establish an inductive correlation between two distinct, externally related phenomena. Where the auditor needs to establish the truth of a proposition expressed in the financial statements, evidence is needed to connect the occurrence of the event expressed in the proposition with the events that constitute the evidence as observed by the auditor. Given a story that establishes a causal connection between the event expressed in the financial statement proposition and the event of observing something that counts as evidence, the auditor has to establish that the financial statement event is the best explanation of the evidence events in the circumstances. This explanation has what was called 'maximal specificity'.

Where the financial statement proposition expresses predictions rather than matters of fact, the auditor needs evidence of the reliability of the predictions by determining whether the premises in the argument upon which the prediction is based are reasonable. This involves determining the acceptability of generalisations upon which the predictions are based. Adopting a sceptical approach implies that the reasoning is not deductive. The process of inductive reasoning 'is a matter of weighing evidence and judging likelihood, not of proof' (Lipton, 1991, p. 412). It involves not only determining the strength of the generalizations needed but also considering whether or not other generalizations and facts may be relevant in the auditing situation that might undermine conclusions previously drawn.

JUDGEMENTS IN RELATION TO MATERIALITY

In Chapter 5 the idea that in order to identify a misstatement as material the auditor needs to determine whether a misstatement could 'reasonably be expected' to influence the economic decisions of users was explored. It was suggested that this was a *counterfactual statement* that depended on inferring what would happen from generalisations. In the absence of universal, law-like statements, the auditor has to rely upon *statistical* generalisations. Inductive reasoning must be used in identifying such generalisations. Such reasoning must also be used in identifying relevant generalisations that have 'maximal specificity' in the context in which they are used to identify material misstatements. It was also suggested that developing the concept of materiality required the auditor to determine what was wanted from such a concept. The concept emerges as a result of practical reasoning from such desires. This analysis suggests that judgement needs to be exercised in deciding what is wanted from a concept of materiality and hence in the development of the concept. It also needs to be exercised in identifying and using generalisations to determine when misstatements are material.

SO, WHAT IS JUDGEMENT?

An examination of these areas where judgement is required to be exercised suggests that what is common to all of these exercises of judgement is that conclusions are drawn in a process of reasoning that is not deductive. This means some choice or decision is required in drawing the conclusions where the conclusion goes beyond the content of the premises and is, hence, 'ampliative'. This appears to offer some support to the CICA definition of judgement as 'making a choice, a decision, leading to action'. The analysis does, however, make clearer the kinds of decisions or choices that are made and that constitute an exercise of judgement. It is important to see that not all of the choices or decisions that constitute exercises of judgement relate to choosing or deciding on actions to be undertaken. Only where the reasoning involved is practical reasoning is the conclusion of the reasoning a desire to act. Judgement must be exercised in determining what is wanted. The beliefs about what actions will fulfil what is wanted involves inductive reasoning. It may involve statistical generalisations where judgement must be exercised in determining which of the generalisations have 'maximal specificity'. Inductive reasoning of this kind does not have a desire to act as its conclusion. Evidential reasoning involves inductive reasoning where the conclusion is a matter of fact or the prediction of what will happen and not an action. Inductive reasoning has relevance to auditing actions even if the conclusion is not a desire to act. If it had no impact on auditing actions, then it would not be relevant to auditing. If reasoning did not, in some sense, 'lead to action', then there would, from the auditing point of view, be no point in undertaking it. However, it is not the case that all exercises of judgement involve practical reasoning to a desire to act.

The IAASB require auditors not only to exercise judgement but to exercise 'professional judgement'. What it is to be professional will now be briefly examined.

ON BEING PROFESSIONAL

The word 'professional' in the expression 'professional judgement' is an adjective. What it means for judgement to be professional is a matter of explaining the characteristics of the reasoning involved in its exercise if it is to be professional. In the literature on professions and professionalism in accountancy, it is acknowledged that 'professional recognition is typically earned and maintained by occupational groups by reference to certain characteristics, behaviour, incentives and constraints on members' activities' (Pierce, 2007, p. 1). The kind of conceptual enquiry into being professional is not always clear in the literature. It is sometimes *descriptive* enquiry into how the term 'professional' is actually used in society by looking at explanations of the term and how it is applied to the behaviour of professionals. This has been called 'naturalism and typology' (Abbott, 1988, p. 4) and focuses on the actual use of the expression whether evidenced by explanations of the word or on the use of the term. Other enquiries are *prescriptive* in that they identify the characteristics that professionals *ought* to exhibit for their behaviour to be professional. The objective of the IAASB project to consider the conceptual aspects of professional judgement is unclear. Is it to identify the characteristics that those who are called professional actually exhibit? Is it to engender behaviour of a certain kind in professionals who do not always exhibit such characteristics in what they do? Is its objective to convince society that professionals in occupational groups do actually exhibit such characteristics in order to protect the economic interests of groups who receive substantial rewards for professional behaviour?

In the CICA report, judgement is said to be professional in so far as it 'implies a more extensive process requiring relevant expertise and knowledge of standards, and following from the requirements and responsibilities of one's job . . . Due care, objectivity and integrity arise from personal values and from society's expectations of professionalism' (CICA, 1988, p. 5). This focuses on some widely recognised characteristics of professional behaviour. These include the use of specialised knowledge that arises out of 'training, examination and licensing' and that is controlled through the development of standards (Pierce, 2007, p. 6). The knowledge is 'abstract' (Abbott, 1988, p. 8). The behaviour is governed by high standards of ethical conduct (Pierce, 2007, p. 7). It involves a commitment to the public interest over and above self-interest or client interests (Pierce, 2007, pp. 7–12). This is also emphasised in the International Ethics Standards Board for Accountants *Code of Ethics* (IESBA, 2013, §100.1). Integrity, objectivity and professional competence and due care are required. Criteria of professionalism also include mastery of a complex body of knowledge and skills used in the service of others (Rice and Duncan, 2006). Some of these characteristics are recognised in the IAASB definition of 'professional judgement' as 'the application of relevant training, knowledge and experience, within the context provided by auditing, accounting and ethical standards, in making informed decisions about the courses of action that are appropriate in the circumstances of the audit engagement' (IAASB, 2010, *Handbook*). Given the analysis in this chapter, the idea of an 'application' needs to be explained further. A better definition would be 'the use of relevant training, knowledge and experience in reasoning to actions that are appropriate in the circumstances of the audit engagement and in accordance with the requirements of auditing, accounting and ethical standards'. What needs to be made clearer is how these requirements relate to the different kinds of reasoning identified in the paper as exercises of judgement.

How this reasoning exemplifies the characteristics of being professional can be seen in evidential reasoning. Finding evidence involves identifying premises about matters of fact that are used to derive conclusions about assertions in financial statements in accordance with inductive reasoning. This requires the use of the 'knowledge and experience' characteristic of professional behaviour. The ethical standards require that other premises, relating to self-interest or client interests, are excluded from this reasoning. Premises that express what the auditor wants or what the client wants where these do not coincide with the desires of the stakeholders for who the audit opinion is given should be excluded. This precludes actions that restrict the search for the most relevant explanation of the evidence that arise because of worries about the amount of work that is required or actions that result from concerns about the reaction of the client and fears of withholding further work. This would be in the interest of the auditor or the client without being in the interests of the stakeholders. The introduction of such additional premises is not accepted given the integrity that is characteristic of professional behaviour, and they should be excluded (CICA, 1995, p. 35). In deciding whether or not to override a standard, the auditor must consider whether doing what is required or whether interpreting the requirement in a certain way will achieve the objectives of the audit. These objectives should exclude those that are self-interested or client interested.

Being professional in exercising judgement is a matter of deriving conclusion from non-deductive reasoning in a 'professional' manner that excludes considering self-interested desires. It involves exercising knowledge and skills in determining factual matters about what actions will bring about a certain end and by exercising scepticism in evidential reasoning. It is important to see that one can only understand what *professional* judgement is by considering different exercises of judgement. Exercising professional judgement is not explained as the exercise of judgement by a professional. This kind of definition is actually given by International Accounting Education Standards Board where a 'professional accountant' is defined as 'an individual who is a member of an IFAC member body' (IAESB, 2013, p. 148). This is not of much help in understanding what it is for judgement to be professional. 'Professional judgement' does not mean 'judgement undertaken by a member of an IFAC member body' or, indeed, of any professional body. If this were the case, then it would not be possible to ask whether any particular judgement of a member of such a body was, indeed, professional, for it would necessarily be the case.

PRACTICAL IMPLICATIONS OF THE SUGGESTED DEFINITION OF 'PROFESSIONAL JUDGEMENT'

Shortcomings in the existing definitions of 'professional judgement' include a failure to identify the nature of the 'process' involved in exercises of judgement. These shortcomings are evident in recent explanations of professional judgement. AICPA acknowledge the importance of judgement in preparing and auditing financial statements and draw attention to developments in producing a 'professional judgement framework' or models of good judgement (AICPA, 2013). The problem with these developments is that they are not underpinned by a clear appreciation of the nature of judgement or the kinds of reasoning that are involved in exercising professional judgement. The ICAS 'professional judgement framework' was developed primarily for financial reporting. It states that professional judgement is a 'key skill' (ICAS, 2012, p. 3) but does not explain what kind of 'skill' is involved. A dictionary definition of 'skill' identifies a range of different kinds of skill including 'expert knowledge' or a 'craft or accomplishment' (*Chambers Dictionary*). This does not make it clear that the 'skill' involved is an ability to undertake reasoning of a certain kind.

The ICAS framework explains that judgement is required in determining the appropriate accounting treatment where there is no specific standard covering the transaction, where there is a standard but no implementation guidance or where more than one set of accounting principles applies to a transaction (ICAS, 2012, p. 4). What is missing in this framework is the acknowledgement that exercises of judgement all arise because the reasoning involved in making a decision about what to do is not deductive. Although the framework is provided to assist preparers in making what is agreed to be exercises of judgement in financial reporting, this framework does not assist in understanding any other exercises of judgement, including those that auditors are likely to face. It says nothing about exercises of judgement involved in reasoning to matters of fact in evidential situations or in determining the materiality of a misstatement. If it spent more time in explaining the nature of the 'skill' that is meant to be involved in making judgements, it might be more useful. Analyses of professional judgement in other areas have similar shortcomings. The SEC discuss professional judgement in a report on financial reporting (SEC, 2008). Although they identify a similar range of examples of situations where professional judgement needs to be exercised, including areas not covered by the ICAS review such as judgements about estimated amounts and evidence which are of relevance to auditor judgements, there is the same lack of appreciation that an exercise of judgement arises through reasoning of certain kinds and that different kinds of reasoning might be involved in different exercises of judgement. A report of the Committee of Sponsoring Organizations of the Treadway Commission (COSO) on judgement processes that are exercised by board members provides a five step professional judgement process that does not explicitly acknowledge the fact that the 'process' involved is one of reasoning. It does not discuss whether the five steps apply in the same way to different kinds of reasoning or whether there may be other steps that apply to certain kinds of non-deductive reasoning.

The auditing profession could learn from the shortcomings of these examinations of judgement when they undertake their own framework of professional judgement in auditing. A conclusion of a prescriptive conceptual enquiry is that exercises of judgement involve undertaking reasoning of a non-deductive kind. Guidance on judgement could then focus on examining what is involved in such reasoning. This would concentrate attention on the reasoning involved in different areas of financial reporting and auditing so that both preparers and auditors understand what is really involved in the 'processes' of judgement. The key to training and guiding the profession in the exercise of judgement is to familiarise them with the kinds of reasoning that are involved in its exercise. Little is said about the need for the skills involved in reasoning in the International Educational Standards. There is nothing about the need for such skills in the ED of the proposed *Entry Requirements to Professional Accounting Education* of IES 1 (IAESB, 2012). They may be implied by the 'intellectual skills' of IES 3 as part of the need for 'broad-minded individuals who think and communicate effectively and who have the basis for conducting inquiry, carrying out logical thinking and undertaking critical analysis' (IAESB, 2012, IES 3, §10). Given that 'logical thinking' involves reasoning, it is important for professionals to realize that different kinds of reasoning are implied by such 'thinking' and that different 'professional skills' may be required in applying professional judgement.

SUMMARY

Although the exercise of judgement is widely held to be important in auditing, little attention has been given to explaining the nature of such judgement. The explanations that have been given talk about judgement as a process of, or an application of knowledge in, making a choice or a decision that leads to action. An examination of decision-making suggest that this is a process of application of practical reasoning of the kind explained in earlier chapters of the book. This kind of reasoning is not deductive, and drawing conclusions requires that decisions or choices be made. Not all exercises of judgement are of this kind. Judging matters of fact, that is, drawing conclusions about what is the case, may require inductive reasoning. This is also not deductive reasoning. A review of the kind of judgement identified in the book, making judgements about financial statements, evidence or materiality, suggests that an exercise of judgement arises whenever reasoning is undertaken that is not deductive. Judgement is drawing conclusions about matters of fact or about what to do where the reasoning involved is not deductive. The characteristics of judgement that render it professional are explored.

REFERENCES

Abbott, A. (1988) *The System of Professions: An Essay on the Division of Expert Labor.* Chicago: University of Chicago Press.

AICPA (2013) *Professional Judgement.* Accessible at: http://www.aicpa.org/intere stareas/frc/pages/professional-judgment.aspx [Accessed 22 March 2013].

Archer, S. (1993) 'On the Methodology of Constructing a Conceptual Framework for Financial Accounting' in M. Mumford and K. Peasnell (eds.) *Philosophical Perspectives on Accounting.* London: Routledge.

Baker, G. & Hacker, P. (1985) *Wittgenstein Rules, Grammar and Necessity.* Oxford: Blackwell.

Bernstein, L. (1967) 'The concept of materiality', *Accounting Review,* January, pp. 86–95.

Bonner, S. (1999) 'Judgement and decision-making research in accounting', *Accounting Horizons,* Vol. 13 (4), pp. 385–398.

CICA (1988) *Professional Judgment in Financial Reporting.* Toronto: CICA.

CICA (1995) *Professional Judgment and the Auditor.* Toronto: CICA.

Dennis, I. (2008) 'A conceptual enquiry into the concept of a "principles-based" accounting standard', *British Accounting Review,* Vol. 40 (3), pp. 260–271.

Dennis, I. (2010) '"Clarity" begins at home: An examination of the conceptual underpinnings of the IAASB's Clarity Project', *International Journal of Auditing,* Vol. 14 (3), pp. 294–319.

Dennis, I. (2014) *The Nature of Accounting Regulation*. New York: Routledge.

FEE (2007) *Selected Issues in Relation to Financial Statement Audits*. Brussels, Belgium: Fédération des Experts Comptables Européens. Accessible at: http://www.fee.be/publications/default.asp?library_ref=4&content_ref=771 [Accessed 27 May 2010].

Hacker, P. (1996) *Wittgenstein Mind and Will*. Oxford: Blackwell.

IAASB (2010) *ISA 200 Overall Objectives of the Independent Auditor and the Conduct of an Audit in Accordance with International Standards*. New York: International Federation of Accountants.

IAASB (2010) *ISA 315 Identifying and Assessing the Risks of Material Misstatement through Understanding the Entity and Its Environment*. New York: International Federation of Accountants.

IAASB (2010) *Handbook of International Standards on Auditing and Quality Control*. New York: International Federation of Accountants.

IAASB (2010) *Preface to the International Standards on Quality Control, Auditing, Review, Other Assurance and Related Services*. New York: International Federation of Accountants.

IAASB (2011) *Proposed IAASB Strategy and Work Program for 2012–2014*. New York: International Federation of Accountants.

IAESB (2012) *Handbook of International Education Pronouncements*. New York: International Federation of Accountants.

ICAS (2006) *Principles Not Rules: A Question of Judgment*. Edinburgh: Institute of Chartered Accountants in Scotland.

ICAS (2012) *A Professional Judgement Framework for Financial Reporting*. Edinburgh: Institute of Chartered Accountants in Scotland. Accessible at: http://icas.org.uk/pjf/ [Accessed 8 March 2013].

IESBA (2013) *Code of Ethics for Professional Accountants*. New York: International Federation of Accountants.

Lipton, P. (1991) 'Inference to the Best Explanation' reprinted in Curd and Cover (eds.) (1998) *Philosophy of Science*. New York: W. W. Norton and Co.

March, J. (1994) *Primer on Decision Making: How Decisions Happen*. New York: The Free Press.

Mattessich, R. (1995) 'Conditional-normative accounting methodology: Incorporating value judgements and means-end relations of an applied science', *Accounting, Organizations and Society*, Vol. 20 (4), pp. 259–284.

Mason, A. & Gibbins, M. (1991) 'Judgment and U.S. accounting standards', *Accounting Horizons*, Vol. 5 (2), pp. 14–24.

Nelson, M. & Tan, H. (2005) 'Judgement and decision making research in auditing: A task, person, and interpersonal interaction perspective', *Auditing: A Journal of Practice and Theory*, Vol. 24, Supplement, pp. 41–71.

Pierce, A. (2007) *Ethics and the Professional Accounting Firm: A Literature Review*. Edinburgh: Institute of Chartered Accountants in Scotland. Accessible at: http://icas.org.uk/pierce [Accessed 8 April 2013].

Rice, V. and Duncan, J. (2006) 'What Does It Mean to Be a "Professional" . . . And What Does It Mean to Be an Ergonomics Professional?' FPE Position Paper. Accessible at: http://citeseerx.ist.psu.edu/viewdoc/download?doi=10.1.1.95.9568&rep=rep1&type=pdf [Accessed 4 April 2013].

SEC (2003) *Study Report Pursuant to Section 108(d) of the Sarbanes-Oxley Act of 2002, SEC*. Accessible at: http://www.sec.gov/news/studies/principlesbasedstand.htm [Accessed 14 November 2011].

SEC (2008) *Final Report of the Advisory Committee on Improvements to Financial Reporting to the United States Securities and Exchange Commission*. Accessible at: http://www.aicpa.org/InterestAreas/FRC/DownloadableDocuments/Professional_Judgment/acifr-finalreport-excerpt.pdf [Accessed 22 March 2013].

Solomon, I. and Trotman, K. (2003) 'Experimental judgment and decision research in auditing: The first 25 years of AOS', *Accounting, Organizations and Society*, Vol. 28, pp. 395–412.

Wedemeyer, P. (2010) 'A discussion of auditing judgment as the critical component in audit quality—A practitioner's perspective', *International Journal of Disclosure and Governance*, Vol. 7 (4), pp. 320–333.

7 Conclusions

This book has presented a theory of auditing. The nature of a theory of auditing as understood in this book was explained. A theory of a practice sets out what is wanted from the practice. The idea of an objective of a practice was examined. It was explained as a rule governed. This kind of theory was said to constitute a conceptual framework for auditing. It starts with the identification of the objectives of auditing. This is identified as something that will increase the credibility of financial statements through the expression of an opinion on them. The nature of the opinion was explored by considering the meaning of the opinion that financial statements 'present fairly' or 'give a true and fair view'. It was suggested that it means that the financial statements fulfil the 'criteria of adequacy' for financial statements that are useful. In order to give an opinion of this kind, evidence is needed that the financial statements meet these criteria. The concept of evidence was explained. Criterial evidence was distinguished from inductive evidence. The nature of probabilities in evidential reasoning was considered. Given that evidence is required to ensure that the financial statements are not materially misstated, the idea of materiality was examined. The insistence that the search for evidence of material misstatements involves the exercise of judgement let to the review of the concept of professional judgement.

This brief description of what is covered in the book illustrates two important strands in the theory of auditing, as conceived in this book. It seeks to identify what is wanted from the practice of auditing and also explains important concepts that have been developed in determining what needs to be done to fulfil the objectives of the practice. This provides some justification for previous writers on auditing theory referring to the areas of enquiry as a philosophy of auditing, namely conceptual enquiry. Explaining the method of conceptual enquiry is itself a conceptual enquiry into the nature of conceptual enquiry. As explained in the book, such enquiries consider the meaning of expressions. This is a form of philosophical investigation. The title of this book could well have been *The Philosophy and Theory of Auditing*, which brings out the two strands in the book. It is important to think about, and seek agreement on, what is wanted from a practice. It is also important that an adequate examination of a practice also includes conceptual enquiry. The book recognises the importance of, in Power's expression, 'conceptual considerations' in practices. One of the starting points of the book is that, to date, there has been little in the way of conceptual enquiry into auditing. Even where it has been undertaken, it has not been recognised as conceptual enquiry. The book has attempted to fill the gap by undertaking enquiry of this kind in the area of auditing. It also explained what is involved and proselytises its importance. If any message is carried over into other areas of enquiry into the practice of accounting, it is that conceptual enquiry is vital to a proper understanding of practices. It is hoped that researchers in these other areas might consider it a worthy objective of future enquiries.

The conception of theory presented in this book is of something that is useful in making decisions about what is required in auditing practices. This means that it is something that standard setters can use in reasoning to standard setting decisions that are used to determine the practices that auditors must undertake. The book does not itself make prescriptions for auditing and does not determine the practices to be adopted by auditors. For this reason it is somewhat divorced from the practices themselves. It is concerned to set out the reasons for adopting practice rather than setting out the practices themselves. This is not intended to reflect a view that determining such practice is not important. It was argued in chapter 1 that academics and practitioners should get involved in standard setting decisions and that the arguments against such involvement were not convincing. The theory presented in this book is meant to make a contribution to the activity of setting standards or rules for a practice and to anyone interested in thinking about what is wanted from the practice and in exploring the concepts that are used in reasoning to such practices.

Index

accounting theory 12–13, 18, 24, 45
agreement on what is wanted from
    a practice 22–3; *see also*
    desirability characterisation
Alexander, D.: on criteria of adequacy
    58, 75; three approaches to true
    and fair 59–61; type A criterion
    of true and fair 66–7; type B
    criterion of true and fair 68–9,
    71; type C criterion of true and
    fair 63, 65
American Institute of Certified Public
    Accountants (AICPA) 44, 65–6,
    90–1, 147
applied science 15, 17
assertions in financial statements 74,
    80–2, 87; and evidence 39,
    93–4; Mautz and Sharaf's
    explanation 87–8; the nature of
    88–90; and relevant and reliable
    information 90–2; *see also*
    scepticism
assurance engagements 2
audit evidence: and descriptive
    conceptual enquiry 80; IAASB's
    conception 80–1; importance
    79–80; and predictions
    and estimates 105–6; and
    probability 96–9; and rational
    argumentation 93–5; and
    reasonable assurance 110–11;
    and stories and generalisations
    in auditing 102–5; and stories
    and generalisations in law
    99–102; that enables the opinion
    81–3; what it is 107–8; *see also*
    criterial evidence, inductive
    evidence, reasonable assurance,
    scepticism

audit opinion: explanations of the
    opinion 57; *see also* descriptive
    conceptual enquiry into 'true
    and fair', evaluative conceptual
    enquiry into 'true and fair'
auditing theory: and the activity of
    theorising 13–14; agreeing on
    objectives or what is wanted
    19–20; descriptive conceptual
    enquiry into 'accounting theory'
    12–13; and the expression of
    what is wanted from a practice
    33–4; need for but lack of
    interest in 1; and reasoning
    15–16; as promulgating rules
    14–15; as something that assists
    standard setters in making
    decisions 4; *see also* CoNAM,
    conceptual frameworks, moral
    reasoning, normative theorising,
    positive theorising, self-interest
Ayer, A. 94, 100, 109

backward argument 31–2, 42, 48, 50
Bayes's rule 97–8
best explanation 102, 103–4, 107,
    110–12, 143
books on auditing theory 2

Canadian Institute of Chartered
    Accountants (CICA) 131–4,
    137, 144, 146–7
Code of Ethics 49–50, 146
Committee of Sponsoring
    Organizations of the Treadway
    Commission (COSO) 148
CoNAM 17
concepts 6–7; of auditing 125,
    131, 153; of evidence 80; of

For Product Safety Concerns and Information please contact our EU
representative GPSR@taylorandfrancis.com
Taylor & Francis Verlag GmbH, Kaufingerstraße 24, 80331 München, Germany